Narra and Poetry

Teaching Guide

Year 6
P7

Heinemann is an imprint of Pearson Education Limited, a company incorporated in England and Wales, having its registered office: Edinburgh Gate, Harlow, Essex, CM20 2JE. Registered company number: 872828

www.pearsonschools.co.uk

Heinemann is the registered trademark of Pearson Education Limited.

First published 2009

12 11 10 09

10 9 8 7 6 5 4 3 2 1

British Library Cataloguing in Publication Data
A catalogue record for this book is available from the British Library.

Literacy Evolve Year 6 Teaching Guide

ISBN 978-0435035846

Copyright notice

Authors: Carol Matchett, Michael Lockwood

Series editor: Janice Pimm

Series Consultant: Michael Rosen

Illustrated by Luke Finlayson

Typeset by Phoenix Photosetting, Chatham, Kent

Printed in the UK by Ashford Colour Press

Acknowledgements

The publisher gratefully acknowledges permission to reproduce copyright material in this book:

Extract from 'Nule' from Nothing to be Afraid of by Jan Mark (Kestrel Books 1980); Moving House from Short and Scary! By Louise Cooper (OUP, 2002); 'Woodpecker' and 'The Warm and the Cold' reprinted from COLLECTED POEMS FOR CHILDREN (Faber 2005) copyright © Ted Hughes 2005; 'The British' reprinted from WICKED WORLD! (Puffin 2000) copyright © Benjamin Zephaniah 2000; 'Talking Turkeys!' reprinted from TALKING TURKEYS (Puffin 1995) copyright © Benjamin Zephaniah 1995; 'Poetics' reprinted from FUNKY CHICKENS (Viking 1996) copyright © Benjamin Zephaniah 1996.

We would like to thank Coppetts Wood Primary School, Winchcombe Abbey Primary, St Mary Magdalen's Catholic Primary, Dorridge Junior School, Fourlanesend CP School, Brookside Primary School, Archbishop of York's CE Jnr School, Lady Modiford's CofE School, Hursthead Jnr School, The Deans Primary School and St Peter's CE Primary School for their invaluable help in the development and trialling of this programme.

Every effort has been made to contact copyright holders of material reproduced in this book. Any omissions will be rectified in subsequent printings if notice is given to the publishers.

To find the latest information about *Literacy Evolve* visit:

www.pearsonschools.co.uk/literacyevolve

Contents

Welcome to *Literacy Evolve*

"If all we mean by literacy is just being able to read one word after another, we're living in a terrible, impoverished world."

Michael Rosen

Sometimes literacy can feel like little more than reading one word after another. *Literacy Evolve* offers a more inspiring way to approach the subject. It is a whole-class resource for narrative and poetry with enjoyment at its heart. It has been influenced by the ideas of former Children's Laureate Michael Rosen and uses whole, 'real' novels, powerful short films and 'single-voice' poetry collections to ignite children's interest in communication and language. If this passion and enjoyment can be inspired at school, then children are likely to read more for pleasure in their own time which in turn will lead to a greater facility with language, increased vocabulary, critical-thinking, personal development and other benefits across the curriculum (UNESCO PISA Report, 2000).

The teaching support has been designed to help you teach literacy in a creative and exciting way. The notes are written by teachers who are passionate about literacy and are packed with ideas that will spark children's creativity and provide imaginative contexts in which to apply their developing literacy skills. The sessions aim to be lively and interactive with an emphasis on speaking and listening, talk for writing and drama. 'Open-ended' questions are used frequently to stimulate meaningful discussion and develop children's confidence in talking about books and ideas. Additionally, its use of film and highly visual books allows great scope for developing children's visual literacy skills.

The units seek to immerse the children in the stimulus piece and move from reading and analysing through to responding and writing. Word and sentence level skills are covered along the way as appropriate to the unit, though the expectation is that a separate spelling programme will also be in place. Assessment for learning practices are embedded throughout, content is matched to Assessment Focuses to help you with Assessing Pupils' Progress, and our interactive planner (I-Planner Online) allows you to track progress.

Welcome to *Literacy Evolve*

Literacy Evolve is correlated to all UK curricula including the new Proposed Primary Curriculum and the Renewed Primary Framework. At Year 6 there are 20 weeks of teaching divided into units of between 1 and 4 weeks. The teaching sessions are intended to last around 1 hour to 1 ½ hours, but they can be extended or contracted as appropriate to the needs of individual classes and timetables.

Progression is built in across the units and therefore, within the narrative or poetry section it is advisable to use the units in the numbered order. However, I-Planner Online allows you to reorder the units and customise them if you so wish.

Literacy Evolve is not a one-size-fits-all programme. I-Planner allows you to teach your way and according to the needs of your class. You can customise the lesson plans as you wish, including moving units around, changing the day-to-day detail of the weekly plans, allocating different independent tasks, evaluating children and changing your future plans according to assessments.

Read on to find out more about what *Literacy Evolve* has to offer.

Literacy Evolve components

Meet the team

Michael Rosen (Series Consultant)

When I ask myself how I got into this world of children's books it all goes back to my mum and dad, who were teachers. One of the most amazing memories I have from my childhood was of when we were on a camping holiday in Yorkshire. Every night we gathered in the tent, my dad pumped up a little lamp and he read us the whole of *Great Expectations* with all the voices and actions. The voices and gestures live with me even now. It's this kind of power – literature in action – that I believe in. It's these 'Golden Moments' that teachers cherish. Every child is entitled to that level of engagement and delight that my father gave us.

A real 'Golden Moment' for me was when I was reading the story of Persephone to my 8 year-old daughter, when we came across the word 'pity'. Here is a difficult, abstract idea but when enacted in the Persephone myth it becomes accessible and concrete. Suddenly we were able to think of other examples of pity from her life and mine and also to juggle it with other abstract words like sympathy, compassion or callousness.

Literature is the most pleasurable way we have access to these difficult ideas, but we will never reach them if we quiz children too closely with closed-ended questions. Literature is a way of opening up a conversation between equals: there is no difference between my daughter's right to talk about 'pity' and mine. So here we have this enormous treasure house of literature stretching back thousands of years, giving us the greatest wisdom that the human race can put together, accessible to all.

Literacy Evolve has evolved out of the ideas that I'm expressing here, so I'm delighted to be a part of the project and hope that teachers and children will enjoy finding their way through its stories and poems. No-one involved in the project is claiming that this is an end in itself – what matters with reading and young people is that we get them hooked, and *Literacy Evolve* strikes me as a great way to do just that. It reaches out into that vast world of books that can never exhaust.

Meet the team

Carol Matchett

During my 17 years as a class teacher, engaging children with reading and writing was always a particular interest. I carried out classroom research projects in this area and shared classroom practice with other teachers. I began to write and create my own materials and that's how I eventually became a full-time writer.

I liked to put 'whole books' and stories at the centre to my literacy teaching. I loved that whole sense of sharing a story with a class – laughing together, sharing the edge-of-seat excitement, feeling moved or uplifted by a story… The shared experience is then such a great starting point for discussion, drama, reading and writing. And working on *Literacy Evolve* has given me the chance to explore a whole new set of exciting books.

Golden Moment

I was reading Bernard Ashley stories to a class. A boy – not really an enthusiastic reader – asked if he could borrow the book to read instead of his 'reading book'. It was actually rather more difficult than his usual 'reading book' so I thought he would soon give up. But he didn't. He read the book to me, he read it in quiet reading time; he even took it home to read. As a young teacher I think I learned more from the experience than he did. It showed me the power of books and what really motivates children to read.

Michael Lockwood

I was a teacher for nearly 10 years, specialising in KS2 and Literacy. I've always believed in the power of whole texts read aloud to hook children into books, with or without the special effects. Since leaving the classroom, I've lectured in teacher training, working with the next generation of teachers to develop their strategies for bringing children and texts together. I've also been able to research and write about the teaching of English. In my most recent book, *Promoting Reading for Pleasure in the Primary School* (Sage 2008), I try to show teachers how they can inspire the reading habit and just how important that is. Poetry has always been a special interest of mine and the chance to work on this strand of Literacy Evolve was too good to miss.

Golden Moment

I was reading aloud Mildred Taylor's *Roll of Thunder, Hear My Cry* to a Year 6 class. I'd reached the climax of the novel where the storm in the title happens – and lo and behold the heavens opened outside and a real thunderstorm broke out. I've never had a more spellbound audience. Even the caretaker who was passing by stayed to listen!

The stimulus materials

Novels

"When a book is written, it's written whole. The point of a book is that it should be fun, it should be exciting, it should tell you more about the world around you, it should open your eyes and open your heart, it should make you joyful, it should make you sad – and you can't get this from just taking little snippets from it."

Michael Morpurgo

The joy of reading whole novels aloud to children is central to *Literacy Evolve*. As the stories spark their imagination and interest, children will feel more confident about reading for themselves – another book by the same author, or a story with a similar theme. As they listen to the story unfold and see characters develop, children are encouraged to ask questions and explore the answers for themselves. This is 'comprehension' in its truest sense.

The novels in *Literacy Evolve* have been selected by children's literature experts and trialled in classrooms across the country. They have been selected for their quality, power and teaching potential.

Literacy Evolve assumes that you will read the book to the children in the first instance and has time built in for reading during the sessions. (It is also recommended that teachers read the novel themselves before sharing in class.) If timetable restrictions occasionally mean that a book has to be read independently, simply written chapter summaries in I-Planner Online have been included for children who may have difficulty accessing the text for themselves.

Year 6 (P7) novels

Fantastic, Funny, Frightening

A treasure trove of wonderful stories from authors like Paul Jennings, Jan Mark and Michael Rosen. Each story is a prime example of its genre, whether it be humour, sci-fi or mystery.

Millions by Frank Cottrell Boyce

When a bag stuffed full of money drops out of the sky Damian and Anthony find themselves rich. Very rich indeed. Suddenly the brothers can buy anything they want except the one thing they really need…

An amazing mixture of poignancy and laugh-out-loud humour this Carnegie medal winning book is the *perfect class reader for Year 6.*

Winner of the Carnegie Medal, 2004, shortlisted for the Guardian Children's Fiction Award, and shortlisted for the Blue Peter Book Award.

The stimulus materials

***Eye of the Wolf* by Daniel Pennac**

Born worlds apart: a wolf from the Far North and a boy from Yellow Africa...The wolf has lost nearly everything on his journey to the zoo. The boy too has lost much and seen many terrible things. They stand eye-to-eye on either side of the wolf's enclosure and, slowly, each makes his own extraordinary story known to the other...

Told in flashbacks, the author has woven a narrative that is magical, mysterious and utterly unforgettable. Look into the Eye of the Wolf and you will be captivated.

Winner of the Marsh Award for Children's Literature in Translation.

Poetry Collections

"With the Literacy Evolve project, what we've got are poets talking about why they wrote a poem, how they wrote a poem and where they come from. So we get the possibility of the child engaging with the poet and the poem and that's very, very important."

Michael Rosen

Literacy Evolve doesn't offer just another yearly anthology of poetry. Instead, the whole collection is dedicated to the voice of one poet, such as Benjamin Zephaniah, Grace Nichols or Ted Hughes.

This 'single voice' collection approach means that children get to know the poets as individuals: they understand their views and their style. Additionally, the collections have a 'personal journal' feel to them, with the poets giving insights into their backgrounds and the inspiration behind their poems. All this helps to bring poetry to life for children and increases their understanding and enjoyment.

There are two poetry collections a year (both contained in a single 'flipover' volume).

"I think it's important that children look at and enjoy a volume of poetry by one poet; then they get the voice and they get the point of view. Rather than, you know, a hundred poems about hedgehogs..."

Roger McGough

The stimulus materials

Multi-media

Multi-media is an interactive way for children to engage in reading and also learn about storytelling. This interactive approach will help raise the reading standards of children, while giving them the skills to tackle both traditional and multi-media texts. *Literacy Evolve* has specially chosen this resource for its quality and multi-stranded plot structure, which will help children in their own writing and in their understanding of how a story is structured.

Year 6 (P7) multi-media text

Prison Planet

In the distant future, the human race has been enslaved by an alien race called the CLAWs. It is up to one girl alone, Cal, who is half human and half CLAW to come to Earth to find her mother and overthrow the evil Chief CLAW, who has enslaved all of humanity.

A colourful and imaginative interactive movie that allows the user to choose the destiny of the character by making simple decisions about what actions she should take. Classic in its narrative, and with slick visuals, the story drives forward with the children very much in control of how the protagonist will complete her mission.

The stimulus materials

Unit stimuli

This chart shows the main stimulus pieces across *Literacy Evolve* Key Stage 2 (P4-P7) and how they are matched to units.

Year 3/P4

Narrative Unit 1: *Storm* – novel (Settings)

Narrative Unit 2: *Dragon Slayer* – film (Myths and legends)

Narrative Unit 3: *Ottoline and the Yellow Cat* – novel (Mystery)

Narrative Unit 4: *The Legend of Spud Murphy* – novel (Author study)

Narrative Unit 5: *Dragon Slayer* – film (Play and film scripts)

Poetry Units 1, 2 and 3: Gina Douthwaite, Roger McGough

Year 4/P5

Narrative Unit 1: *Invasion* – novel (Historical settings)

Narrative Unit 2: *The Spiderwick Chronicles* – novel (Fantasy)

Narrative Unit 3: *Christophe's Story* – novel (Other cultures)

Narrative Unit 4: *Lard* – film (Issues)

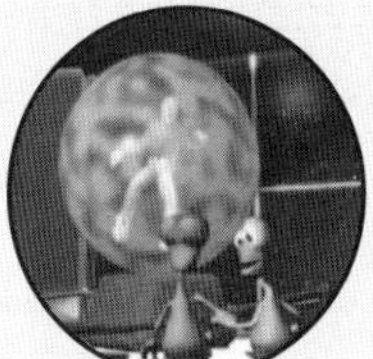

Narrative Unit 5: *Bicho* – film (Play and film scripts)

Poetry Units 1 and 2: Grace Nichols, James Carter

Year 5/P6

Narrative Unit 1: *Friend or Foe* – novel (Author study)

Narrative Unit 2: *The Book* – film (Traditional stories)

Narrative Unit 3: *Oranges in No Man's Land* – novel (Other cultures)

Narrative Unit 4: *Tales of the Family from One End Street* – novel (Classic literature)

Narrative Unit 5: *Magik Circus* – film (Film narrative)

Narrative Unit 6: *News and adverts* – film (Media scripts)

Poetry Units 1, 2 and 3: Michael Rosen, Charles Causley

Year 6/P7

Narrative Unit 1: *Fantastic, Funny, Frightening!* – stories (Genres)

Narrative Unit 2: *Planet Prision* – multi-media text (Multi-modal reading)

Narrative Unit 3: *Millions* – novel (Author study)

Narrative Unit 4: *Eye of the Wolf* – novel (Narrative technique)

Narrative Unit 5: *Fantastic, Funny, Frightening!* – stories (Revision)

Poetry Units 1, 2 and 3: Benjamin Zephaniah, Ted Hughes

The teaching approach

Visual literacy
A focus on visual literacy skills gives children another access point to understanding and responding to the texts.

Open questions
Open-ended questions stimulate meaningful discussion and develop children's confidence in talking about books and ideas.

Active strategies and talk for writing
Talk for writing, speaking, listening and drama strategies mean that the children are active and engaged all through the lesson and are continually preparing for writing. The strategies are highlighted and a glossary is provided on page xvii.

Differentiation
Where appropriate, tasks are differentiated three ways, with three dots indicating tasks for the more able. Often the differentiation ideas are offered in the supporting T/TA notes on I-Planner Online.

Session 12

We are learning to …	Resources
• use drama to explore characters • understand different points of view and how this affects characters' behaviour (PNS Strands 4.1, 7.2) **Assessment Focuses** AF (R): 3	*Lord* (film) PCM: 4.11

Shared teaching

- Share the learning objectives.
- Review Thought Tracking from Session 11 to recap Jake's thoughts and motives in *Lord*.
- Recap the thinking point from Session 11. Take feedback.
- Organise a Forum Theatre activity to show how the other characters in the film felt. Explain that the film follows the main character Jake, but the children will focus on the viewpoint of the other characters.
- Watch the film again. Ask the children to nominate peers to act out the roles of the characters in the film: the two boys, Jake's mum, the neighbour, the old man, the young girl and the shopkeepers. The rest of the children act as directors and explain to the characters what they should do. Use props if appropriate.
- Guide the children while the Forum Theatre takes shape and remind them of the ground rules for large group work. If possible, film the activity to review in the plenary.
- After the Forum Theatre, use Hot-Seating to focus on the two boys. Show 'Quality questions' (PCM 4.11) as a prompt to ask the children playing those characters to explain how they felt and what they thought about what Jake did.

Independent and Guided

- In small groups, Hot-Seat the rest of the characters in *Lord*: Jake's mum, the shopkeepers, the young girl, the neighbour and the old man.

••• Take turns to play a character and answer questions from the rest of the group to explain what they saw and what they thought about it.

•• As above. Focus on Jake's mum and the shopkeepers first. (TA+)

• As above. Use PCM 4.11 as a prompt. (T)

Plenary

- Remind the children that their actions can be perceived differently by different people, depending on their point of view.
- Recap the learning objectives.
- If you filmed the Forum Theatre activity, show the highlights.
- Discuss the viewpoints of the other characters in the film. *Were you surprised by what they thought? Have you changed your view of what happened in the film? How did the hot-seating help you explore the characters?*
- Explain that in Session 13, the children will look more closely at the other characters and what they know about them.

Assessment pointers

- S&L: drama activities will show how far the children can sustain roles and understand the characters.
- AF3 (R): the forum theatre and hot-seating activities show how well the children can interpret information and events from different viewpoints.

Session 13

We are learning to …	Resources
• explore shots, music, words and images in film • explore how film directors use film techniques • choose words and images for particular effects (PNS Strands 2.2, 8.3, 9.5) **Assessment Focuses** AF (R): 5, 6; AF (W): 1, 7	*Lord* (film) ITP: 4.10, 4.11, 4.12 PCM: 4.12

Shared teaching

- Show 'Film shots' (ITP 4.10) to recap film vocabulary learned in Year 3.
- Share the learning objectives. Explain that this session will focus on how the director made the film in order to convey meaning to the viewer, e.g. the choices made about what camera shots and music to use, how the characters should speak and look, etc.
- Watch *Lord* from the beginning to Marker 1. *What do you notice about the way the clip is filmed? How does the director portray the tall boy playing football?* Focus on the way the director films the ball rolling across the road. *Why is the ball rolling filmed at ground level? What effect does this have? What is the effect of the colour of the ball?*
- *As an author how might you write about the ball rolling?* Reflect on work from Phase 1 about expressive and figurative language. Encourage the children to suggest adverbs.
- Watch *Lord* from Marker 1 to Marker 2. Note the camera angles, the close-up of the boy's face and the way he walks towards Jake. *What is the effect of these shots?*
- Show 'How does Jake feel?' (ITP 4.11). Ask for words to describe how Jake felt about the ball while he watched the other boys playing. *Jake obviously wanted to play with the ball. Why? How does he feel when he is bouncing the ball? How does he feel after the ball is flattened?*
- Explain that you're going to put the film sequence into written words. Use Modelled Writing to create a model text or show 'The golden ball' (ITP 4.12) example text.
- Use Think Alouds to show your thought processes while developing the model text, e.g. *Jake was very excited about the ball … how can I convey that? How could I describe the ball? What does it look like? Sound like?* Show or create your own model text.

Independent and Guided

- The children watch *Lord* from Marker 3 to Marker 4 and describe the scene in written words.

••• Write a description of the incident in the shop from the moment Jake enters until he leaves.

•• As above. Use prompts from 'Jake's dilemma in the shop' (PCM 4.12) to structure writing. (T)

• As above. Use PCM 4.12 as a writing frame (TA)

Plenary

- Take feedback and ask for volunteers to share their writing.
- Recap the learning objectives and explain that just like a film director, an author makes choices to get the reader to think and feel certain things. *What tools can an author use?* (E.g. powerful vocabulary, suspense, descriptive and expressive language, etc.)
- Discuss the tools a film director has to work with. *How do music, sound, images and different camera shots change how you feel when watching a film?*

Assessment pointers

- AF5, 6 (R): shared discussions will indicate how far the children understand the effect an author's choice of language has on a reader.
- AF1, 7 (W): written outcomes show how far the children can write imaginatively and use effective vocabulary.

80 Narrative Unit 4: *Lord*

The teaching approach

Objectives
Clear objectives for sharing with the class and evaluating against. Assessment Focuses are also clearly flagged.

PHASE 3: PLANNING AND WRITING A STORY WITH A DILEMMA (7 DAYS)

Session 14

We are learning to …	Resources
• plan writing using planning tools • work together to plan writing (PNS Strands 9.1) **Assessment Focuses** AF (W): 3	ITP: (4.1) PCM: (4.1, 4.2)

Shared teaching

- Recall annotated 'Story mind map' (ITP 4.1). Remind the children of the work they did when they planned their oral stories. *How did the storymaker cards help you to plan?*
- Share the learning objectives. Explain that the children are going to write a story with issues based on a structure like *Lord*, so that the ending opens up another issue or dilemma and leaves the main character on a cliffhanger.
- Discuss what the story should include, e.g. a beginning, middle, end and twist.
- Discuss the audience for the children's stories, e.g. their peer group, and the purpose of a story with a dilemma, e.g. to make people think carefully about the issues raised as well as to entertain.
- As a starting point for ideas, read through the dilemmas collected on the Learning Wall and recall dilemmas in films and stories from earlier sessions.

Independent and Guided

- The children plan in groups, pairs or individually, using a technique of their own choice, e.g. Mind Mapping, Improvisation, etc. Give the children time to explore dilemmas and solutions and provide support according to their needs.

Use 'Storymaker cards 1' (PCM 4.1) and 'Storymaker cards 2' (PCM 4.2) to plan a new dilemma story.

As above. (TA+)

As above. (T+)

Plenary

- Play Just a Minute. Talk Partners take turns to tell the rough sequence of their story.
- Encourage the children to give positive verbal feedback about what they liked in each other's story and why.
- Ask the children to give peer assessment, using thumbs up, down, or half way. *Has your partner got a clear idea of their own story with a dilemma?* Make a note of any thumbs down and support these children in Session 15.
- Recap the learning objectives. *How did you plan your story? Did anyone help you develop your ideas? How?*

Assessment pointers

- S&L: group or pair work will show how far the children can adopt group roles, drawing ideas together and promoting effective discussion.
- AF3 (W): peer assessment and independent planning work will show how far the children can generate imaginative ideas and structure their stories.

Reference to the Interactive Teaching Resource
Interactive teaching pages which support and enliven your shared teaching are clearly referenced.

Session 15

We are learning to …	Resources
• plan writing using planning tools • choose words and images for particular effects (PNS Strands 9.1, 9.5) **Assessment Focuses** AF (W): 3, 4, 7	ITP: 4.13 PCM: (4.1, 4.2), 4.13, 4.14

Shared teaching (1)

- Share the learning objectives. Explain that in this session, the children will continue to develop plans for their stories with a dilemma. Explain that they will need to have a clear plan for your story and know the order in which things happen in the plot before you start writing.
- Recap the notes made in the independent and guided activity in Session 14 and explain that the children are going to take these notes and develop a story plan.

Independent and Guided (1)

- The children work independently to complete 'Dilemma story planner' (PCM 4.13), using notes from 'Storymaker cards 1' (PCM 4.1) and 'Storymaker cards 2' (PCM 4.2). Encourage the children to add figurative and expressive language and adverbs to the plan, that they can use in their story.

Use PCM 4.13. Complete all sections, including the final 'Twist'.

As above. Provide support with the 'Vocabulary' column. (TA+)

As above. If necessary, allow the children to draw scenes from their story plan instead of writing. (T+)

Shared teaching (2)

- Remind the children of the work they did on story structure in Session 10. *How did the director structure the film to make it interesting?*
- Show 'Story plan' (ITP 4.13). Ask for a volunteer to share their ideas from PCM 4.13. Model how to transfer these ideas onto the first screen of ITP 4.13, thinking about the order in which events happen. *What comes next, after I have opened my story and set the scene?*
- Discuss chapters in a story and how they are used. Explain that each step on ITP 4.13 could form a chapter.
- Model completing the second screen of ITP 4.13. Show the children how to use the Learning Wall and other sources to find interesting opening sentences and connectives to use.

Independent and Guided (2)

- The children use annotated PCM 4.13 to complete their 'Story plan' (PCM 4.14).

Complete PCM 4.14 and start thinking about openings and connectives to use in their story. (T)

As above, thinking about openings to use in their story.

As above, concentrating on completing their story plans. (TA+)

Plenary

- Talk Partners peer review each other's plans using thumbs up, down or half way. *Does the story build up to the most exciting part?* Allow the children time to respond to the feedback.
- Recap the learning objectives. *What opening sentences and connectives have you made a note of?*

Assessment pointers

- S&L: pair work will show how well the children can express and respond to opinions.
- AF3, 4, 7 (W): story plans will show how far the children can sequence and structure their stories.

Narrative Unit 4: *Lord* 81

Teaching Assistant or Teacher notes
(T) or (TA) indicates the recommended support for each Independent Activity. A + sign indicates that additional notes are available on I-Planner Online.

Assessment for Learning
Assessment for learning is embedded throughout, including peer review, self-review, marking ladders and success criteria.

Assessment Pointers
Assessment pointers identify relevant evidence for each Assessment Focus, including Speaking and Listening, and help with APP.

Interactive Teaching Resource

The Interactive Teaching Resource (ITR) is the one-stop shop for all the supporting materials you will need to use *Literacy Evolve*. All resources are accessed using a 'player' which provides a range of annotation and editing tools.

The ITR contains:

- Films (up to three per year for Key Stage 2 (P4–P7))
- Videos of author interviews
- Videos of poetry performances by the original poet
- Additional stimulus materials (short stories, extracts, photos, artwork, audio, etc.)
- PDF versions of PCMs (editable versions can be found on I-Planner)
- A wealth of interactive teaching pages which structure and support your lesson in an engaging and interactive way

Navigating the DVD

The ITR is very simple to navigate. You will find references to the pages you require in the teaching notes. These are the Interactive Teaching Pages (ITPs).

To access your desired electronic resource:

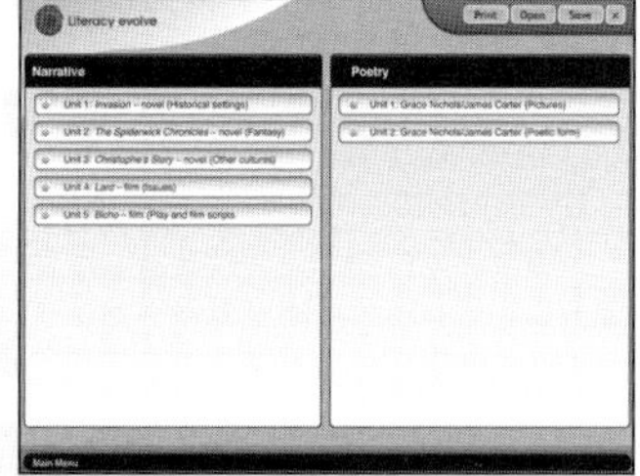

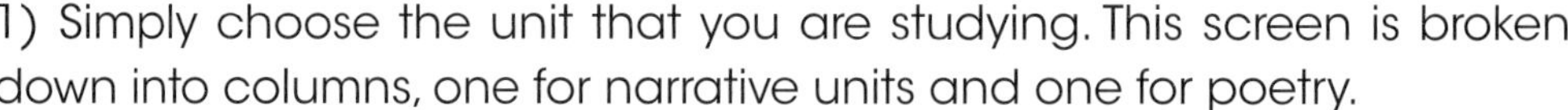

1) Simply choose the unit that you are studying. This screen is broken down into columns, one for narrative units and one for poetry.

2) Once you have opened your chosen unit, you can then select the resource type that you require (as indicated in the lesson plans). From this screen you can access video resources, ITPs and electronic versions of PCMs. (Please note that the Storybooks option is only available for Key Stage 1 units.)

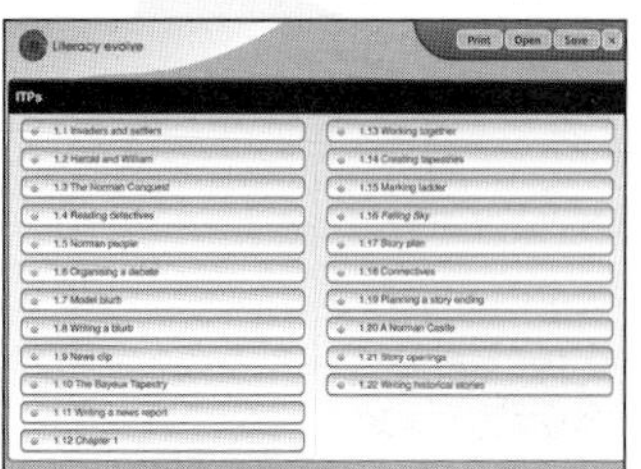

3) When you have clicked on the type of resource that you need, you can then select the specific ITP, film or PCM that you require by checking the relevant number and name of the resource against the lesson plan. Once clicked, the resource will load automatically and is ready to use. You can then navigate to the previous menus via the 'breadcrumb' navigation toolbar at the bottom of the screen.

Interactive Teaching Resource

Toolbar

At the bottom of any activity or video, you will find a toolbar full of features for you to use to annotate the screen.

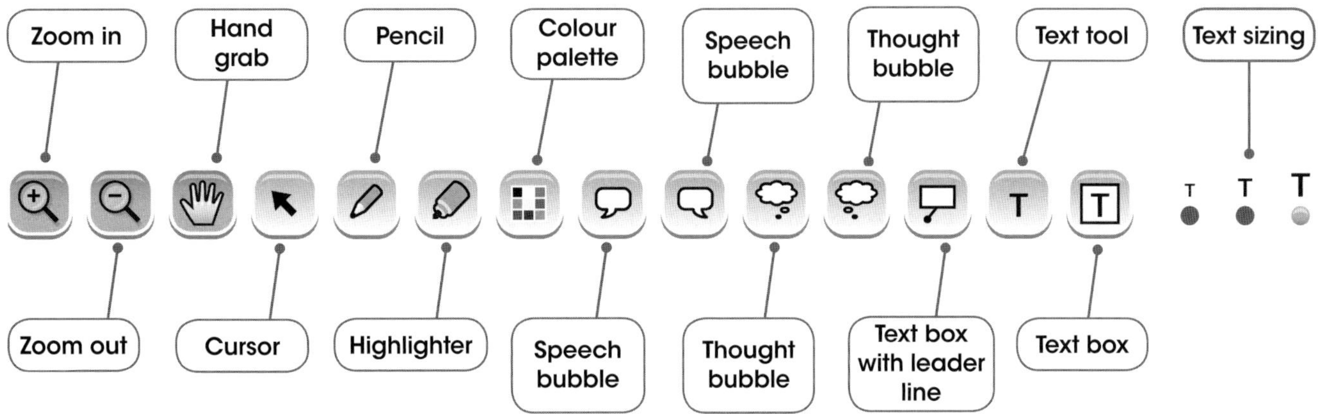

Film Tools (situated next to the annotation toolbar)

There are also a range of film tools available, including film markers, which let you add your own stop/start points to the film.

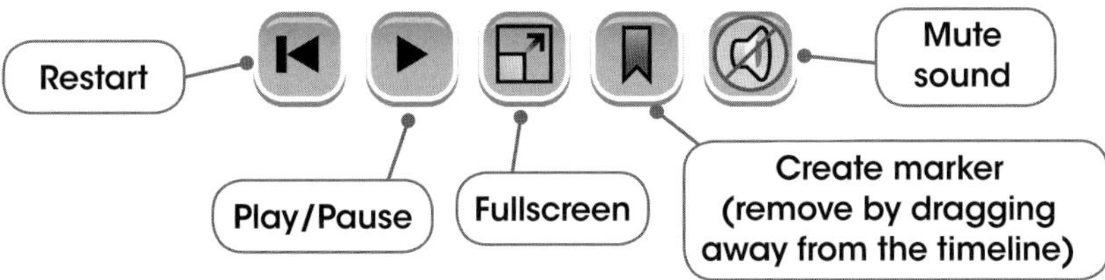

Printing

There is a print button located in the top right-hand corner of the player. Clicking this button will print the current page in view. You simply need to select the printer you wish to use from the list, as with your normal operating system.

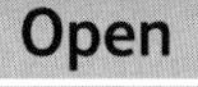

Loading

To load a previously saved screen, simply click the open button in the top right-hand corner of the player. This will then bring up a list of locations on your computer. Find the file that you wish to use and open as normal. This new file will then replace the screen currently open.

Open

Saving

To save your work on a current screen, click the save button located in the top right-hand corner of the player. You can then save the screen to a desired location on your computer.

Exit

This button will close the program completely.

Assessment and I-Planner

Assessment for Learning practices are embedded through *Literacy Evolve*. Objectives are shared and reviewed at the beginning and end of every session. There are many opportunities for self- and peer-assessment, and success criteria are used for children to evaluate their work at each stage of its development.

All the lesson content is matched to Assessment Focuses. Assessment pointers are provided for every session which help you to identify what evidence has been identified for each Assessment Focus.This matches the approach of Assessing Pupil Progress and will help fulfil the requirements of this initiative.

I-Planner Online allows you to record evaluations of your children's learning, and from this will generate 'alerts' to remind you when your assessments are next relevant to your planning.

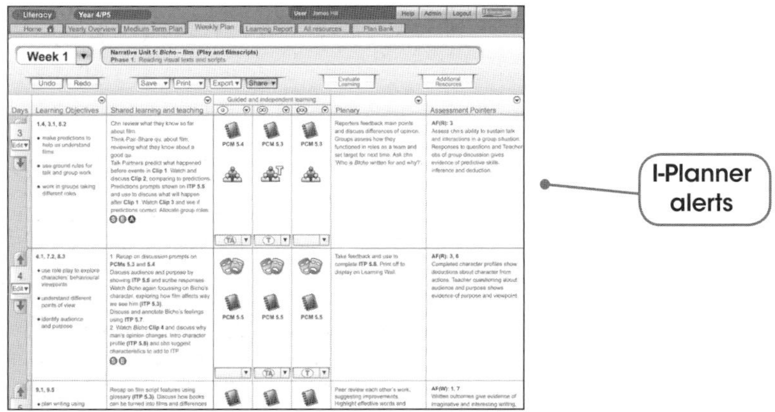

In addition, I-Planner Online will create an ongoing Learning Report to summarise where the class are and which pupils you have identified as needing further support or extension.

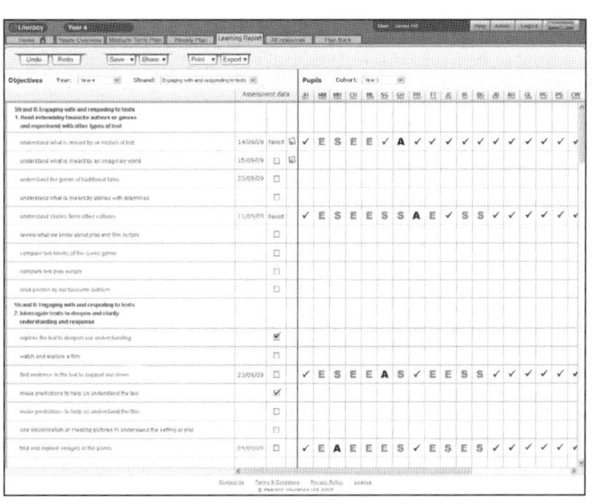

Detailed information on how I-Planner works can be found on the Help tab of I-Planner.

The Learning Report is based on the Renewed Framework objectives. Underneath each of the Framework objectives are the *Literacy Evolve* 'We are learning to …' statements or learning objectives. These break down the broader Framework objectives into smaller chunks. You can use the Evaluate Learning feature in I-Planner Online to quickly assess these objectives and the Learning Report will then show at a glance how much progress your pupils are making towards the overall Framework objectives.

Teaching strategy glossary

Babble Gabble: The children work in pairs to retell a story they have just listened to. One child retells the story as fast as they can, whilst still including as much detail as possible, changing after a minute so their partner continues the tale.

Conscience Alley: One child takes on the role of the character whilst the other children create each side of the alley, putting forth their opposing views as the character walks down. The child in role listens to his 'conscience' before making a decision about the course of action to take.

Envoys: One member of each group moves between the other groups, sharing information and collecting ideas.

Expert Groups: Groups each focus on a specific subject, researching and discussing to become experts on it. (Leads to Jigsawing.)

Fortunately/Unfortunately: Players take it in turns to tell a story which begins alternately with these words, e.g. unfortunately I lost my dinner money on the way to school. Fortunately I don't like school dinners!

Forum Theatre: A small group of children act out a scene, while the rest of the class work as directors.

Freeze Frame: A drama activity where the children use their bodies to form a still image to illustrate a specific incident or event.

Grammar Poetry: Groups try to make up nonsense sentences consisting of an adjective, noun and verb all beginning with the same letter or sound, e.g. angry aardvarks amble.

Hot-Seating: A drama technique where a child takes on the role of a character in the 'hot seat', while the other children ask the character either prepared or improvised questions.

Improvisation: A drama activity that is not planned in any way. The children take on roles and make up the dialogue, actions, etc. as they go along.

Jigsawing: Home groups are given a task to complete. Each member is then given a number and groups of children with the same number are formed (i.e. all the number 1s together) to undertake investigations, discuss their work and agree on the main points to report back to the home group.

Just a Minute: The children speak for one minute on a chosen subject, trying not to hesitate or repeat themselves.

Learning Wall: A place where key ideas, information and success criteria are stored in the classroom, so that children can easily refer to it throughout the sessions.

Mind Map: The children think of ideas about a particular topic, such as the personality traits of a character, the features of a story type, etc. Then they write down these ideas, usually in the form of a diagram.

Modelled Writing: The teacher models the writing process by orally rehearsing before writing, making and explaining out loud decisions and changes, while encouraging the children to share the writing process.

Rainbowing: Discussion is paused and each group is given a different colour. The class is reorganised into colour groups so that the children share ideas with children from other groups.

Role Play: The children take on the roles of different characters to act out a scene.

Role on the Wall: Key words and phrases are placed inside and outside an outline of a character, e.g. character's thoughts placed inside, other characters' opinions on the outside.

Signifier: A drama technique where a prop or item of clothing is used to signify a role being played.

Snowballing: Pairs discuss a subject then join with another pair to form a group and share ideas. Two groups then join together and so on until there is a whole-class discussion.

Statement Game: The children are given a set of cards on which statements are written. They then use the cards to discuss in groups or with a partner to decide how to categorise the statements.

Talk Partners: Pairs talk through and develop ideas together.

Teacher in Role: The teacher takes on the role of a character who is being focused on, in order to introduce, control or develop drama activities.

Think Alouds: Out loud, the teacher explains their thought processes during the writing process. This also includes aspects such as rereading the text to check for sense and making changes to the text, e.g. crossing out, improving words for effect.

Think-Pair-Share: The children are given think time, then talk though ideas with a partner, before sharing ideas with a larger group or the rest of the class.

Think Time: The children are given a brief amount of time to think about a question before answering.

Thought Tracking: The action in a novel or a film is frozen at a key moment and the thoughts of the character are spoken aloud, either by the child in role or by the rest of the group.

Two Stars and a Wish: When reviewing each other's work, the children identify two positive aspects and one negative aspect to feed back on.

Walking Bus: Music is played while the children walk around the classroom. When the music stops, the teacher asks a question which the children discuss with those nearest to them.

Word Tennis: In pairs, each child takes it in turn to say one word or phrase. This either makes up a continuous sentence or is used as a form of word association.

Curriculum Correlation – Proposed Primary Curriculum

Understanding English, communication and languages curriculum progression

	Narrative					Poetry		
LATER	Unit 1 *Fantastic…* (Genres)	Unit 2 *Prison Planet* (Multi-modal reading)	Unit 3 *Millions* (Author study)	Unit 4 *Eye of the Wolf* (Narrative technique)	Unit 5 *Fantastic…* (Revision)	Unit 1 Zephaniah/ Hughes (Imagery)	Unit 2 Zephaniah/ Hughes (Poetic voice)	Unit 3 Zephaniah/ Hughes (Revision)
1. Speaking and listening								
Convey complex ideas, using different techniques for clarity and effect	✔	✔	✔	✔	✔	✔	✔	✔
Select relevant ideas and use appropriate vocabulary to engage and maintain the interest of listeners	✔	✔	✔	✔		✔	✔	✔
Organise and adjust what they say, including the use of spoken standard English, according to the formality of the context, the needs of their listeners and any communication technology being used	✔	✔	✔	✔	✔	✔	✔	✔
Evaluate their own and others' speech and identify how it varies							✔	✔
Sustain different roles, deal with disagreement and vary contributions in group discussion	✔	✔	✔	✔		✔	✔	✔
Extend and justify their opinions and ideas, building on what they have heard	✔	✔	✔	✔	✔	✔	✔	✔
Use dialogue and discussion to build up and refine ideas, move groups on and reach agreement collaboratively	✔	✔	✔	✔		✔	✔	✔
To identify differences between spoken and written language, both on paper and on screen, taking account of context, purpose and audience.		✔	✔		✔		✔	✔
2. Reading								
Use inference and deduction to understand layers of meaning	✔	✔	✔	✔	✔	✔	✔	✔
Make connections and comparisons between different parts of a text and with other texts they have read	✔	✔	✔	✔	✔	✔	✔	✔
Verify the accuracy and reliability of information, including from online sources, detect bias and distinguish evidence from opinion								
Search for information using ICT and other methods and make choices about the appropriateness of the information								
Evaluate techniques used by authors and poets commenting on how effective they are	✔	✔	✔	✔	✔	✔	✔	✔
Recognise and use some conventions for conveying meaning in moving-image and multimodal texts		✔						
Evaluate structural and organisational features, including the use of different presentational devices, layouts and combinations of formats, and their effects	✔	✔	✔	✔	✔	✔	✔	✔
Evaluate ideas and themes that broaden perspectives and extend thinking	✔		✔	✔			✔	✔
Express and justify preferences by referring to the texts	✔	✔	✔	✔	✔	✔	✔	✔
Identify the use of specialist vocabulary and of structures and techniques associated with different forms and purposes of writing	✔	✔		✔	✔	✔	✔	✔

Curriculum Correlation – Proposed Primary Curriculum

Understanding English, communication and languages curriculum progression

	Narrative					Poetry		
LATER	Unit 1 *Fantastic…* (Genres)	Unit 2 *Prison Planet* (Multi-modal reading)	Unit 3 *Millions* (Author study)	Unit 4 *Eye of the Wolf* (Narrative technique)	Unit 5 *Fantastic…* (Revision)	Unit 1 Zephaniah/ Hughes (Imagery)	Unit 2 Zephaniah/ Hughes (Poetic voice)	Unit 3 Zephaniah/ Hughes (Revision)
Critique views, opinions and arguments								
Reflect on viewpoints in narratives and distinguish between those of the characters and those of the author	✔		✔	✔	✔	✔	✔	✔
3. Writing								
Plan, create, shape and review their work, knowing when and how to improve it including the use of ICT	✔	✔	✔	✔	✔	✔	✔	✔
Select form, content, style and vocabulary to suit particular purposes and readers	✔	✔	✔	✔	✔	✔	✔	✔
Combine written text and illustration, moving image and sound, integrating different effects to add power to the words and meanings	✔	✔						
Synthesise ideas using ICT by combining a variety of information from different sources								
Communicate and collaborate with others remotely and in locations beyond the school by selecting and using appropriate ICT								
Use features of layout, presentation and organisation effectively in written and on-screen media	✔	✔	✔	✔	✔	✔	✔	✔
Understand how paragraphs, bullets, hyperlinks, screen layout and headings are used to organise and link ideas, and to use these in their own work	✔	✔	✔	✔	✔			
Explore how ideas are linked within and between sentences	✔		✔	✔	✔			
Function of punctuation within sentences and how to use it to clarify structure and development in what they write	✔	✔		✔	✔			
Recognise and apply common spelling patterns for regular and irregular words, using conventions and spellchecking techniques as well as their knowledge of the origins of words and how spelling has changed over time		✔					✔	
Gain fluency in handwriting and keyboard use	✔	✔	✔	✔			✔	

Curriculum Correlation – Primary Framework

	Narrative					Poetry		
	Unit 1 *Fantastic...* (Genres)	Unit 2 *Prison Planet* (Multi-modal reading)	Unit 3 *Millions* (Author study)	Unit 4 *Eye of the Wolf* (Narrative technique)	Unit 5 *Fantastic...* (Revision)	Unit 1 Zephaniah/ Hughes (Imagery)	Unit 2 Zephaniah/ Hughes (Poetic voice)	Unit 3 Zephaniah/ Hughes (Revision)
1. Speaking								
Use a range of oral techniques to present persuasive arguments and engaging narratives	✔		✔	✔				
Participate in whole-class debate using the conventions and language of debate, including Standard English						✔		
Use the techniques of dialogic talk to explore ideas, topics or issues	✔	✔	✔		✔	✔	✔	✔
2. Listening and responding								
Make notes when listening for a sustained period and discuss how note-taking varies depending on context and purpose								
Analyse and evaluate how speakers present points effectively through use of language and gesture						✔		
Listen for language variation in formal and informal contexts								
Identify the ways spoken language varies according to differences in context and purpose of use								
3. Group discussion and interaction								
Consider examples of conflict and resolution, exploring language used								
Understand and use a variety of ways to criticise constructively and respond to criticism	✔							✔
4. Drama								
Improvise using a range of drama strategies and conventions to explore themes such as hopes, fears, desires	✔	✔	✔	✔	✔			
Consider the overall impact of a live or recorded performance, identifying dramatic ways of conveying characters' ideas and building tension								✔
Devise a performance considering how to adapt the performance for a specific audience								✔
5. Word recognition (objectives covered by the end of Year 2)								
6. Word structure and spelling								
Spell familiar words correctly and employ a range of strategies to spell difficult and unfamiliar words								
Use a range of appropriate strategies to edit, proofread and correct spelling in own work, on paper and on screen								
7. Understanding and interpreting texts								
Appraise a text quickly, deciding on its value/quality/ usefulness	✔							
Understand underlying themes, causes and points of view	✔		✔	✔	✔			✔
Understand how writers use different structures to create coherence and impact	✔	✔		✔	✔			

Curriculum Correlation – Primary Framework

	Narrative					Poetry		
	Unit 1 *Fantastic…* (Genres)	Unit 2 *Prison Planet* (Multi-modal reading)	Unit 3 *Millions* (Author study)	Unit 4 *Eye of the Wolf* (Narrative technique)	Unit 5 *Fantastic…* (Revision)	Unit 1 Zephaniah/ Hughes (Imagery)	Unit 2 Zephaniah/ Hughes (Poetic voice)	Unit 3 Zephaniah/ Hughes (Revision)
Explore how word meanings change when used in different contexts								
Recognise rhetorical devices used to argue, persuade, mislead and sway the reader								
8. Engaging with and responding to texts								
Read extensively and discuss personal reading with others, including in reading groups	✔		✔					
Sustain engagement with longer texts, using different techniques to make the text come alive		✔	✔	✔	✔			
Compare how authors from different times and places present experiences and use language	✔	✔	✔		✔	✔	✔	✔
9. Creating and shaping texts								
Set own challenges to extend achievement and experience in writing	✔	✔	✔	✔	✔			
Use different narrative techniques to engage and entertain the reader	✔	✔	✔	✔	✔			
In non-narrative, establish, balance and maintain viewpoints								
Select words and language drawing on their knowledge of literary features and formal and informal writing	✔			✔	✔			
Integrate words, images and sounds imaginatively for different purposes						✔	✔	
10. Text structure and organisation								
Use varied structures to shape and organise texts coherently	✔	✔	✔					
Use paragraphs to achieve pace and emphasis	✔			✔	✔			
11. Sentence structure and punctuation								
Express subtle distinctions of meaning, including hypothesis, speculation and supposition, by constructing sentences in varied ways	✔	✔	✔	✔	✔			
Use punctuation to clarify meaning in complex sentences	✔	✔		✔	✔			
12. Presentation								
Use different styles of handwriting for different purposes with a range of media, developing a consistent and personal legible style				✔		✔	✔	
Select from a wide range of ICT programs to present text effectively and communicate information and ideas				✔		✔	✔	

Curriculum Correlation – Wales

The National Curriculum for Wales, English correlation chart

	Narrative					Poetry		
Wales Key Stage 2 Programme of Study	Unit 1 *Fantastic…* (Genres)	Unit 2 *Prison Planet* (Multi-modal reading)	Unit 3 *Millions* (Author study)	Unit 4 *Eye of the Wolf* (Narrative technique)	Unit 5 *Fantastic…* (Revision)	Unit 1 Zephaniah/ Hughes (Imagery)	Unit 2 Zephaniah/ Hughes (Poetic voice)	Unit 3 Zephaniah/ Hughes (Revision)
Skills Pupils should be given opportunities to:								
1. listen and view attentively, responding to a wide range of communication	✔	✔	✔	✔	✔	✔	✔	✔
2. identify key points and follow up ideas through question and comment, developing response to others in order to learn through talk	✔	✔	✔	✔	✔	✔	✔	✔
3. communicate clearly and confidently, expressing opinions, adapting talk to audience and purpose, using appropriate gesture, intonation and register in order to engage the listener	✔	✔	✔	✔	✔	✔	✔	✔
4. develop their awareness of the social conventions of conversation and discussion	✔	✔	✔	✔	✔	✔	✔	✔
5. develop their ability to use a range of sentence structures and vocabulary with precision, including terminology that allows them to discuss their work	✔	✔	✔	✔	✔	✔	✔	✔
6. develop their understanding of when it is necessary to use standard English, and use formal and informal language appropriately	✔	✔	✔	✔	✔	✔	✔	✔
7. evaluate their own and others' talk and drama activities and develop understanding of how to improve, considering how speakers adapt their vocabulary, tone, pace and style to suit a range of situations.	✔	✔	✔	✔	✔	✔	✔	✔
Range Pupils should be given opportunities to develop their oral skills through:								
1. seeing and hearing different people talking, including people with different dialects		✔				✔	✔	✔
2. experiencing and responding to a variety of stimuli and ideas: visual, audio and written	✔	✔	✔	✔	✔	✔	✔	✔
3. communicating for a range of purposes, *e.g. presenting information, expressing opinions, explaining ideas, questioning, conveying feelings, persuading*	✔	✔	✔	✔	✔	✔	✔	✔
4. speaking and listening individually, in pairs, in groups and as members of a class	✔	✔	✔	✔	✔	✔	✔	✔
5. using a variety of methods to present ideas, including ICT, *e.g. drama approaches, discussion and debate*	✔	✔	✔	✔	✔	✔	✔	
6. presenting, talking and performing for a variety of audiences	✔	✔	✔	✔	✔	✔	✔	✔
7. increasing their confidence in language use by drawing on their knowledge of English, Welsh and other languages	✔	✔	✔	✔	✔	✔	✔	✔
8. engaging in activities that focus on words, their derivation, meanings, choice and impact.	✔	✔	✔	✔	✔	✔	✔	✔

Curriculum Correlation – Wales

The National Curriculum for Wales, English correlation chart

	Narrative					Poetry		
Wales Key Stage 2 Programme of Study	Unit 1 *Fantastic...* (Genres)	Unit 2 *Prison Planet* (Multi-modal reading)	Unit 3 *Millions* (Author study)	Unit 4 *Eye of the Wolf* (Narrative technique)	Unit 5 *Fantastic...* (Revision)	Unit 1 Zephaniah/ Hughes (Imagery)	Unit 2 Zephaniah/ Hughes (Poetic voice)	Unit 3 Zephaniah/ Hughes (Revision)
Reading Pupils should be given opportunities to:								
1. develop phonic, graphic and grammatical knowledge, word recognition and contextual understanding within a balanced and coherent programme	✔	✔	✔	✔	✔	✔	✔	✔
2. develop their ability to read with fluency, accuracy, understanding and enjoyment	✔	✔	✔	✔	✔	✔	✔	✔
3. read in different ways for different purposes, including:	✔	✔	✔	✔	✔	✔	✔	✔
• skimming, scanning and detailed reading	✔	✔	✔	✔	✔	✔	✔	✔
• using prediction, inference and deduction	✔	✔	✔	✔	✔	✔	✔	✔
• distinguishing between fact and opinion, bias and objectivity in what they read/view								
4. recognise and understand the characteristics of different genres in terms of language, structure and presentation	✔	✔	✔	✔	✔	✔	✔	✔
5. consider what they read / view, responding orally and in writing to the ideas, vocabulary, style, presentation and organisation of image and language, and be able to select evidence to support their views	✔	✔	✔	✔	✔	✔	✔	✔
6a. use a range of appropriate information retrieval strategies including ICT, *e.g. the alphabet, indexes and catalogues*								
6b. retrieve and collate information and ideas from a range of sources including printed, visual, audio, media, ICT and drama in performance	✔							
7. use the knowledge gained from reading to develop their understanding of the structure, vocabulary, grammar and punctuation of English, and of how these clarify meaning	✔	✔	✔	✔	✔			
8. consider how texts change when they are adapted for different media and audiences.		✔	✔	✔	✔			
Range Pupils should be given opportunities to develop their reading / viewing skills through:								
1. becoming enthusiastic and reflective readers	✔	✔	✔	✔	✔	✔	✔	✔
2. reading individually and collaboratively	✔	✔	✔	✔	✔	✔	✔	✔
3. experiencing and responding to a wide range of texts that include:	✔	✔	✔	✔	✔	✔	✔	✔
• information, reference and other non-literary texts, including print, media, moving image and computer-based materials		✔						
• poetry, prose and drama, both traditional and contemporary	✔	✔	✔	✔	✔	✔	✔	✔

Curriculum Correlation – Wales

The National Curriculum for Wales, English correlation chart

	Narrative					Poetry		
Wales Key Stage 2 Programme of Study	Unit 1 *Fantastic…* (Genres)	Unit 2 *Prison Planet* (Multi-modal reading)	Unit 3 *Millions* (Author study)	Unit 4 *Eye of the Wolf* (Narrative technique)	Unit 5 *Fantastic…* (Revision)	Unit 1 Zephaniah/ Hughes (Imagery)	Unit 2 Zephaniah/ Hughes (Poetic voice)	Unit 3 Zephaniah/ Hughes (Revision)
• texts with a Welsh dimension and texts from other cultures				✔		✔	✔	✔
4. reading / viewing extracts and complete texts:	✔	✔	✔	✔	✔	✔	✔	✔
• with challenging subject matter that broadens perspectives and extends thinking, *e.g. environmental issues, sustainability, animal rights, healthy eating*		✔	✔	✔			✔	
• with a variety of structural and organisational features	✔	✔	✔	✔	✔	✔	✔	✔
• that show quality and variety in language use	✔	✔	✔	✔	✔	✔	✔	✔
• that reflect the diversity of society in the twenty-first century	✔		✔	✔	✔	✔	✔	✔
• that reflect individual pupils' personal choice of reading matter.	✔	✔	✔	✔	✔	✔	✔	✔
Writing Pupils should be given opportunities to communicate in writing and to:								
1. use the characteristic features of literary and non-literary texts in their own writing, adapting their style to suit the audience and purpose	✔	✔	✔	✔	✔	✔	✔	
2. use a range of sentence structures, linking them coherently and developing the ability to use paragraphs effectively	✔	✔	✔	✔	✔		✔	✔
3. use punctuation to clarify meaning including full stop, exclamation and question marks, comma, apostrophe, bullet points, speech marks	✔	✔		✔	✔			
4. choose and use appropriate vocabulary	✔	✔	✔	✔	✔	✔	✔	✔
5. use the standard forms of English: nouns, pronouns, adjectives, adverbs, prepositions, connectives and verb tenses	✔	✔	✔	✔	✔			✔
6. develop and use a variety of strategies to enable them to spell correctly		✔					✔	
7. use appropriate vocabulary and terminology to consider and evaluate their own work and that of others	✔	✔	✔	✔	✔	✔	✔	✔
8. draft and improve their work, using ICT as appropriate, to:	✔	✔	✔	✔	✔	✔	✔	✔
• plan	✔	✔	✔	✔	✔	✔	✔	
• draft	✔	✔	✔	✔	✔	✔	✔	✔
• revise	✔	✔	✔	✔	✔	✔	✔	✔
• proofread	✔	✔	✔	✔	✔	✔	✔	
• prepare a final copy	✔	✔		✔		✔	✔	
9. present writing appropriately:	✔	✔	✔	✔		✔	✔	
• developing legible handwriting	✔		✔	✔		✔	✔	

Curriculum Correlation – Wales

The National Curriculum for Wales, English correlation chart

	Narrative					Poetry		
Wales Key Stage 2 Programme of Study	Unit 1 *Fantastic…* (Genres)	Unit 2 *Prison Planet* (Multi-modal reading)	Unit 3 *Millions* (Author study)	Unit 4 *Eye of the Wolf* (Narrative technique)	Unit 5 *Fantastic…* (Revision)	Unit 1 Zephaniah/ Hughes (Imagery)	Unit 2 Zephaniah/ Hughes (Poetic voice)	Unit 3 Zephaniah/ Hughes (Revision)
• using appropriate features of layout and presentation, including ICT.	✔	✔	✔	✔		✔	✔	
Range Pupils should be given opportunities to develop their writing skills through:								
1. writing for a range of purposes, *e.g. to entertain, report, inform, instruct, explain, persuade, recount, describe, imagine and to generate ideas*	✔	✔	✔	✔	✔	✔	✔	✔
2. writing for a range of real or imagined audiences	✔	✔	✔	✔	✔	✔	✔	✔
3. writing in a range of forms	✔	✔	✔	✔	✔	✔	✔	✔
4. writing in response to a wide range of stimuli: visual, audio and written.	✔	✔	✔	✔	✔	✔	✔	✔

Curriculum Correlation – NI

The Northern Ireland Curriculum, Language and Literacy correlation chart

	Narrative					Poetry		
Teachers should enable pupils to develop knowledge, understanding and skills in:	Unit 1 *Fantastic…* (Genres)	Unit 2 *Prison Planet* (Multi-modal reading)	Unit 3 *Millions* (Author study)	Unit 4 *Eye of the Wolf* (Narrative technique)	Unit 5 *Fantastic…* (Revision)	Unit 1 Zephaniah/ Hughes (Imagery)	Unit 2 Zephaniah/ Hughes (Poetic voice)	Unit 3 Zephaniah/ Hughes (Revision)
Talking and listening Pupils should be enabled to:								
listen and respond to a range of fiction, poetry, drama and media texts through the use of traditional and digital resources	✔	✔	✔	✔	✔	✔	✔	✔
tell, re-tell and interpret stories based on memories, personal experiences, literature, imagination and the content of the curriculum	✔	✔	✔	✔	✔	✔	✔	
participate in group and class discussions for a variety of curricular purposes	✔	✔	✔	✔	✔	✔	✔	✔
know, understand and use the conventions of group discussion	✔	✔	✔	✔	✔	✔	✔	✔
share, respond to and evaluate ideas, arguments and points of view and use evidence or reason to justify opinions, actions or proposals	✔	✔	✔	✔	✔	✔	✔	✔
formulate, give and respond to guidance, directions and instructions	✔	✔	✔	✔	✔	✔	✔	✔
participate in a range of drama activities across the curriculum	✔	✔	✔	✔	✔	✔	✔	✔
improvise a scene based on experience, imagination, literature, media and/or curricular topics			✔	✔	✔			
describe and talk about real experiences and imaginary situations and about people, places, events and artefacts	✔	✔	✔	✔	✔	✔	✔	✔
prepare and give a short oral presentation to a familiar group, showing an awareness of audience and including the use of multimedia presentations	✔		✔	✔	✔	✔	✔	✔
identify and ask appropriate questions to seek information, views and feelings	✔	✔	✔	✔	✔	✔		✔
talk with people in a variety of formal and informal situations	✔	✔	✔	✔	✔	✔	✔	✔
use appropriate quality of speech and voice, speaking audibly and varying register, according to the purpose and audience	✔		✔	✔	✔	✔	✔	✔
read aloud, inflecting appropriately, to express thoughts and feelings and emphasise the meaning of what they have read	✔		✔	✔	✔	✔	✔	✔
recognise and discuss features of spoken language, including formal and informal language, dialect and colloquial speech.	✔	✔	✔	✔	✔	✔	✔	✔
Reading Pupils should be enabled to:								
participate in modelled, shared, paired and guided reading experiences	✔	✔	✔	✔	✔	✔	✔	✔
read, explore, understand and make use of a wide range of traditional and digital texts	✔	✔	✔	✔	✔	✔	✔	✔
engage in sustained, independent and silent reading for enjoyment and information								

Curriculum Correlation – NI

The Northern Ireland Curriculum, Language and Literacy correlation chart

	Narrative					Poetry		
Teachers should enable pupils to develop knowledge, understanding and skills in:	Unit 1 *Fantastic…* (Genres)	Unit 2 *Prison Planet* (Multi-modal reading)	Unit 3 *Millions* (Author study)	Unit 4 *Eye of the Wolf* (Narrative technique)	Unit 5 *Fantastic…* (Revision)	Unit 1 Zephaniah/ Hughes (Imagery)	Unit 2 Zephaniah/ Hughes (Poetic voice)	Unit 3 Zephaniah/ Hughes (Revision)
extend the range of their reading and develop their own preferences	✔	✔	✔	✔	✔	✔	✔	✔
use traditional and digital sources to locate, select, evaluate and communicate information relevant for a particular task								
represent their understanding of texts in a range of ways, including visual, oral, dramatic and digital	✔	✔	✔	✔	✔	✔	✔	✔
consider, interpret and discuss texts, exploring the ways in which language can be manipulated in order to affect the reader or engage attention	✔	✔	✔	✔	✔	✔	✔	✔
begin to be aware of how different media present information, ideas and events in different ways		✔	✔	✔	✔	✔	✔	✔
justify their responses logically, by inference, deduction and/or reference to evidence within the text	✔	✔	✔	✔	✔	✔	✔	✔
reconsider their initial response to texts in the light of insight and information which emerge subsequently from their reading	✔		✔	✔	✔			✔
read aloud to the class or teacher from prepared texts, including those composed by themselves, using inflection to assist meaning	✔		✔	✔	✔	✔	✔	✔
use a range of cross-checking strategies to read unfamiliar words in texts								
use a variety of reading skills for different reading purposes.	✔	✔	✔	✔	✔	✔	✔	✔
Writing Pupils should be enabled to:								
participate in modelled, shared, guided and independent writing, including composing onscreen	✔	✔	✔	✔	✔	✔	✔	✔
discuss various features of layout in texts and apply these, as appropriate, within their own writing		✔	✔		✔	✔	✔	
experiment with rhymes, rhythms, verse structure and all kinds of word play and dialect			✔			✔	✔	
write for a variety of purposes and audiences, selecting, planning and using appropriate style and form	✔	✔	✔	✔	✔	✔	✔	✔
use the skills of planning, revising and redrafting to improve their writing, including that which they have composed digitally	✔	✔	✔	✔	✔	✔	✔	✔
express thoughts, feelings and opinions in imaginative and factual writing	✔	✔	✔	✔	✔	✔	✔	✔
use a variety of stylistic features to create mood and effect	✔	✔	✔	✔	✔	✔	✔	
begin to formulate their own personal style	✔	✔	✔	✔	✔	✔	✔	✔
create, organise, refine and present ideas using traditional and digital means, combining text, sound or graphics	✔	✔	✔	✔	✔	✔	✔	✔

Curriculum Correlation – NI

The Northern Ireland Curriculum, Language and Literacy correlation chart

	Narrative					Poetry		
Teachers should enable pupils to develop knowledge, understanding and skills in:	Unit 1 *Fantastic…* (Genres)	Unit 2 *Prison Planet* (Multi-modal reading)	Unit 3 *Millions* (Author study)	Unit 4 *Eye of the Wolf* (Narrative technique)	Unit 5 *Fantastic…* (Revision)	Unit 1 Zephaniah/ Hughes (Imagery)	Unit 2 Zephaniah/ Hughes (Poetic voice)	Unit 3 Zephaniah/ Hughes (Revision)
understand the differences between spoken and written language		✔	✔	✔	✔	✔	✔	✔
use a variety of skills to spell words correctly		✔				✔	✔	
develop increasing competence in the use of grammar and punctuation to create clarity of meaning	✔	✔	✔	✔	✔			
develop a swift and legible style of handwriting.	✔	✔	✔	✔		✔	✔	

Curriculum Correlation – Scotland

The Curriculum for Excellence, Literacy and English correlation chart

	Narrative					Poetry		
SECOND	Unit 1 *Fantastic…* (Genres)	Unit 2 *Prison Planet* (Multi-modal reading)	Unit 3 *Millions* (Author study)	Unit 4 *Eye of the Wolf* (Narrative technique)	Unit 5 *Fantastic…* (Revision)	Unit 1 Zephaniah/ Hughes (Imagery)	Unit 2 Zephaniah/ Hughes (Poetic voice)	Unit 3 Zephaniah/ Hughes (Revision)
Experiences and outcomes The development of literacy skills plays an important role in all learning.								
I develop and extend my literacy skills when I have opportunities to:								
– communicate, collaborate and build relationships	✔	✔	✔	✔	✔	✔	✔	✔
– reflect on and explain my literacy and thinking skills, using feedback to help me improve and sensitively provide useful feedback for others	✔	✔	✔	✔	✔	✔	✔	✔
– engage with and create a wide range of texts in different media, taking advantage of the opportunities offered by ICT	✔	✔	✔	✔	✔	✔	✔	✔
– develop my understanding of what is special, vibrant and valuable about my own and other cultures and their languages				✔		✔	✔	✔
– explore the richness and diversity of language, how it can affect me, and the wide range of ways in which I and others can be creative	✔	✔	✔	✔	✔	✔	✔	✔
– extend and enrich my vocabulary through listening, talking, watching and reading.	✔	✔	✔	✔	✔	✔	✔	✔
In developing my English language skills:								
– I engage with a wide range of texts and am developing an appreciation of the richness and breadth of Scotland's literary and linguistic heritage	✔	✔	✔	✔	✔	✔	✔	✔
– I enjoy exploring and discussing word patterns and text structures.	✔	✔	✔	✔	✔	✔	✔	✔
Listening and talking **Enjoyment and choice** – within a motivating and challenging environment, developing an awareness of the relevance of texts in my life								
I regularly select and listen to or watch texts which I enjoy and find interesting, and I can explain why I prefer certain sources.	✔	✔	✔	✔	✔	✔	✔	✔
I regularly select subject, purpose, format and resources to create texts of my choice. ***LIT 1-01a / LIT 2-01a***	✔	✔	✔	✔	✔	✔	✔	
Tools for listening and talking – to help me when interacting or presenting within and beyond my place of learning								
When I engage with others, I can respond in ways appropriate to my role, show that I value others' contributions and use these to build on thinking. ***LIT 2-02a***	✔	✔	✔	✔	✔	✔	✔	✔
I can recognise how the features of spoken language can help in communication, and I can use what I learn.	✔	✔	✔	✔	✔	✔	✔	✔

Curriculum Correlation – Scotland

The Curriculum for Excellence, Literacy and English correlation chart

	Narrative					Poetry		
SECOND	Unit 1 *Fantastic…* (Genres)	Unit 2 *Prison Planet* (Multi-modal reading)	Unit 3 *Millions* (Author study)	Unit 4 *Eye of the Wolf* (Narrative technique)	Unit 5 *Fantastic…* (Revision)	Unit 1 Zephaniah/ Hughes (Imagery)	Unit 2 Zephaniah/ Hughes (Poetic voice)	Unit 3 Zephaniah/ Hughes (Revision)
I can recognise different features of my own and others' spoken language. ***ENG 2-03a***						✔	✔	✔
Finding and using information – when listening to, watching and talking about texts with increasingly complex ideas, structures and specialist vocabulary								
As I listen or watch, I can identify and discuss the purpose, main ideas and supporting detail contained within the text, and use this information for different purposes. ***LIT 2-04a***								✔
As I listen or watch, I can make notes, organise these under suitable headings and use these to understand ideas and information and create new texts, using my own words as appropriate. ***LIT 2-05a***								
I can select ideas and relevant information, organise these in an appropriate way for my purpose and use suitable vocabulary for my audience. ***LIT 2-06a***								✔
Understanding, analysing and evaluating – investigating and/or appreciating texts with increasingly complex ideas, structures and specialist vocabulary for different purposes								
I can show my understanding of what I listen to or watch by responding to literal, inferential, evaluative and other types of questions, and by asking different kinds of questions of my own. ***LIT 2-07a***	✔	✔	✔	✔	✔	✔	✔	✔
To help me develop an informed view, I can distinguish fact from opinion, and I am learning to recognise when my sources try to influence me and how useful these are. ***LIT 2-08a***								
Creating texts – applying the elements others use to create different types of short and extended texts with increasingly complex ideas, structures and vocabulary								
When listening and talking with others for different purposes, I can:	✔	✔	✔	✔	✔	✔	✔	✔
– share information, experiences and opinions	✔	✔	✔	✔	✔	✔	✔	✔
– explain processes and ideas	✔	✔	✔	✔	✔	✔	✔	✔
– identify issues raised and summarise main points or findings	✔	✔	✔	✔	✔	✔	✔	✔
– clarify points by asking questions or by asking others to say more. ***LIT 2-09a***	✔	✔	✔	✔	✔	✔	✔	✔

Curriculum Correlation – Scotland

The Curriculum for Excellence, Literacy and English correlation chart

	Narrative					Poetry		
SECOND	Unit 1 *Fantastic...* (Genres)	Unit 2 *Prison Planet* (Multi-modal reading)	Unit 3 *Millions* (Author study)	Unit 4 *Eye of the Wolf* (Narrative technique)	Unit 5 *Fantastic...* (Revision)	Unit 1 Zephaniah/ Hughes (Imagery)	Unit 2 Zephaniah/ Hughes (Poetic voice)	Unit 3 Zephaniah/ Hughes (Revision)
I am developing confidence when engaging with others within and beyond my place of learning. I can communicate in a clear, expressive way and I am learning to select and organise resources independently.	✔	✔	✔	✔	✔	✔	✔	✔
Reading **Enjoyment and choice** – within a motivating and challenging environment, developing an awareness of the relevance of texts in my life								
I regularly select and read, listen to or watch texts which I enjoy and find interesting, and I can explain why I prefer certain texts and authors. ***LIT 1-11a / LIT 2-11a***	✔	✔	✔	✔	✔	✔	✔	✔
Tools for reading – to help me use texts with increasingly complex or unfamiliar ideas, structures and vocabulary within and beyond my place of learning								
Through developing my knowledge of context clues, punctuation, grammar and layout, I can read unfamiliar texts with increasing fluency, understanding and expression.	✔	✔	✔	✔	✔	✔	✔	
I can select and use a range of strategies and resources before I read, and as I read, to make meaning clear and give reasons for my selection. ***LIT 2-13a***								
Finding and using information – when reading and using fiction and non-fiction texts with increasingly complex ideas, structures and specialist vocabulary								
Using what I know about the features of different types of texts, I can find, select and sort information from a variety of sources and use this for different purposes. ***LIT 2-14a***								
I can make notes, organise them under suitable headings and use them to understand information, develop my thinking, explore problems and create new texts, using my own words as appropriate. ***LIT 2-15a***								
Understanding, analysing and evaluating – investigating and/or appreciating fiction and non-fiction texts with increasingly complex ideas, structures and specialist vocabulary for different purposes								
To show my understanding across different areas of learning, I can identify and consider the purpose and main ideas of a text and use supporting detail. ***LIT 2-16a***	✔	✔	✔	✔	✔	✔	✔	✔

Curriculum Correlation – Scotland

The Curriculum for Excellence, Literacy and English correlation chart

	Narrative					Poetry		
SECOND	Unit 1 *Fantastic…* (Genres)	Unit 2 *Prison Planet* (Multi-modal reading)	Unit 3 *Millions* (Author study)	Unit 4 *Eye of the Wolf* (Narrative technique)	Unit 5 *Fantastic…* (Revision)	Unit 1 Zephaniah/ Hughes (Imagery)	Unit 2 Zephaniah/ Hughes (Poetic voice)	Unit 3 Zephaniah/ Hughes (Revision)
To show my understanding, I can respond to literal, inferential and evaluative questions and other close reading tasks and can create different kinds of questions of my own. ENG 2-17a	✔	✔	✔	✔	✔	✔	✔	✔
To help me develop an informed view, I can identify and explain the difference between fact and opinion, recognise when I am being influenced, *and have assessed how useful and believable my sources are.* ***LIT 2-18a***								
I can:								
– discuss structure, characterisation and/or setting	✔	✔	✔	✔	✔	✔	✔	✔
– recognise the relevance of the writer's theme and how this relates to my own and others' experiences	✔	✔	✔	✔	✔	✔	✔	✔
– discuss the writer's style and other features appropriate to genre. ENG 2-19a	✔	✔	✔	✔	✔	✔	✔	✔
Writing **Enjoyment and choice** – within a motivating and challenging environment, developing an awareness of the relevance of texts in my life								
I enjoy creating texts of my choice and I regularly select subject, purpose, format and resources to suit the needs of my audience. ***LIT 1-20a / LIT 2-20a***	✔	✔	✔	✔	✔	✔	✔	
Tools for writing – using knowledge of technical aspects to help my writing communicate effectively within and beyond my place of learning								
I can spell most of the words I need to communicate, using spelling rules, specialist vocabulary, self-correction techniques and a range of resources. ***LIT 2-21a***		✔					✔	
In both short and extended texts, I can use appropriate punctuation, vary my sentence structures and divide my work into paragraphs in a way that makes sense to my reader. ***LIT 2-22a***	✔	✔	✔	✔				
Throughout the writing process, I can check that my writing makes sense and meets its purpose. ***LIT 2-23a***	✔	✔	✔	✔	✔	✔	✔	✔
I consider the impact that layout and presentation will have and can combine lettering, graphics and other features to engage my reader. ***LIT 2-24a***	✔			✔	✔	✔	✔	
Organising and using information – considering texts to help create short and extended texts for different purposes								

Curriculum Correlation – Scotland

The Curriculum for Excellence, Literacy and English correlation chart

	Narrative					Poetry		
SECOND	Unit 1 *Fantastic…* (Genres)	Unit 2 *Prison Planet* (Multi-modal reading)	Unit 3 *Millions* (Author study)	Unit 4 *Eye of the Wolf* (Narrative technique)	Unit 5 *Fantastic…* (Revision)	Unit 1 Zephaniah/ Hughes (Imagery)	Unit 2 Zephaniah/ Hughes (Poetic voice)	Unit 3 Zephaniah/ Hughes (Revision)
I can use my notes and other types of writing to help me understand information and ideas, *explore problems, make decisions, generate and develop ideas or create new text.*			✔	✔				
I recognise the need to acknowledge my sources and can do this appropriately. ***LIT 2-25a***								
By considering the type of text I am creating, I can select ideas and relevant information, organise these in an appropriate way for my purpose and use suitable vocabulary for my audience. ***LIT 2-26a***			✔					✔
Creating texts – applying the elements which writers use to create different types of short and extended texts with increasingly complex ideas, structures and vocabulary								
I am learning to use language and style in a way which engages and/or influences my reader. ***ENG 2-27a***	✔	✔	✔	✔	✔	✔	✔	
I can convey information, describe events, explain processes or combine ideas in different ways. ***LIT 2-28a***	✔	✔	✔	✔	✔	✔	✔	✔
I can persuade, argue, explore issues or express an opinion using relevant supporting detail and/or evidence. ***LIT 2-29a***	✔		✔		✔		✔	✔
As I write for different purposes and readers, I can describe and share my experiences, expressing what they made me think about and how they made me feel. ***ENG 2-30a***	✔				✔	✔	✔	✔
Having explored the elements which authors use in different genres, I can use what I learn to create stories, poems and plays with an interesting and appropriate structure, interesting characters and/or settings which come to life. ***ENG 2-31a***	✔	✔	✔	✔	✔	✔	✔	

Narrative Unit 1

FANTASTIC, FUNNY, FRIGHTENING! – stories (Genres)

Medium term plan (4 weeks)	
Phase	**Learning Outcomes**
Phase 1: Exploring genre; speaking and listening (2 days)	• Children can identify different fiction genres and explain some of their key features. • Children can explain reading preferences in terms of different genres.
Phase 2: Reading and analysing short stories in different genres (10 days)	• Children can use different strategies to engage with stories from a variety of genres. • Children can analyse the language and structure of a range of fiction genres.
Phase 3: Writing a short story in a chosen genre (8 days)	• Children can plan, write and improve a short story in a particular genre that engages the reader and uses appropriate language and structural features.

Narrative Unit 1

FANTASTIC, FUNNY, FRIGHTENING!

Big picture

The children begin to explore the idea of genre, identifying typical genre features by looking at a range of story openings, covers, titles and blurbs. They discuss the genre expectations set up by these features and begin to classify examples. They then extend their understanding by reading, responding to and then analysing short stories in five different genres from the anthology *Fantastic, Funny, Frightening!* This analysis of key features, characters, themes, structure and language then feeds into their own writing when they write a short story in a genre of their choice.

Prior learning

This unit assumes that the children can already:

- identify and discuss characters, dilemmas, settings, simple themes and the author's intentions
- use different techniques to plot out the structure of stories.
- identify some of the ways language is used for effect
- discuss their responses to stories in groups
- use a range of strategies to explore their understanding of stories
- plan the main stages of a story and use their plan to write the story.

Key aspects of learning

Communication: Work collaboratively in pairs and groups.
Creative thinking: Use powerful language to create a specific effect.
Empathy: Empathise with characters in stories.
Enquiry: Respond to puzzles in stories by asking questions; question meanings and implications of story details.
Evaluation: Justify their views and opinions; evaluate stories, their own work and that of others against agreed success criteria.
Reasoning: Give reasons for opinions, making inferences from the text.

Progression in narrative

In this unit the children will:

- identify genre features and recognise challenges to stereotypes.
- write and evaluate effective story endings.
- understand how the time of writing and the intended audience influence style; and how authors use language to influence readers.
- recognise how authors use dialogue to create various effects.
- experiment with different narrative styles.
- plan and structure their own narrative writing.

Cross-curricular links

Art: The children could produce artwork conveying the different moods of different genres.
Citizenship: Link with themes of rules, laws and responsibility.
Design and Technology: Produce a class anthology of stories.
Science and ICT: Explore how the science fiction genre is based on real science and technology ideas.

PHASE 1: EXPLORING GENRE; SPEAKING AND LISTENING (2 DAYS)

Session 1

We are learning to …	Resources
• use talk to explore story genres • identify different story genres (PNS Strands 1.3, 7.3) **Assessment Focuses** AF (R): 7	ITP: 1.1 PCM: 1.1, 1.2

Shared teaching

- Introduce 'The Big Picture' for the unit and share the learning objectives.
- Introduce the idea of fiction genres by discussing how fiction books are classified in bookshops, libraries or databases. *What genres can you think of?* (E.g. adventure, crime, romance, humour.) Start a list on the Learning Wall.
- *Let's think about what we mean by a genre.* Allow Think Time and then invite responses, encouraging the children to reflect on their contributions and extend their thinking. *Do you agree with that? Is there anything else you'd like to add? So if two stories are set on a farm, do we put them in a 'farm genre'?*
- Show 'Story openers' (ITP 1.1). *Let's be reading detectives and decide what genre these books might be.* Discuss any predictions based on the titles and the reasons for these.
- Click on one or two of the titles to display the opening of the story. Talk Partners discuss what type of story it is. *How do you know?* Take feedback; identifying features that provide clues or evidence that suggest the genre, e.g. details about setting, characters, the event, the mood, etc. Repeat with the other title.
- Explain that stories don't always fit neatly into one genre and can fit into more than one, e.g. a fantasy adventure and a 'rom-com'. *Can anyone think of examples of books that could be classified into more than one genre?*

Independent and Guided

- Provide groups with a selection of books or 'Story openers' (PCM 1.1) to classify into genres. If groups are using real books, they use the cover, blurb, opening paragraph and chapter headings to help classify the books. The children discuss ideas and support their views with reference to the books or the book blurbs.

(ooo) Choose a genre and make notes of the evidence of typical features on 'Genre bookmarks' (PCM 1.2).

(oo) As above. (T+)

(o) Record evidence on sticky notes attached to the books. (TA+)

Plenary

- Recap the learning objectives. Share classifications and the reasons for them.
- Add more genres to the list on the Learning Wall, together with examples from the discussion or the children's own reading.
- *What have you learned about genre?* (E.g. a genre is a set of texts with a number of similarities.)
- Add work from this session to the Learning Wall for future reference.

Assessment pointers

- S&L: group work will show how far the children can engage with others, draw ideas together and promote discussion.
- AF7 (R): response to questions, group discussions and completed PCMs or sticky notes show how far the children are able to identify and comment on typical features of a range of genres.

Session 2

We are learning to ...	Resources
• use talk to explore story genres • explain our personal preferences for particular genres (PNS Strands 1.3, 8.1) **Assessment Focuses** AF (R): 6, 7	ITP: (1.1), 1.2 PCM: 1.3, 1.4

Shared teaching (1)

- Recap the genres listed in Session 1 and share the learning objectives.
- Take a vote on the most popular genre(s). *What makes genre stories enjoyable to read? What do you want from a good genre story?* Allow Think Time, then invite feedback, encouraging discussion of expectations, key features, author's purpose and effect on the reader.
- Recall 'Story openers' (ITP 1.1), recapping how the children classified the books in Session 1. *Which would you most like or least like to read?*
- Focus the discussion on expectations set up by the opening lines and the genre. *What might you expect to find in this type of story? What do you think it will be about? What might happen? How might it end? What about the style and how the story is told? Does this influence your choice? Would it make you want to read it?*
- Show 'Genre ingredients' (ITP 1.2). Use the children's ideas so far and their notes from Session 1 to fill in features for the first genre: traditional fairy tales. *What are the key features of books in this genre?*

Independent and Guided (1)

- Give each group 'Genre ingredients' (PCM 1.3) to complete, each with a different genre written in the middle: dilemma stories, sci-fi/fantasy, horror and humour. Support the children with an identified need. (T/TA)

Shared teaching (2)

- Invite each group to feed back and fill in the relevant charts on ITP 1.2. Encourage the rest of the class to offer further suggestions to add to the chart.
- Explain that they are now going to discuss their favourite genres and choose one more genre to look at in detail.

Independent and Guided (2)

- Groups are given 'Genre cards' (PCM 1.4) to use for discussion.

ooo Select a genre and prepare a presentation of annotated extracts to represent the chosen genre. (TA+)

oo Select a genre and make a list of reading suggestions for the chosen genre, with notes relating to key features.

o Explore the preferred genres, discussing those on PCM 1.4. (T+)

Plenary

- Recap the learning objectives.
- Groups present their work, explaining their preferred genre and choice of extracts or recommendations. Add any further features to ITP 1.2.
- Discuss how our preference for a particular genre often leads our choice of books. *Is this always a good thing?*

Assessment pointers

- S&L: group work will show how far the children can adopt group roles, drawing ideas together and promoting effective discussion.
- AF6, 7 (R): group discussion and completed PCMs show how far the children understand an author's purpose and effect and show their appreciation of context and traditions of different genres.

PHASE 2 READING AND ANALYSING SHORT STORIES IN DIFFERENT GENRES (10 DAYS)

Session 3

We are learning to ...	Resources
• use talk to explore story genres • explore themes in stories and poems • express personal response, saying why and how a text affects us (PNS Strands 1.3, 7.2, 8.1) **Assessment Focuses** AF (R): 2, 3, 6, 7	*Fantastic, Funny, Frightening!* PCM: 1.5

Shared teaching

- Recap 'The Big Picture' and share the learning objectives.
- Show the contents page of *Fantastic, Funny, Frightening! What type of story is* The Glass Cupboard*? What do you expect from a traditional tale?* Recap key features, e.g. typical characters, events, endings, often an old story with no known author.
- *Do you enjoy traditional stories and fairy tales?* Encourage extended answers, e.g. not just saying 'boring'. *What makes you say that?*
- Read *The Glass Cupboard* (pages 1–7) from *Fantastic, Funny, Frightening!*, with the children following in their own books. Pause for thought at the end, then take responses. *What do you think now? Was it what you expected? Did you enjoy it more or less than you thought? Did anything surprise you?* Take feedback.
- Talk Partners discuss the last page of the story, beginning at 'And when the King heard ... ' (page 7). *Was this a surprising ending? What does it mean? How is the Earth like the glass cupboard? Can you think of some real-life examples that show how the Earth is fragile?*
- Discuss whether the children think this is a traditional tale. *Many traditional tales have a message or theme, but is this a traditional tale? When do you think it was written? What makes you say that?* Point out the original publication date on the acknowledgements page at the back of the book. *How has the author updated the typical theme?*
- *Although it is a modern tale it uses familiar ingredients from traditional tales.* Talk Partners look back and list familiar ingredients they noticed. Take feedback, e.g. magic object, character types, themes, etc.

Independent and Guided

- Pairs explore characters, themes or events in *The Glass Cupboard* and make comparisons with other traditional tales, looking for similarities and differences. Pairs Snowball to compare findings within groups.

ooo Look for themes in the story. (T+)

oo Look at words that describe typical fairy tale characters. See 'Traditional tales' (PCM 1.5).

o Compare the characters in the story with the characters in another familiar fairy tale. (TA+)

Plenary

- Recap the learning objectives. Share ideas about characters, themes and events. *How is* The Glass Cupboard *similar or different from traditional fairy tales? How does it develop the genre? Do the characters fit the usual stereotypes?* (E.g. kings are traditionally cruel.) *How has the author adapted the traditional tale format to make it suitable for older readers?*

Assessment pointers

- S&L: pair work will show how well the children can express and explain relevant ideas.
- AF2, 3 (R): responses to questions and group work show how far the children are able to retrieve and interpret information from texts.
- AF6, 7 (R): responses to questions and feedback show how far the children understand the author's purpose and the effect on the reader and how far they can make comparisons between texts.

Session 4

We are learning to …	Resources
• explain how time is conveyed in traditional tales • identify style and language features of traditional tales • talk about how authors of the past used language differently (PNS Strands 7.3, 8.3) **Assessment Focuses** AF (R): 2, 4, 5, 7	*Fantastic, Funny, Frightening!* ITP: (1.2), 1.3, 1.4, 1.5

Shared teaching

- Use 'Genre ingredients' (ITP 1.2) to recap and note key traditional tale features, e.g. characters, events, themes.
- Share the learning objectives and explain that, today, the children are going to focus on how the author uses a traditional tale story structure and style to create a fairy-story feel.
- Show 'Story track' (ITP 1.3). Invite a child to put the events in order. Explain that traditional tales have simple structures to make them easy to remember, e.g. an event to start the story off, a sequence of follow-up events, some repeated. Discuss other fairy tale structures. *How do they start? Is there anything that connects the different stories?*
- Look at *The Glass Cupboard* (pages 1–7) from *Fantastic, Funny, Frightening!* and discuss the sequence of events. *How much time passes in* The Glass Cupboard*? How is time conveyed?* Talk Partners look for time-related phrases in the story, e.g. 'And all that day and all that night' (page 5); 'Sometime later' (page 6). Share findings and add to the Learning Wall.
- Show '*The Glass Cupboard*' (ITP 1.4) and focus on style. *What makes it effective? Why does it sound like a fairy tale? What clues are there in the language or style?* Talk Partners identify features.
- Take feedback and use Modelled Writing to highlight and annotate the text on ITP 1.4, e.g. typical opening ('There was once'); addressing the reader ('If you wanted'); sentence openers ('Now … '); repeated patterns and building up ideas in threes ('If you wanted … ', 'Or if you wanted … ', 'Even if you wanted … ').
- Read '*Rumpelstiltskin*' (ITP 1.5). *Does it have the same style and language features? What language features give clues to the age of the story?* (E.g. 'he had not two farthings … '; 'on the morrow'.)

Independent and Guided

- Pairs analyse passages from *The Glass Cupboard* and *Rumpelstiltskin*, making notes on style and language features.

(ooo) Make notes on *Rumpelstiltskin* from ITP 1.5, another passage from *The Glass Cupboard* and, if possible, another fairy tale. (TA+)

(oo) Make notes on another passage from *The Glass Cupboard* and, if possible, another fairy tale.

(o) Make notes on another passage from *The Glass Cupboard*. (T)

Plenary

- Take feedback. Add any new ideas or examples to ITP 1.2.
- Recap the learning objectives and summarise key ideas from ITP 1.2. *What makes a good modern fairy tale?*

Assessment pointers

- S&L: pair work will show how well the children can express relevant ideas.
- AF2, 4 (R): pair work will indicate how far the children can understand structure and identify organisational features.
- AF5, 7 (R): response to questions and pair work show how far the children are able to comment on language features and relate texts to literary traditions.

Session 5

We are learning to …	Resources
• use drama to understand characters • comment on the impact and effectiveness of a story • discuss themes, motives and feelings in stories (PNS Strands 4.1, 7.1, 7.2) **Assessment Focuses** AF (R): 2, 3, 6	*Fantastic, Funny, Frightening!* ITP: (1.2) PCM: 1.6

Shared teaching

- Ask the children to open their copies of *Fantastic, Funny, Frightening!* and turn to the contents page. *What type of story is* The Balaclava Story*? What do we expect to find in this type of story? What sort of dilemmas might characters face? Do you usually enjoy this type of story? What's the appeal?* (E.g. familiar real-life issues and situations; interesting characters you can relate to.) *What do you feel or think when you read this type of story?* (E.g. empathise with characters; relate the story to personal experiences and feelings.)
- Read *The Balaclava Story* to 'Oh heck.' (page 39), encouraging the children to empathise with the characters and relate the story to personal experiences and feelings.
- At page 39, encourage empathy. *Imagine how he feels. What if it were you? What is his biggest fear? What is the worst thing that could happen?* Talk Partners take turns to make statements, thinking in role and referring closely to the text.
- Explore the main character's motives. *Why did he do it? Why does he want to be a Balaclava Boy?* Extend simple answers, e.g. 'because Barry and Tony were Balaclava Boys', to develop thinking about themes such as friendship and peer pressure.
- Model relating events to personal experience, e.g. *I remember when I was at school, everyone had … , apart from me. Does the story remind you of something that has happened to you? Can you relate to any of it?* Think-Pair-Share ideas, taking care to be sensitive to individual children's personal experiences and circumstances.
- Encourage predictions. *What could, should or will the main character do? What might happen then?* Think-Pair-Share ideas.
- Read to the end of the story.

Independent and Guided

- In pairs, or small groups, the children explore the central character and themes of *The Balaclava Story*.

(ooo) Hot-Seat the main characters to explore the themes.

(oo) Track the thoughts and feelings of the main character in the scene back at home (pages 41–44). (T+)

(o) Complete 'Thought tracking' (PCM 1.6). (TA)

Plenary

- Share ideas about the main character and themes. Note these on the appropriate screen of 'Genre ingredients' (ITP 1.2).
- Recap the learning objectives.
- Discuss the story as a whole. *Is this a good story? Why do we empathise with the main character and relate to the situations? Did you enjoy this type of story?*

Assessment pointers

- S&L: drama activites will show how well the children can create and sustain roles to explore issues.
- AF2, 3 (R): responses to questions and group and pair work show how far the children can make inferences.
- AF6 (R): discussion will show the children's understanding of the author's purposes and the intended effect on the reader.

Session 6

We are learning to …	Resources
• identify typical style and language features of real-life stories • identify language clues that suggest when a text was written (PNS Strands 8.3) **Assessment Focuses** AF (R): 4, 5	*Fantastic, Funny, Frightening!* ITP: (1.2) 1.6 PCM: 1.7

Shared teaching

- Talk Partners play Just a Minute, retelling *The Balaclava Story* (pages 31–46) from *Fantastic, Funny, Frightening!*
- Take feedback. *What did you like best? What was your favourite part?*
- Share the learning objectives and explain that, today, the children will look at how the style and story structure added to its effectiveness.
- Read '*The Balaclava Story*' (ITP 1.6). *Why is this paragraph crucial? How is the idea developed in the paragraph*? (E.g. the event is introduced and the response/thoughts of the character shown.)
- *The story has a distinctive style and tone. How would you describe it? How is this effect created?*
- Highlight key language features on ITP 1.6, discussing the effects. *Why did the author use 'pinch' rather than 'steal'? Why has the author used dashes and ellipses?*
- Talk Partners find and read a new section of dialogue from *The Balaclava Story*, with appropriate expression. *What do you notice about the language used in the dialogue?* (E.g. informal; natural; shortened forms; phrases and single words; slang; dialect.)
- *What clues does the language give about when and where the story was written? Did you think the age of the story spoilt it in any way?*
- Begin to focus on the story structure. *How does the author keep us interested and on tenterhooks?* Reread the opening few lines. *What makes it a good opening*? (E.g. we are thrown straight into the story; it introduces the problem straight away; the first sentence is intriguing.)
- Reread the ending. *Why is this so effective*? (E.g. a sudden surprise; the punchline is humorous and relieves the tension.)

Independent and Guided

- The children work in pairs to analyse the plot structure of *The Balaclava Story* and Snowball to compare findings.

ooo Plot the events of the story on a tension graph or, if possible, compare the structure of *The Balaclava Story* with other stories in this genre. (T+)

oo Plot the events of the story on a tension graph. (TA)

o Plot the events of the story on 'Story plan' (PCM 1.7).

Plenary

- Take feedback and add responses to the Learning Wall. *How has the author built up the story for maximum impact?* (E.g. making us wait right to the end; introducing further complications.)
- Recap the learning objectives. Summarise language and structural features of the genre on 'Genre ingredients' (ITP 1.2).
- *What made this a good example of a dilemma story? Are there any new points you can add?*

Assessment pointers

- S&L: pair work will show how well the children can express and explain relevant ideas.
- AF4, 5 (R): discussion and independent work show how far the children understand plot structure and the author's use of language.

Session 7

We are learning to …	Resources
• see how an author creates interest through how they reveal events • analyse how authors use language and other techniques to create particular settings and worlds (PNS Strands 7.3, 8.3) **Assessment Focuses** AF (R): 5, 6, 7	*Fantastic, Funny, Frightening!* ITP: (1.2)

Shared teaching

- Ask the children to turn to the contents page in their copies of *Fantastic, Funny and Frightening! What type of story is* Virtually True*? Who prefers sci-fi or fantasy stories to dilemma stories?*
- Take predictions based on the title and genre expectations. *What might this story be about? Where do you think it will be set?*
- Read *Virtually True* (pages 47–68) from *Fantastic, Funny, Frightening!*, as far as '… the crazier the situation seemed to be' (page 49). Encourage responses. *Is it what you expected? Does it sound like a sci-fi or fantasy story so far?*
- Share the learning objectives and discuss the effectiveness of the opening and any puzzles. Encourage the children to Think-Pair-Share questions raised by the opening using 'I wonder … ' sentences, e.g. *I wonder how the narrator knows Sebastian Schultz.* Save for later.
- Discuss how the intrigue has been created, e.g. starting in the middle of the story, hooking us in with a puzzle, showing the narrator's immediate thoughts and reactions.
- Read as far as '… *Dragonquest* would have to wait' (page 55). *This is more like what we expected. What sci-fi or fantasy elements have you noticed? Does it remind you of any other stories?*
- *Have any of our questions been answered? What do you think is happening?* The children exchange views, referring back to the text.
- Take predictions and add them to the Learning Wall. *What might happen in the 'Dragonquest' game?*
- Read the 'Dragonquest' and 'Jailbreak' episodes, from page 55 as far as 'GAME OVER' (page 61), encouraging the children to look for answers to their puzzles.

Independent and Guided

- Pairs collect examples of descriptive and emotive language used to create fantasy worlds and build excitement in *Virtually True*.

ooo Focus on the 'Dragonquest' and 'Jailbreak' episodes.

oo As above. (T+)

o As above, working only on the 'Dragonquest' episode (pages 55–58). (TA+)

Plenary

- Take feedback. *What details helped you to visualise the events, places or creatures?* Make a note of descriptive and emotive language and add to the Learning Wall.
- Recap the learning objectives. Summarise language and make notes of structural features of the genre on 'Genre ingredients' (ITP 1.2).
- Take feedback. *Have any of your puzzles been answered? How do you think it will end?* Take note of predictions and add to the Learning Wall.

Assessment pointers

- S&L: pair work will show how well the children can recount ideas and listen and respond to others.
- AF5, 6 (R): discussion and independent work show how far the children understand the author's use of language, its impact on the reader and the cultural context.

Session 8

We are learning to …	Resources
• recognise how the author has played with time to reveal events in different ways • analyse how authors use language and other techniques to create suspense, tension and excitement (PNS Strands 7.3, 8.3) **Assessment Focuses** AF (R): 4, 5	*Fantastic, Funny, Frightening!* ITP: (1.2), 1.7 PCM: 1.8

Shared teaching (1)

- Recap *Virtually True* (pages 47–68) from *Fantastic, Funny, Frightening!* so far and share the learning objectives.
- Discuss examples of descriptive language identified in Session 7 that helped create settings. *Why were these important?* (E.g. picturing invented settings/creatures and making them seem real.) *What other effect did the descriptive language have?* (E.g. built up excitement, suggested danger.) Discuss examples of this from the 'Dragonquest' or 'Jailbreak' episodes from pages 55–61.
- Explain that another way of building excitement is by varying sentence structures.
- Show '*Virtually True*' (ITP 1.7). Read the extract, emphasising the excitement. How does the author use different sentence types to create suspense and tension? Talk Partners identify examples in the extract. *What is the effect of the connectives?* (E.g. surprise/suggesting speed, immediacy.) *What about the exclamation and the short sentence?* (E.g. shows high emotion, reflects the character's state of mind, sudden impact.) *Why has the author reordered the clauses?* (E.g. it puts the focus on the character's feelings.)

Independent and Guided

- The children work in pairs to complete 'Sci-fi sentences' (PCM 1.8), recording examples of sentence structures from the story so far. Encourage the children to explain the effect created. Support the children with an identified need. (T/TA)

Shared teaching (2)

- Recap the story so far and remind the children of the predictions they made in Session 7 on the Learning Wall. *Would you like to change any of your predictions?*
- Read the rest of the story from 'As I removed the visor … ' (page 61) to the end.
- Discuss the story as a whole. *What do you think about how the story is resolved? Does it answer all our puzzles? Is there anything you don't understand? What do you make of the final sentence?*

Plenary

- Recap the learning objectives. *How is the story like a quest adventure? Why has the author revealed events out of order? What have you learnt about a sci-fi or fantasy story?*
- Show 'Genre ingredients' (ITP 1.2). *What made this a good example of a sci-fi story? Are there any new points we can add?*

Assessment pointers

- S&L: pair work will show how far the children can collaborate and develop ideas.
- AF4,5 (R): completed PCMs and oral responses show how far the children can identify and comment on the author's structural choices and the use of language and sentence features.

Session 9

We are learning to …	Resources
• understand how moods, feelings and ideas are conveyed in horror/mystery stories (PNS Strands 7.2) **Assessment Focuses** AF (R): 2, 3, 6	*Fantastic, Funny, Frightening!*

Shared teaching

- Ask the children to look at the contents page of *Fantastic, Funny, Frightening! What type of story is* Nule? *What is the fun of reading, listening to or viewing this type of story?* (E.g. enjoying the suspense, waiting for the expected surprise or shock, experiencing fear from a safe distance.) *What goes on in your head when reading this type of book?* (E.g. interacting, feeling, responding, anticipating, etc.)
- Share the learning objectives.
- Read *Nule* (pages 73–92) from *Fantastic, Funny, Frightening!* as far as '… for a time' (page 75). *What does it make you think?*
- Discuss how the genre shapes expectations through setting, characters and events, e.g. describing the old house as not being interesting actually suggests that something interesting might happen.
- Continue reading as far as 'Libby said nothing' (page 85) with the children noting any suspicious hints on sticky notes.
- Discuss words and phrases that suggest rather than tell. *What makes you think there's something scary about Nule?* (E.g. Nule starts to be described as a person and Libby acts differently towards it.)
- Encourage inferences about characters' feelings from the text. *How do the different characters respond to Nule? Would you feel like Libby does, or more like Martin?*
- Encourage predictions based on these hints and knowledge of the genre. *What do you think might happen?*
- Read as far as '… to see where its feet were going' (page 88). *How has the author made it more scary?* (E.g. by making more suggestions: strange noises, dead ladies' clothes, dry rot and danger, adding details about Nule.) *What might happen next?*
- Continue reading from 'That night … ' (page 88) as far as '… and believed in ghosts' (page 90).

Independent and Guided

- In pairs, the children respond to Martin's night-time scene in *Nule*, from 'That night' (page 88) as far as '… and believed in ghosts' (page 90).

Create Freeze Frames to explore Martin's thoughts and feelings.

Read aloud and re-enact the scene, using appropriate expression and actions. (TA+)

Read the scene aloud, using appropriate expression. (T+)

Plenary

- Recap the learning objectives. Listen to or watch a re-enactment. *What did you feel as we were reading? How does the author create these feelings?* (E.g. suggesting rather than saying; through the setting; by creating uncertainty; describing characters' responses; creating suspense by leading up to the scariest part a bit at a time.)

Assessment pointers

- S&L: drama activites will show how far the children can sustain roles and understand the characters.
- AF2, 3 (R): response to questions and group work shows how far the children can make inferences.
- AF6 (R): responses to questions show how far the children can identify the author's purpose and effect on the reader.

Session 10

We are learning to …	Resources
• identify the typical structure of a horror/mystery story • analyse how authors use language and other techniques to create suspense, tension and excitement (PNS Strands 7.3, 8.3) **Assessment Focuses** AF (R): 4, 5, 6	*Fantastic, Funny, Frightening!* ITP: (1.2), 1.8, 1.9 PCM: 1.9, 1.10

Shared teaching (1)

- Recap *Nule* (pages 73–92) from *Fantastic, Funny, Frightening!* so far and continue reading from 'Were you reading in bed last night?' (page 90) to the end. *What do you think? Did Nule walk? Is this a good ending?* (E.g. it leaves things open and retains a sense of uncertainty.)
- Share the learning objectives. *What makes a good mystery story? What is the author's purpose?* (E.g. to create fear, suspense and tension.)
- Talk Partners discuss the success of *Nule. Did it have a good sense of suspense, fear and uncertainty?* Pairs Snowball responses. Encourage comments and reference to specific details such as the setting, characters, events, language, build-up of tension. *If the author asked you how to make it scarier, what would you say?*

Independent and Guided (1)

- In groups, the children complete 'Fear factor' (PCM 1.9). Support the children with an identified need. (T/TA)

Shared teaching (2)

- Show 'Fear factor' (ITP 1.8). Take feedback to create the graph. Ask the children to explain their decisions with reference to the text.
- *How has the narrative been structured for maximum impact?* (E.g. it starts quietly, builds up, peaks at the encounter, dips in tension then increases at the end.)
- Show '*Nule*' (ITP 1.9). Discuss the first three sentences one at a time. *How is suspense built up? Which details are important?* (E.g. the middle of the night, alone, dull/low light, expressive language.) *Why have 'shone coldly' and 'broody telephone' been chosen?*
- Read the final two sentences. *What is the impact? What techniques have been used?* (E.g. delaying the moment, the sudden punch of short sentences following the long previous sentence.)

Independent and Guided (2)

- The children work in pairs, noting examples of style and language features in mystery stories.

ooo Read and compare *Moving House* (pages 69–72) with *Nule.* (T+)

oo Analyse another scene from *Nule* with a passage from *Moving House.*

o Annotate 'Language features' (PCM 1.10). (TA+)

Plenary

- Share and discuss findings and add to the Learning Wall.
- Recap the learning objectives.
- *How do different sentence lengths and features affect the build-up of suspense in the story?* Show the appropriate screen of 'Genre ingredients' (ITP 1.2). *What made this a good example of a mystery story? Are there any new points to add?*

Assessment pointers

- S&L: pair work will show how far the children can listen and respond to others.
- AF4, 5, 6 (R): responses show how far the children can respond to an author's language, relating it to purpose and context.

Session 11

We are learning to …	Resources
• present scenes from humorous stories, conveying characters and events • comment on what makes a humorous text funny (PNS Strands 1.1, 8.1) **Assessment Focuses** AF (R): 2, 6	*Fantastic, Funny, Frightening!*

Shared teaching

- Ask the children to look at the contents page of *Fantastic, Funny, Frightening! What type of story is* In the Shower with Andy? Explain that many stories have humorous moments but for stories in this genre it is the main purpose.
- Share the learning objectives. Talk Partners discuss stories that have made them smile or laugh out loud. *What made them funny?*
- Share some suggestions, focusing on features that create humour, e.g. a character's behaviour or events.
- Read *In the Shower with Andy* (pages 15–30) from *Fantastic, Funny, Frightening!* with an appropriately lively tone, as far as 'I can't just leave it' (page 27). The children follow in their books, marking parts they find amusing with sticky notes.
- Discuss the children's response. *Which parts did you find amusing? What is your favourite part? Was there anything you would have liked more of, or any bits you didn't find funny?* Take feedback, using responses to focus on different elements that contribute to humour, e.g. behaviour of the main character, the situation, the dialogue, the narrator's comments on events, the description of events, the style of the story and how it is told.
- Recap the story so far and explain that Andy is up in the roof of the house. The shower is still full of water and his parents are downstairs having dinner with Mr and Mrs Bainbridge. *What do you think might happen next? If you were the author, how would you end the story?* Think-Pair-Share suggestions, encouraging discussion of ideas.
- Continue reading as far as '… to weigh me down' (page 28). *What about now? Does this confirm or change your predictions?*
- Read to the end of the story. *Were any of your predictions right? Did the ending surprise you in anyway? Did you find it funny?*

Independent and Guided

- The children discuss their responses to the story, first in pairs and then in small groups. In their groups, they work on a drama activity or read the story aloud to convey the story's humour.

ooo Select a section of the story to present, reading aloud and using mime. Focus on actions, gesture and facial expression. (TA+)

oo Freeze Frame the story ending.

o Read the story aloud expressively. (T+)

Plenary

- Recap the learning objectives. Watch some of the children's mimes. *Have you conveyed the humour of the situation? What made the ending funny? What were the main humorous features of this story?*

Assessment pointers

- S&L: drama pieces will show how far the children can sustain roles and scenarios to explore the text.
- AF2 (R): drama activities show how far the children can refer to the text.
- AF6 (R): responses in shared teaching and group work show how far the children are able to comment on the author's purpose and the overall effect of the text.

Session 12

We are learning to …	Resources
• explain how humorous stories are structured for maximum effect • analyse language and techniques that authors use to create humour (PNS Strands 7.3, 8.3) **Assessment Focuses** AF (R): 4, 5	*Fantastic, Funny, Frightening!* ITP: (1.2), 1.10 PCM: (1.7)

Shared teaching

- Share the learning objectives and recap the story of *In the Shower with Andy* so far. *What laughter rating would you give it? Was it a smile book or a side-splitter? What were the main things that made it amusing?* Talk Partners discuss and then feed back.
- *What sort of humour is this? What other sorts of humour can you think of?* (E.g. humour based on real-life situations, word play, slapstick, jokes)
- *Apart from being funny, do humorous stories have anything in common?* Show 'Genre ingredients' (ITP 1.2). *Which ingredients are important in a humorous story? Are characters or events more important than the setting or theme?*
- Read *Thank Goodness!* (pages 13–14) from *Fantastic, Funny, Frightening!*. *What laughter rating would you give it? What made it funny? Why was the ending effective?* (E.g. it has a good, short, sharp punchline; no explanation; it's a surprise.)
- Show '*Thank Goodness*: the bare bones' (ITP 1.10). *How does the story build up to the ending?* (E.g. encourages anticipation of the joke, clues are given early on, just when you thought he was safe …)
- Explain that an important feature of humorous stories is the style and the way the story is told. Read the 'bare bones' version from ITP 1.10. *Does this sound as funny? Why does the story version get a bigger laugh? What makes it so effective? How would you describe the style?* (E.g. comic, jokey; uses everyday language like a comedian telling a joke.) *What techniques does the author use?* (E.g. embellishing the story with details to make the events come alive, building up the anticipation of what is to come, using dialogue and direct speech.) Add these features on ITP 1.2.

Independent and Guided

- Pairs analyse the structure, style and language techniques in a humorous story.

OOO Map the structure of *In the Shower with Andy*, using 'Story plan' (PCM 1.7), noting style and language techniques.

OO As above. (T)

O In a guided group, read *Water, Water, Water!* (pages 9–11) from *Fantastic, Funny, Frightening!*. Pairs then identify the 'bare bones', noting style and language techniques used. (TA+)

Plenary

- Recap the learning objectives. Share the groups' findings, identifying similarities and differences in styles, techniques and structures. Add the work to the Learning Wall. *What have you learnt about what makes a good humorous story?* Add any additional points to ITP 1.2.

Assessment pointers

- S&L: pair work will show how well the children can express and explain relevant ideas.
- AF4, 5 (R): pair work and responses to questions show how far the children can identify structural choices, appreciate the author's use of language and literary features and explain the effect on the reader.

PHASE 3: WRITING A SHORT STORY IN A CHOSEN GENRE (8 DAYS)

Session 13

We are learning to …	Resources
• use talk to explore story genres • choose the genre and main idea for our stories (PNS Strands 1.3, 9.1) **Assessment Focuses** AF (W): 1, 2	ITP: (1.2), 1.11 PCM: 1.11, 1.12

Shared teaching (1)

- Share the learning objectives and explain that the children are going to write a short story in a chosen genre. Discuss a specific purpose or audience, e.g. a genre-based anthology for readers aged 9–12.
- Explain that in this session, the children will develop their story ideas. Explain that authors find inspiration in many different places, such as a real person, a familiar place, a news story, a personal experience, etc.
- Show 'Story web' (ITP 1.11). Explain that the prompts will help the children to explore and develop story ideas. Model selecting a story idea from 'Story ideas' (PCM 1.11) and use the prompts on ITP 1.11 to explore possibilities. Add ideas to the pop-up boxes. Select another story idea and encourage the children to suggest possibilities.
- Select one of the suggested story ideas and change the genre. *How does your story plan change?*

Independent and Guided (1)

- In groups the children use PCM 1.11 and ITP 1.11 to explore ideas for their stories orally. They cut up the cards on PCM 1.11 and choose different aspects to include in their story. When they have decided on a story idea, they complete 'Story web' (PCM 1.12). Support the children with an identified need. (T+/TA+)

Shared teaching (2)

- Form Expert Groups to share ideas.
- Explain that the children are now going to produce a checklist relating to one genre to help them write their stories. They first need to decide on the overall purpose of a story in their genre. *What will the reader want or expect? What is your main aim as writers?*
- Refer to 'Genre ingredients' (ITP 1.2) and demonstrate using it as a reminder for the checklist.

Independent and Guided (2)

- Expert Groups work together to make checklists for their chosen genres, using printouts of appropriate screens from ITP 1.2. Support the children with an identified need. (T/TA)

Plenary

- Ask groups to feed back a few points from their checklists. Add to the Learning Wall.
- Recap the learning objectives. *Are you happy with your ideas? If not, what can you do? How will the checklist help you?*

Assessment pointers

- S&L: group work will show how far the children can engage with others, draw ideas together and promote discussion.
- AF1, 2 (W): completed PCMs, checklists and group discussions show how far the children can write thoughtfully, for a specific purpose with appropriate genre features.

Session 14

We are learning to …	Resources
• make and respond to comments constructively • use a narrative structure that fits with the genre (PNS Strands 3.2, 10.1) **Assessment Focuses** AF (W): 1, 2, 3	ITP: 1.12 PCM: (1.7, 1.12)

Shared teaching

- Share the learning objectives and explain that in this session, the children are going to plan their stories.
- Focus on different features of the genres, e.g. initiating and following up events in fairy tales; problem resolution in dilemma stories; the series of challenges in sci-fi; the build-up to an encounter in mystery stories; possible structures for a humorous story.
- Recap different planning techniques, e.g. story track, story web, flowchart.
- Identify the main structural stages as found on 'Story plan' (PCM 1.7).
- Show 'Story plan' (ITP 1.12) and a genre checklist from Session 13, to plan a story in a particular genre. (E.g. *This is a mystery story about a family who discover something unusual in the cellar of their new house.*)
- Explain that in the opening, they need to introduce the characters and setting, and get the story going. Use Modelled Writing to show the children where to add their notes on ITP 1.12. *Now the story must build up, so to begin with I want everything to seem to be going well. Let's have … .* Ask for contributions. *Now I need a problem to begin building tension and get the reader wondering.* Comment on the suggestions, encouraging ideas for improvements. (E.g. *Good idea, but I wonder if that would give it away a bit too much? I wonder how we could make it more subtle?*)
- Add notes in a different colour, to identify key points in the story, e.g. 'the crisis (most exciting) point'; 'suspense sections before this'. Explain why this is important, e.g. *This will remind me to build up the suspense as I write.*
- When the flowchart is complete, use Think Alouds to give a story outline using the plan. *Does it work? Can you suggest any improvements?* Respond to the comments, making changes, seeking clarification and asking for further suggestions.

Independent and Guided

- The children work individually to plan their stories, referring to completed 'Story web' (PCM 1.12). Pairs then share plans and offer feedback, referring to genre checklists from Session 13.

ooo Select their own planning techniques.

oo As above. (T+)

o Complete 'Story plan' (PCM 1.7). (TA+)

Plenary

- Encourage pairs to feed back. *What did you like about your partner's plan? Does the structure fit with the features of the genre? What feedback did you give? How did you use the checklist to help you?*
- Recap the learning objectives.

Assessment pointers

- S&L: pair work will show how sensitively the children can express and respond to opinions.
- AF1, 2, 3 (W): story plans show how far the children are able to select appropriate genre features, organise and structure stories and maintain overall direction.

Session 15

We are learning to …	Resources
• write an effective opening that will appeal to the reader • select style and language features suitable for the genre and purpose (PNS Strands 9.2, 9.4) **Assessment Focuses** AF (W): 1, 2, 3, 7	*Fantastic, Funny, Frightening!* ITP: (1.1)

Shared teaching

- Share the learning objectives.
- Recall 'Story openers' (ITP 1.1) and recap different types of openings, e.g. a setting description; a dramatic event; dialogue; a question; something intriguing, etc. Discuss the effect of different openings on the reader in the stories from *Fantastic, Funny, Frightening! What is the effect of the setting description in* Nule*; the puzzle in* Virtually True*; the opening statement in* The Balaclava Story? (E.g. making the reader feel something, drawing the reader in, intriguing the reader, etc.)
- Select a genre and discuss ways of starting a story to achieve a particular effect. *What effect might I want at the start of a mystery story? How could I do that?* (E.g. a setting description to establish mood or an intriguing statement.) Encourage the children to offer suggestions and write the first sentence. (E.g. 6 Crusader Terrace seemed a perfectly normal old house – at first.) *What is the effect?*
- Talk Partners discuss how to start a story in another genre using a different type of opening appropriate to the genre, e.g. *'Stop right there, Samuel Jacobs!' I stopped – right there.*
- Talk Partners read out their sentences. Encourage the class to guess the genre and comment on the effectiveness of the opening.
- Use Modelled Writing to create an opening paragraph to follow your first sentence, feeding in information about characters (through descriptive details, actions, reactions and dialogue); setting (details or sensory description for mood); and getting the plot moving (hinting at a problem or puzzle).
- Discuss the style and language appropriate to the genre. Use Think Alouds to rehearse sentences, orally redrafting before writing. *Does that sound right?* Model referring to the genre checklist on the Learning Wall.
- Reread the opening. *Is it engaging? Does it sound like a genre story? How would you change or improve anything?*

Independent and Guided

- Pairs orally rehearse and then write their individual story openings, referring to their story plans from Session 14. They read their work to each other, improving the sound and effectiveness of sentences and vocabulary chosen. Encourage the children to use the genre checklists to help them. Support the children with an identified need. (T+/TA)

Plenary

- Recap the learning objectives. Ask some of the children to share their openings. *Why did you choose that?* Encourage the children to offer feedback. *What do you like about the opening? What effect have they created? How could it be improved?*

Assessment pointers

- S&L: pair work will show how sensitively the children can express and respond to opinions.
- AF1, 2, 3, 7 (W): written openings show how far the children are able to establish viewpoint and include detail, use features and style appropriate to the genre, create a suitable opening and select appropriate language.

Session 16

We are learning to …	Resources
• build up events in the middle of our story • organise our writing into paragraphs to show the stages in our story • use different ways of introducing and connecting paragraphs (PNS Strands 10.1, 10.2) **Assessment Focuses** AF (W): 3, 4	*Fantastic, Funny, Frightening!* ITP: (1.8, 1.12)

Shared teaching

- Explain that, in this session, the children will write the middle of their stories. Recap the story structure and remind the children that in this section, the story must build up towards the most exciting point. Recall annotated 'Fear factor' (ITP 1.8) if necessary.
- Share the learning objectives. Use *Virtually True* (pages 47–68) from *Fantastic, Funny, Frightening!* to focus on how paragraphs are used. Use the sequence of paragraphs starting 'It all started a month ago' (page 49). Discuss the purpose of each paragraph. *What is this paragraph about? What is its purpose? Why is a new paragraph needed?* (E.g. a change of subject.)
- Discuss how the opening sentences introduce the subject of each paragraph and link them together. Identify different types of link, e.g. 'It all started a month ago' (page 49), 'Anyway, back at home …' (page 51), 'That's why we …' (page 50).
- Talk Partners locate other paragraph starters in the story (or a story from a different genre) to add to the Learning Wall.
- Recall annotated 'Story plan' (ITP 1.12). Refer to the notes in the 'build-up' box and develop these ideas into paragraphs, e.g. *I think two paragraphs are needed: one about how everyone wants to be in the pantomime and one to show Alisha's feelings about this.*
- Use Modelled Writing to create the first sentences for each of these paragraphs, showing what the paragraph is about and making links between them, e.g. *Everyone wanted to be … , That's why I knew … .*
- Refer to the 'problem' box on ITP 1.12. *What might the next paragraph be about? How could we open the paragraph?* (E.g. *On the day of the auditions …* .) *How many paragraphs might we need?*
- The children look at the 'build-up' box on their own story plans from Session 14 and develop these ideas into paragraphs. *How many paragraphs will you need? What will they be about?*
- Talk Partners share ideas.

Independent and Guided

- The children work independently to write the middle section of their stories, using paragraphs to build the story to a climax. At intervals, pairs check each other's ideas and refer to the genre checklists on the Learning Wall. Support the children with an identified need. (T+ / TA+)

Plenary

- Recap the learning objectives. Ask the children to share some of their opening sentences. *Why did you decide to start like that?* Discuss the effects of the different paragraph openers and improvements that could be made. Add more examples to the Learning Wall.

Assessment pointers

- S&L: pair work will show how far the children can listen and respond to others.
- AF3, 4 (W): response to questions and written work show how far the children can use paragraphs to support story structure and overall direction and show clear links between paragraphs.

Session 17

We are learning to …	Resources
• use feedback to improve our work • use techniques appropriate to the genre to keep the reader's interest • improve language choices to create effects that fit the genre (PNS Strands 3.2, 9.2, 9.4) **Assessment Focuses** AF (W): 1, 2, 7	ITP: (1.2), 1.13

Shared teaching

- Share the learning objectives and explain that, today, the children are going to revise and improve their stories, focusing on making them fit their genre.
- Show and read 'Writing sample' (ITP 1.13) and explain that this is an extract from a fantasy story about a boy who is transported to another world and must find the answer to a puzzle in order to return home. This part of the story is building up to the point where the boy meets the person who will tell him the answer.
- Read the extract. *How does the author want us to feel? Does it have that effect? Can you visualise the fantasy world? Has the author used the fantasy style and language? How could these be improved?*
- Allow Think Time. *How could we build up the tension or make it sound menacing? What language features could we use?* (E.g. add descriptive details to help the reader visualise the setting or the Ice Creature; use language to create a hostile setting/build tension; use actions/dialogue/response to show rather than tell Leo's fear.)
- Encourage the children to offer suggestions to improve the text and make changes on ITP 1.13. Use Think Alouds to explain the changes you make. (E.g. *Let's add details to help the reader visualise the setting and build up a sense of danger. Do you have any suggestions* for *adjectival phrases or similes?*) Discuss suggestions in terms of the effect created. Amend the text, rereading to check the overall effect.
- Talk Partners redraft a sentence to achieve a particular effect, e.g. using words to make the creature seem more menacing, e.g. *With a voice as icy as the north wind.*
- Recall the appropriate screen of 'Genre ingredients' (ITP 1.2). Focus on how the ingredients, particularly the style/language, have been added.

Independent and Guided

- In Expert Groups the children comment on each other's stories, referring to the learning objectives and genre checklists. Individually, the children make improvements in response to the comments, referring to the Learning Wall. Support the children with an identified need. (T+/ TA+)

Plenary

- Recap the learning objectives. *What do you like about your group's stories so far? What feedback did you give them? How did your group's feedback help you to improve your story? What changes did you make? Do you think you have achieved the effect you wanted? What language features have you used? Is there anything you still need help with?*

Assessment pointers

- S&L: group work will show how far the children can express and respond to opinions.
- AF1, 2 (W): response to questions and written work show how far the children can select style and features appropriate to genre detail.
- AF7 (W): redrafted writing and peer assessment show how well the children can choose vocabulary for effect.

Session 18

We are learning to ...	Resources
• add and move phrases and clauses in sentences • use punctuation to clarify complex sentences (PNS Strands 11.1, 11.2) **Assessment Focuses** AF (W): 5, 6	ITP: (1.7, 1.9), 1.14

Shared teaching

- Share the learning objectives and explain that, in this session, the children are going to continue revising their stories, this time focusing on sentence construction.
- Recap the work from Phase 2, reminding the children that sentence variation is a clever trick authors use to achieve particular effects, such as varying pace, building tension and avoiding repetition.
- Recall '*Virtually True*' (ITP 1.7) and briefly recap the structures and the effect they helped to achieve in the passage.
- Use some of the sentences as models for practising sentence construction, e.g. the reordered clauses sentence.
- Talk Partners orally rehearse sentences starting with a conjunction, e.g. 'As I …', 'Although he …', 'While they …'. They then write the sentences, remembering to use a comma to separate the two clauses.
- Take feedback and add example sentences to the Learning Wall.
- If there is time, recall '*Nule*' (ITP 1.9) and discuss the different sentence structures and the effect achieved, e.g. long sentences that deliberately delay and build up suspense, followed by short sentences for surprise and instant impact. Also highlight conjunctions that link and commas that separate the different parts.
- Read 'Sentence improvement' (ITP 1.14). *How does the author want us to feel?* (E.g. panic) *How could varying sentence structures help improve this?*
- Use the on-screen prompts and the children's suggestions to change the sentence construction to achieve the effect required. Explain decisions in terms of the effect, e.g. using questions to suggest the character's state of mind; long sentences combining actions for a sense of pace.
- Talk Partners revise a sentence, e.g. moving the subordinate clause/adverbial phrase to the start of the sentence.
- Take feedback and ask the children to explain the effect achieved.
- Reread the final version and discuss changes in the overall effect. For an example of rewritten text, go to Screen 2.

Independent and Guided

- The children improve sentence structures in their story.
- ●●● Work independently and look at the examples on ITP 1.14 for help.
- ●● Work as a group. (T+)
- ● Improve sentences already identified. (TA+)

Plenary

- Recap the learning objectives and ask the children to share examples of their rewritten sentences. *How did you change the sentence? What effect have you created?*

Assessment pointers

- AF5, 6 (W): revised sentences and response to questions show how far the children are able to vary length and structure of sentences, form and handle complex sentences and use commas.

Session 19

We are learning to ...	Resources
• discuss stories in a writers' workshop • write an effective ending for our story • check that the story ideas link together logically (PNS Strands 3.2, 9.2, 10.1) **Assessment Focuses** AF (W): 3	PCM: 1.13

Shared teaching (1)

- Prior to the session, select one child's writing to use in the shared session.
- Share the learning objectives and explain that a writers' workshop is a group of writers who support each other by giving opinions, offering constructive criticism and helpful advice. In this session, the writers' workshop will help the children to bring their stories to a good end.
- Introduce the main idea of the selected story, or invite the writer to do so, e.g. *This is a story about …* .
- Explain that the ending must fit the overall structure of the story, so invite the writer to read the story so far. Listen and check that the story has a clear sense of direction and keeps to its main idea. *Does it build up to an exciting point? Does anything seem out of place or not needed?*
- Encourage the children to offer helpful comments and ask others if they agree. Encourage the writer to respond, e.g. explaining his or her reasons, asking questions to clarify points, saying how they might adjust the content in response, etc.
- Give the children 'Story ending' (PCM 1.13). Ask the chosen writer to explain the resolution and ending planned for their story. Encourage the children to use the prompts on PCM 1.13 to help comment on the idea. *As a reader, what would you think of this ending? If you were the writer, how would you end it?*
- Encourage a dialogue between the children and the writer. *What do you think of that idea? Are you going to change your planned ending?*

Independent and Guided

- Expert Groups hold a writers' workshop, discussing endings for their stories, using PCM 1.13 and their original story plans from Session 14. The children then work independently to write the ending to their stories. Support the children with an identified need. (T+/TA+)

Shared teaching (2)

- Explain that stories need a 'great last line', a sudden surprise or punchline, that makes you smile or leaves you thinking, e.g. *The Balaclava Story* and *Thank Goodness!* have punchlines; *Virtually True*, *Nule* and *The Glass Cupboard* make you think.
- Use the prompts on PCM 1.13 to discuss possibilities for great last lines.
- Talk Partners orally rehearse their 'great last lines' before adding them to their stories.

Plenary

- Recap the learning objectives. *What have you learnt about ending stories effectively? Did you find the writers' workshop helpful?*

Assessment pointers

- S&L: group work will show how well the children can adopt group roles and express relevant ideas.
- AF3 (W): written endings and group discussion show how well the children can check the overall direction and bring their stories to a suitable close.

Session 20

We are learning to ...	Resources
• offer constructive criticism to other writers • use response from an audience to help evaluate our writing • evaluate the success of our story in terms of genre and purpose (PNS Strands 3.2, 9.1) **Assessment Focuses** AF (W): 1, 2, 3	ITP: 1.15 PCM: 1.14, 1.15, 1.16

Shared teaching (1)

- Share the learning objectives and explain that it's good for authors to get audience feedback so they can find out what works and what doesn't, and make changes or store information away for the future.
- Talk Partners share their stories and offer feedback. Use the questions in 'Your thoughts' (PCM 1.14) to prompt feedback. Discuss the writer's role in the activity. *What should the writer be thinking about? How should they respond to comments?* (E.g. assessing whether it is a useful suggestion; noting points to act on; asking questions to follow up a point; seeking advice, etc.)

Independent and Guided (1)

- The children work in pairs with someone they have not worked with previously. Writers introduce their story, giving the genre, the main idea and saying what they were trying to achieve. They then read their story to their partner, who use 'Discussing ideas' (PCM 1.15) to respond to the story. Support the children with an identified need. (T/TA)

Shared teaching (2)

- Allow Think Time for the children to reflect on what they have learnt from the audience response session before taking feedback. *What comments did your partner make? What points did you discuss? What decisions did you agree on? How will you use these comments to improve your work?*
- *What other information could you use to evaluate your stories?* Show 'Marking ladder' (ITP 1.15). Model how to assess a volunteer's story against the first few points.

Independent and Guided (2)

- The children evaluate their own stories referring to their genre checklists and 'Marking ladder' (PCM 1.16). They then make the final changes to their stories.

Work in a writing conference. (T+)

Work in pairs, using PCM 1.16. (TA+)

As above.

Plenary

- Recap the learning objectives. *How did talking about your work and trying it out on an audience help you to identify ways of improving it? What did you find most useful? How could the discussion have been more useful?*
- Discuss how to polish the stories, e.g. proofreading, and how to prepare a final version, e.g. producing a neat/typed copy; illustrating.
- Reflect on the unit as a whole, identifying areas for development. *What did you enjoy about the unit? Which were your favourite stories? What will you remember next time you write a short story?*

Assessment pointers

- S&L: pair work will show how well the children can adopt group roles and express and respond to opinions.
- AF1, 2, 3 (W): completed stories show how well the children can develop ideas and content, maintain purpose, features and style in relation to genre, and structure and organise their story for effect.

Name: ______________________ Date: ______________

Story openers

Discuss which genre each story is.

The Magic Feather

There was once a king who had three beautiful daughters. Now, two of the daughters were vain and foolish creatures, but the youngest daughter was as wise as she was beautiful …

The Life and Times of Sadie Diamond

Who wants to be in the rotten school pantomime anyway? I tried to convince myself I didn't. But I did.

The Purple Planet

'Inter-Space Shuttle Flight 507 coming in to land.'
The voice activated the luggage control robots, which immediately buzzed into life.

Shadow House

The house had been empty and undisturbed for many years. No one had crossed the threshold or dared disturb the silence within. It had been boarded up all that time, gathering dust and gathering stories.

Danger if you Dare

Splash! Troy Masters landed in the ocean clutching the briefcase as the helicopter blades swirled overhead.

Don't Choose an Alligator for a Pet

His name was Ally. Well, it would be. He was an alligator.

Goal Mouth

The crouched figure dived full length, landing with a splatter of mud. 'Come on Michael. That's six-nil,' groaned Jason, reclaiming the ball from the back of the net. 'It's the cup match on Saturday. You'll have to do better than that.'

The Case of the Broken Mirror

The telephone rang early in the morning. It was Inspector Evans. There had been another break-in, this time at the Manor House.

Genre bookmarks

Make notes about typical features for your chosen genre.

Genre bookmark

Name: ____________________

Book title: ____________________

Author: ____________________

Genre: ____________________

Evidence of typical features

Characters: ____________________

____

____

____

____

Setting: ____________________

____

____

____

____

Plot: ____________________

____

____

____

Main events: ____________________

____

____

____

Themes: ____________________

____

____

____

Mood: ____________________

____

____

____

Language: ____________________

____

____

____

Other points: ____________________

____

____

____

Fold

Genre ingredients

Complete the chart about one genre.

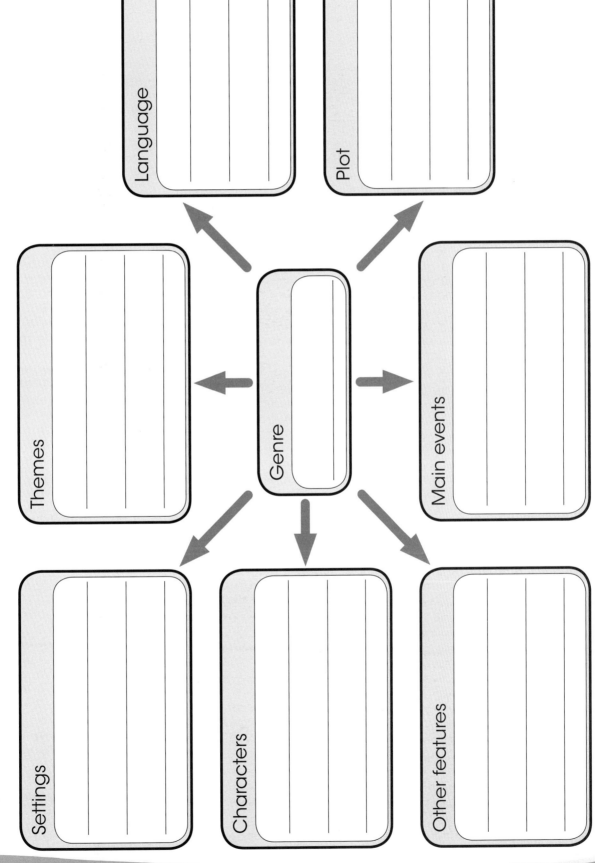

Settings

Themes

Language

Characters

Genre

Plot

Other features

Main events

Genre cards

Cut up the cards and discuss the different genres. Choose one to discuss in more detail.

Adventure	Animal stories	Crime	Fantasy
Ghost stories	Horror	Historical stories	Humour
Mystery stories	Fairy tales	Myths and legends	Dilemma stories
Romance	Science fiction	Sport stories	War stories

Name: ____________________ Date: ____________

Traditional tales

Write words on the targets to describe fairy tale characters.

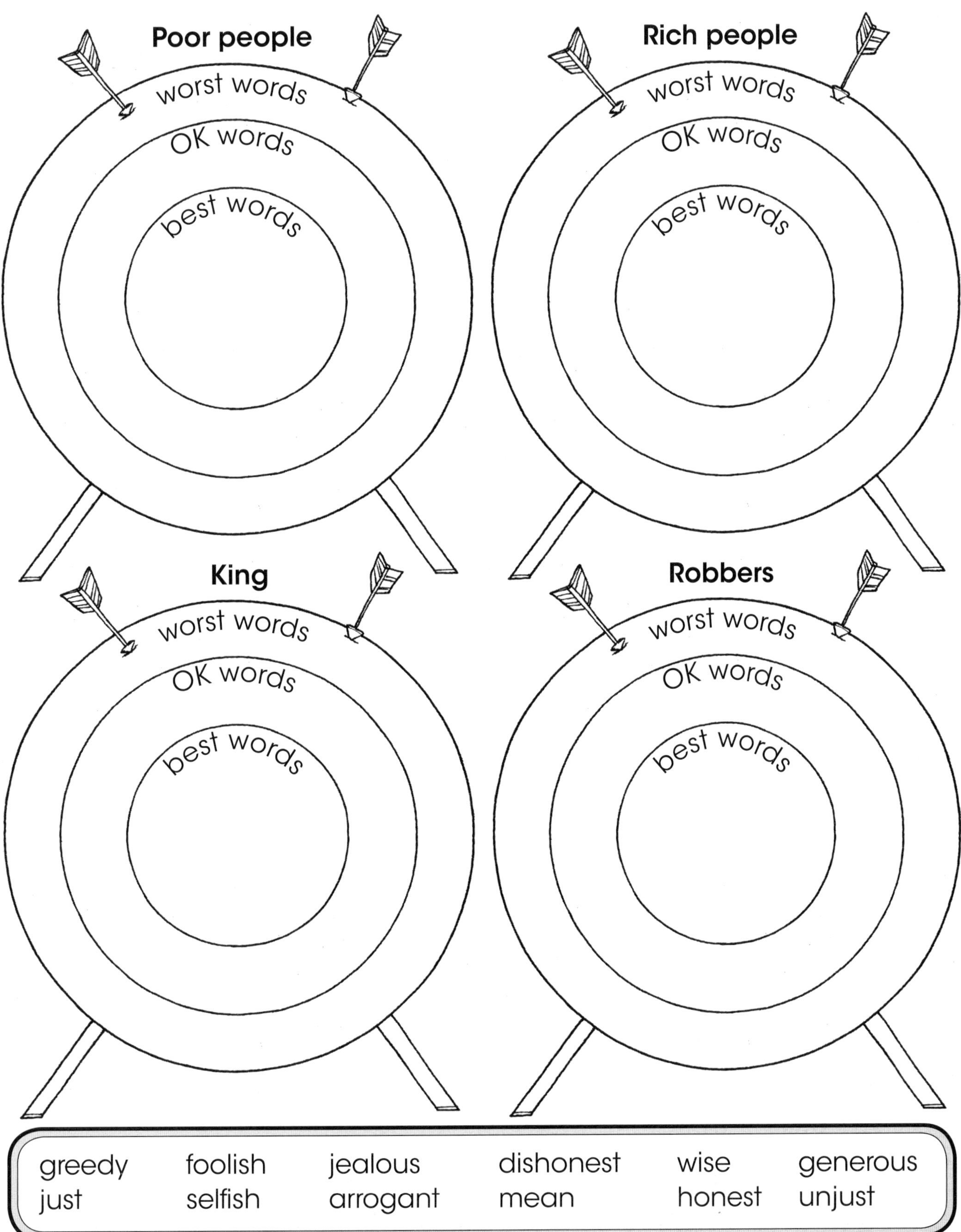

greedy	foolish	jealous	dishonest	wise	generous
just	selfish	arrogant	mean	honest	unjust

Thought tracking

Thought-track the main character. Look for clues in the text that show what the character is thinking.

In the playground …
(pages 33–36)

Back in the classroom …
(page 39)

In the cloakroom …
(page 38)

On the way home …
(pages 40–41)

Name: ____________________ Date: ____________

Story plan

Add notes to map the events in *The Balaclava Story*.

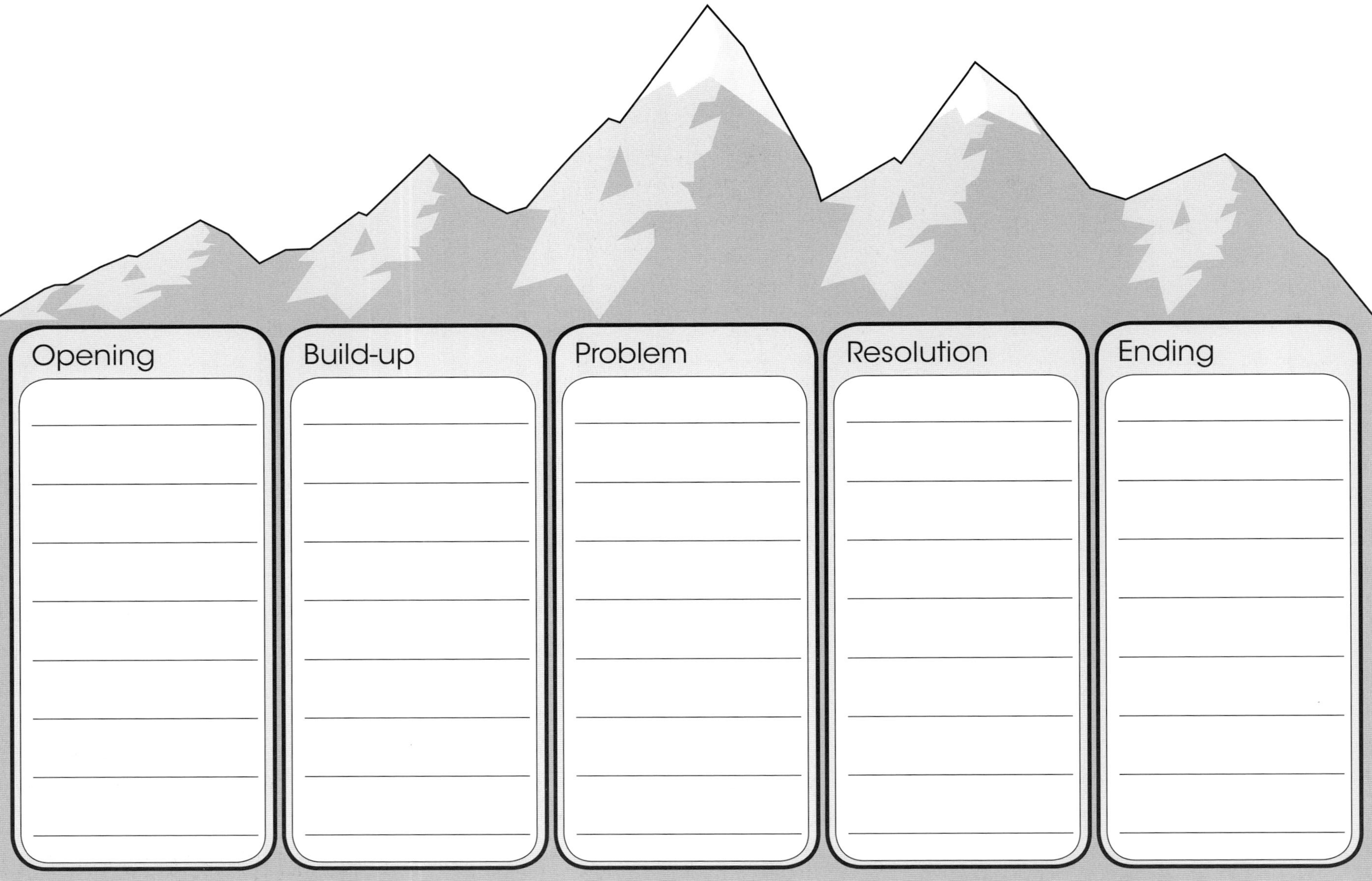

Sci-fi sentences

Find examples of the structures in the story.

Opening sentences:

- adverbial starters
- *-ing*/*-ed* starters
- time connectives, e.g. At that moment …
- prepositional phrases, e.g. Across the moonlit battlements …

____

____

____

____

Reordering clauses

e.g. As I watched in horror, the guards bent down and unclicked the dogs' leads.

____

Long sentences combining actions and events

e.g. We dodged the guards, we fled the dogs, we made it to a staircase and pounded upwards.

____

____

Short, punchy sentences

e.g. It was too late.

____

Exclamations and questions

e.g. 'NOOOOOO!' I screamed.

e.g. 'What was happening?'

____

____

Name: ______________________ Date: ______________ **1.9**

Fear factor

Draw a graph to show how frightening the different parts of *Nule* are.

Extremely scary

Not at all scary

1 2 3 4 5 6 7 8 9 10

Event number

Events

1. The house was not old enough to be interesting, just old enough to be starting to fall apart. (page 73)
2. … the house stopped being interesting altogether for a time. (page 75)
3. When she talked to it she just called it Nule. (page 80)
4. … in the darkness of the hall, it looked just like a person, waiting … (page 83)
5. … Nule stared once more without eyes, and smiled without a mouth. (page 85)
6. … as if Nule had turned its head to see where its feet were going. (page 88)
7. Then he realised that the creaks were coming not from above but from below. (page 88)
8. It did not shine on Nule. Nule was not there. Nule was half-way up the stairs … (page 90)
9. He looked down into the hall where the sun shone through the frosted glass … (page 91)
10. … if he left Nule alone, Nule might walk again. (page 92)

Name: ______________________ Date: ______________ **1.10**

Language features

1. Read the extract from *Nule*.

Then he realised that the creaks were coming not from above but from below.

He held his breath. Downstairs didn't creak.

His alarm clock gleamed greenly in the dark and told him that it had gone two o'clock. Mum and Dad were asleep ages ago. Libby would sooner burst than leave her bed in the dark. Perhaps it *was* a burglar. Feeling noble and reckless he put on the bedside lamp, slid out of bed, trod silently across the carpet. He turned on the main light and opened the door. The glow shone out of the doorway and saw him as far as the landing light switch at the top of the stairs, but he never had time to turn it on.

2. Highlight examples of the language used to build suspense.

Language

1. Description of setting
2. Use of senses: sights and sounds
3. Low light and darkness
4. Expressive adjectives and verbs
5. Character's response
6. Longer descriptive sentences.
7. Sudden, short sentences
8. Sentence structures to delay

Story ideas

Use the cards to think of story ideas. Add your own ideas to the blank cards.

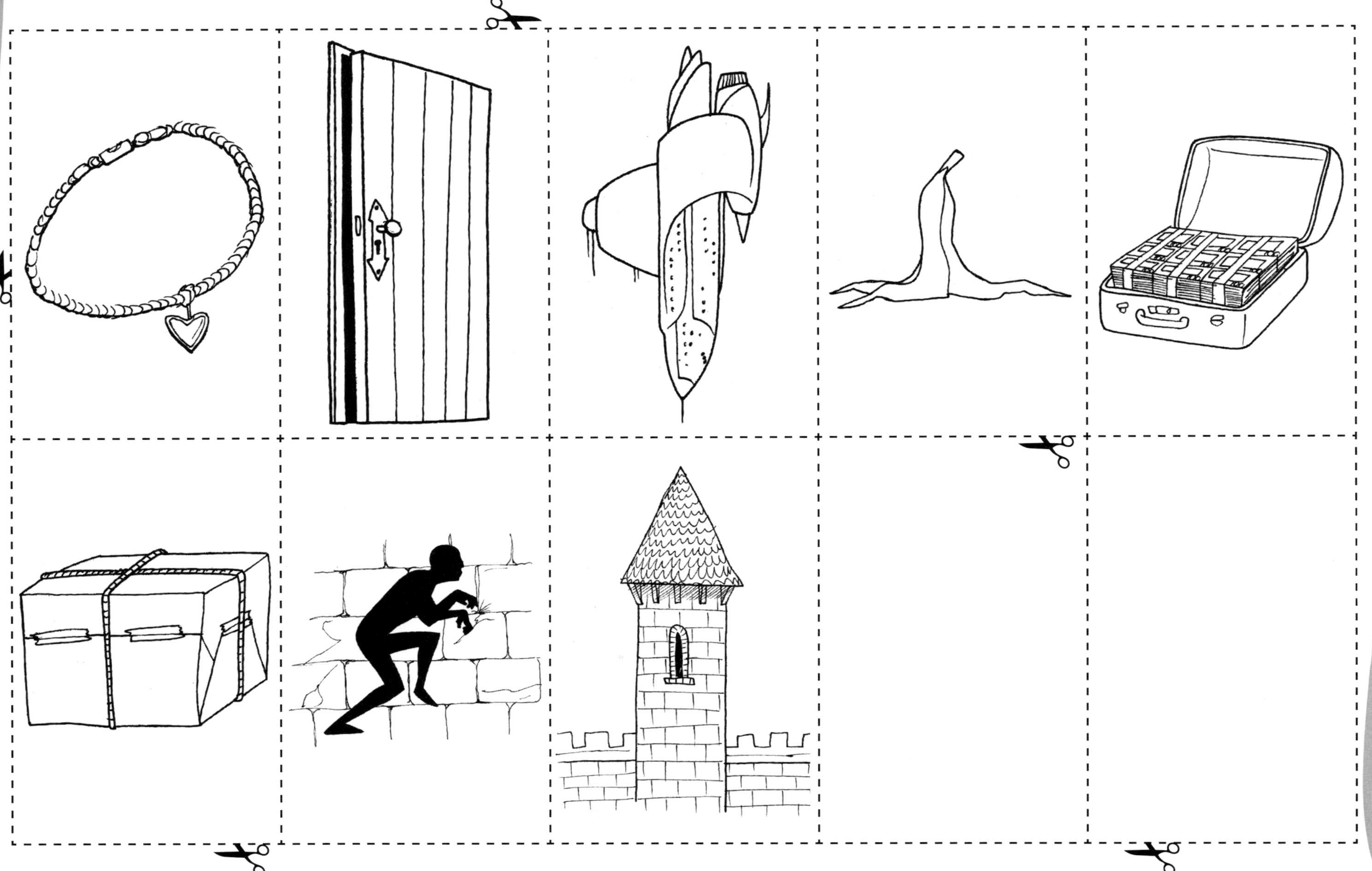

Story web

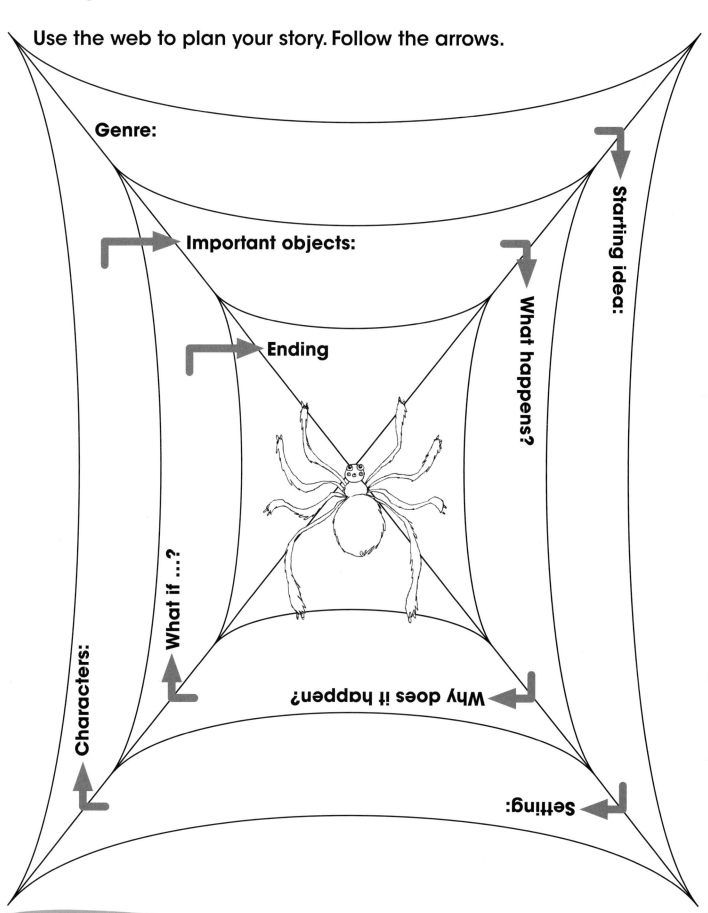

Use the web to plan your story. Follow the arrows.

Story ending

Check your resolution and ending.

	Yes	No
• Are they believable?	☐	☐
• Do they round things off?	☐	☐
• Are dilemmas and problems resolved?	☐	☐
• Will they surprise the reader?	☐	☐
• Are they too predictable?	☐	☐
• Does the ending fit with the story?	☐	☐

Improve your story

Try to make your story original.

Try ...

- a comment from your narrator
- a thought from the main character
- a line of dialogue
- an intriguing or mysterious remark
- a sentence to show that a character or something has changed
- building the story up so that a final effort achieves success

Great last line

Give your reader something to smile or think about at the end.

Try ...

- a question, perhaps addressed to the reader
- a message or warning to the reader
- a link back to the start of the story
- using an unexpected event (like *The Balaclava Story*)
- only partly solving the story and leaving your reader guessing (like *Nule*)

Your thoughts

1. Use the questions to help you comment on your partner's story.

a. Is it clear what genre the story is? Why or why not?

____

____

b. Which parts work well?

____

____

c. Is the story clear? Why or why not?

____

____

d. Does it achieve the writer's purpose? Why or why not?

____

____

e. Does it keep you interested? How?

____

____

2. Think of two stars and a wish for your partner's story.

☆ ______________________________

☆ ______________________________

wish ______________________________

Discussing ideas

Use the mind map to give and respond to feedback.

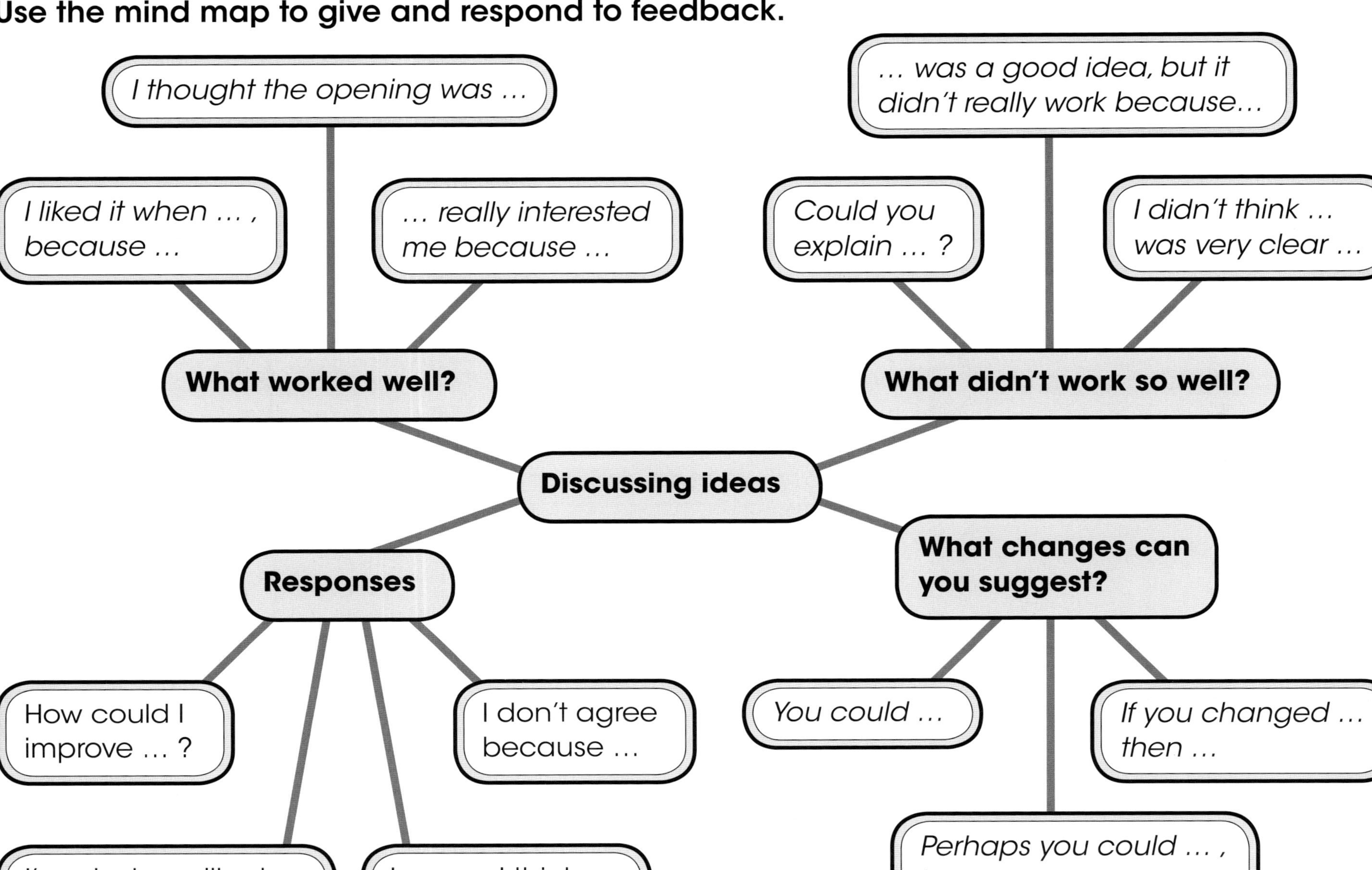

Marking ladder

Use the marking ladder to check your work.

My comments		My partner's comments
	My story includes details about the characters, setting or events to keep the story interesting.	
	My story opening grabs the reader's attention.	
	My story has a build-up, resolution and ending.	
	My story is written in paragraphs to show the main events and my paragraphs link together.	
	I have used style and language features suitable to the genre.	
	I have varied some of my sentences to achieve a particular effect, e.g. long sentences to build suspense.	

Narrative Unit 2

PLANET PRISON – multi-media text (Multi-modal reading)

Medium term plan (3 weeks)	
Phase	**Learning Outcomes**
Phase 1: Reading and exploring the text (4 days)	• Children can use a range of reading techniques and dialogic talk to engage with a contemporary interactive fiction text. • Children can follow, track and compare multiple story routes.
Phase 2: Analysing structure and features (3 days)	• Children can identify the features and structure of the interactive adventure and use this as a model for writing.
Phase 3: Planning and writing (8 days)	• Children can work collaboratively to develop, plan, write and present an interactive text adventure with multiple reading routes. • Children can write an adventure story within the conventions of the genre.

Narrative Unit 2

PLANET PRISON

Big picture

The children read *Prison Planet*, an interactive multi-media adventure with multiple storylines. Working in reading groups, they follow the various routes and use a variety of reading techniques and dialogic talk to discuss and compare the effectiveness of the different alternatives. The children identify genre features and analyse the structure of the text, using a variety of devices to clarify its organisation. They explore how the story is told using a combination of narration, spoken dialogue and visuals. They work collaboratively in groups to plan and write an interactive adventure story with multiple reading routes, developing sections and episodes that are then linked together as a text.

Prior learning

This unit assumes that the children can already:

- identify and discuss characters, dilemmas, settings, simple themes and the author's intentions
- use storyboards and story mapping to organise and structure a story
- navigate an interactive ICT text
- discuss their responses to stories in groups
- plan a story and dialogue from a particular character's point of view.

Key aspects of learning

Communication: Working collaboratively, listening to others; share and build on ideas cooperatively and constructively; communicate outcomes in writing and using other modes and media.
Enquiry: Take an enquiry approach to exploring an interactive fiction text; ask questions, seek answers and make decisions.
Evaluation: Share and evaluate ideas and possibilities; think through consequences; evaluate own and other's work against success criteria.
Information processing: Make comparisons; select information.
Reasoning: Construct reasoned responses to the text.
Self-awareness: Reflect on personal responses and preferences.

Progression in narrative

In this unit the children will:

- identify story and paragraph structures in a non-linear narrative
- identify genre features, e.g. stock characters, settings and problems
- plan and write own non-linear adventure narrative; use genre features to set up puzzles and possible solutions; vary sentence length, pace and emphasis of narrative and dialogue for effect; use dialogue to progress, reveal character or motivation and introduce information.

Cross-curricular links

ICT, Art and design: The suggested outcome could be developed into a simple multimodal text, integrating illustrations, videos and sound clips.
Music: The children could create a music sound clip to accompany the opening of the story.

PHASE 1: READING AND EXPLORING THE TEXT (4 DAYS)

Session 1

We are learning to ...	Resources
• use dialogic talk to discuss the story and respond to the views of others • use active reading strategies to explore the text (PNS Strands 1.3, 8.2) **Assessment Focuses** AF (R): 2, 3	*Planet Prison* ITP: 2.1 PCM: 2.1, 2.2

Shared teaching

- Introduce the 'Big Picture' and explain that the children will be reading and exploring the interactive story *Planet Prison*.
- Share the learning objectives.
- Read the introductory screen of *Planet Prison* (screen 1, Level 1a). Model activating prior knowledge, e.g. *This reminds me of ... .*
- Read screens 2–5 (Level 1a) of *Planet Prison*. (Use Planet Prison Layout AR 2.2 to help you navigate the story structure.) Reinforce how to navigate and play the screens, using hot spots, arrows and links.
- Model clarifying or monitoring information, e.g. *Let's just pause so I can check I have this clear. Cad's mother is on Earth, is that right?*
- Encourage speculation about future events using the information already given, e.g. *It says her father gave her two gifts. I wonder if they might be significant later? Did you notice anything else like that?*
- Read screen 6 (Level 1a) of *Planet Prison. What should Cad do?* Talk Partners discuss ideas, referring to information from the story. Encourage them to think about the consequences of their choices.
- Take feedback and discuss ideas. Encourage class discussion, balancing different viewpoints before reaching a decision.
- Choose a route and continue reading. Pause after screen 7 (Level 3a/b) of *Planet Prison*, 'On the third morning ... ' or screen 11 (Level 2b), 'Dialling Petra'.
- Show 'Key questions' (ITP 2.1) and 'Talk to develop thinking' (PCM 2.1). Demonstrate answering one of the questions on ITP 2.1 using PCM 2.1 to explore your ideas. Encourage the children to discuss what happens as a result of Cad's choice using PCM 2.1. *Was it a good choice? What might have happened if she had made the other choice?*
- Show 'Reading strategies' (PCM 2.2) and discuss.

Independent and Guided

- In groups, the children explore the alternative route through the story, taking the other choice at screen 6 (Level 1a). Stop at screen 7 (Level 3a/b), or screen 11 (Level 2b), depending on the route taken. Use PCM 2.1 and refer to the key questions on ITP 2.1 to encourage discussion. If possible, provide each group with a computer, or work through the route as a class, pausing to allow groups to discuss their ideas. Support the children with an identified need. (T+/TA+)

Plenary

- Take feedback and ask groups to summarise significant events in the alternate route through the story, comparing events in the two routes.
- Pairs discuss the reading strategies they used and complete PCM 2.2.
- Take feedback. *What strategies did you use? When did you use them? How did they help you understand the story?*
- Recap the learning objectives.

Assessment pointers

- S&L: group work will show how far the children can express and respond to opinions.
- AF2 (R): discussions show how far the children are able to support comments by selecting relevant quotations or details from the text.
- AF3 (R): comments on relevant textual clues will show how far the children can draw inferences and deduce meanings.

Session 2

We are learning to …	Resources
• use dialogic talk to comment on the structure of interactive texts • understand the structure of interactive texts • use active reading strategies to explore the text (PNS Strands 1.3, 7.3, 8.2) **Assessment Focuses** AF (R): 2, 3, 4	*Planet Prison* ITP: 2.2 PCM: (2.1, 2.2)

Shared teaching

- Share the learning objectives.
- Show 'Story locations' (ITP 2.2). Encourage the children to summarise the key events that happen in each location. Click on each location to reveal summaries.
- Focus on the key differences and any similarities between the two routes. *What happens in one route that doesn't in the other? What are the similarities?* (E.g. both involve a number of challenges, both are heading towards Zolta Park.)
- Talk Partners discuss how the structure differs from that of other kinds of stories, e.g. there are multiple routes through the story; the reader controls the main character's decisions and influences events and possibly the ending.
- Take feedback. *What are the differences? What is the effect on the reader? How does this structure add to the reading experience?*
- Remind the children of where they got to in each of the story routes in *Planet Prison. What will happen next in each case? Will the different storylines have the same ending? What makes you say that?* Encourage the children to explain their predictions, referring to events so far and other stories of a similar genre.
- Read from screen 7 (Level 3a/b) or screen 11 (Level 2b), depending on the route followed in Session 1. Reinforce active reading strategies, e.g. encouraging the children to predict, clarify and question.
- When Cad faces a decision, encourage the children to discuss and justify their choices before reaching a collective decision.
- Stop just before the story reaches a climax, e.g. on screen 14 (Level 3a/b) 'Cad descended the ladder … ', screen 4 (Level 3c), 'The boosters fired up … ' or screen 4 (Level 3d), at the end of the scene where the train falls off the bridge.
- Show ITP 2.2 again. *What events and places can we add to show the latest events?* Add the children's suggestions to ITP 2.2.

Independent and Guided

- In groups, the children explore the alternative story route, continuing from Session 1. Use 'Talk to develop thinking' (PCM 2.1) to encourage discussion. Ensure all possible story routes are explored and stop groups just before the story reaches a climax. Support the children with an identified need. (T+/TA+)

Plenary

- Take feedback. *How do the different story routes compare? What is the impact on the reader of having multiple routes? Do you like it?*
- Recap the learning objectives. Pairs work together to complete 'Reading strategies' (PCM 2.2) for the guided session. *Did you use any different strategies today? How did they help you understand the story?*

Assessment pointers

- S&L: group work will show how far the children can engage with others, draw ideas together and promote discussion.
- AF2, 3 (R): work from the shared teaching shows how far the children can retrieve and interpret events from the text.
- AF4 (R): oral response to teacher questioning shows how far the children understand the structure of the text.

Session 3

We are learning to …	Resources
• use drama to reflect on and explore the ending • understand the structure of interactive texts (PNS Strands 4.1, 7.3) **Assessment Focuses** AF (R): 2, 3, 4, 6	*Planet Prison* PCM: (2.1), 2.3

Shared teaching (1)

- Share the learning objectives and recap the shared reading route in *Planet Prison*. Encourage the children to summarise the story, including the problems overcome and any challenges, depending on the route taken.
- Continue reading the story to the end of the chosen route. *How does the mood or pattern of the story suddenly change*? (E.g. from near disaster or despair to triumph or joy.) *What key event brings about this change*? Highlight the significance of facts identified earlier, e.g. the weaknesses of the CLAWs and the importance of objects such as the grenade and the locket. *What happens as a result?*
- Show the final screen from the chosen route again. *What technique does the author use to end the story? Would you say it is a good or satisfying ending?*
- Talk Partners discuss whether they think Cad succeeds in her mission. *Is everything resolved? Is the ending final? What is left open?*
- Take feedback and discuss the children's ideas.

Independent and Guided (1)

- In groups, the children explore the alternative story endings for the route taken in Session 2, completing 'Story ending' (PCM 2.3). The children to discuss their ideas as they progress using 'Talk to develop thinking' (PCM 2.1). Support the children with an identified need. (T+/TA+)

Shared teaching (2)

- Encourage the children to summarise the endings. *How are the endings similar or different?* (E.g. in all of them the CLAWs are defeated but this is done in different ways.) *Which ending do you think is the most or least satisfying*? The children Think-Pair-Share responses, referring to the problems resolved, the success of Cad's mission, the open ending and the questions that remain.
- Take feedback. *Do problems have to be resolved at the end of a story?*

Independent and Guided (2)

- In groups, the children Freeze Frame a flash forward to show what happened next. This should fill in the gaps and answer some of the questions, explaining what has happened and how the characters feel. Support the children with an identified need. (T/TA)

Plenary

- Recap the learning objectives. Watch the freeze frames. *Why did you choose to show this?* Encourage the children to explain where they got their ideas for the progression of the plot. *Why do you think this would happen? What in the story gave you this idea? Would* Planet Prison *be better if 'flash forwards' like these were added?*

Assessment pointers

- S&L: freeze frames will show how well the children can convey ideas about the story.
- AF2, 3 (R): oral responses show how far the children can support ideas with evidence from the text and make inferences and deductions.
- AF4, 6 (R): group discussion shows how far the children understand the structural features of the genre and identify effects on the reader.

Session 4

We are learning to ...	Resources
• use active reading strategies to explore the text • say how authors create certain effects and explore the impact on the reader (PNS Strands 8.2, 8.3) **Assessment Focuses** AF (R): 4, 7	*Planet Prison* ITP: 2.3 PCM: (2.2), 2.4, 2.5

Shared teaching

- Share the learning objectives. Recall 'Reading strategies' (PCM 2.2) and recap the strategies for reflecting on a text.
- Show '*Planet Prison*' (ITP 2.3). Talk Partners discuss which of the terms they would use to describe *Planet Prison.* Encourage them to think of the key features of the story and their knowledge of other stories to help them.
- Take feedback and drag the words into place. Encourage the children to explain their choices. *Why do you think it's modern? What other modern stories have you read? Can you explain what 'interactive' means? How is* Planet Prison *interactive? Does interactive fiction have to be on-screen? Have you read anything else like this?*
- Discuss why particular words have not been chosen and draw on the children's knowledge of other texts. *Why is this not a classic or a traditional text? What would be an example of that? How is this different?* Discuss any uncertainties about terms, e.g. *What does non-linear mean? Is* Planet Prison *non-linear? Can you think of other examples of non-linear texts?*
- Look at the terms selected on ITP 2.3. *What does this suggest about who the author is and when the story was written? Does it remind you of any other types of story – in a book or on-screen? In what way is* Planet Prison *like a computer adventure game or a 'choose your own adventure' story?*
- Talk Partners discuss reasons for presenting stories in this way. *Why do you think some authors write stories that are interactive*?
- Take feedback on examples of interactive and multimedia elements that engage the reader, e.g. sound, graphics, parts you can click on.
- Show screens 6–11 (Level 2b) of *Planet Prison* (the cabin scene) and explore the different features using 'Multimedia prompts' (PCM 2.4).

Independent and Guided

- The children work in groups, with each group focusing on a different element from PCM 2.4. Show screens 1–5 (Level 3c) and screen 1 (Level 4e/f) of *Planet Prison,* pausing before the choice is made. Pause after each screen to allow the children time to complete 'Multimedia storyboard' (PCM 2.5), making notes about their given element as it appears on each screen. Support the children with an identified need. (T+/TA+)

Plenary

- Take feedback. Encourage the other children to ask questions about the group's notes and the impact of the elements on the reader.
- Recap the learning objectives. Discuss the genre. *Would you like to read more texts like this?*

Assessment pointers

- S&L: group work will show how far the children can express and respond to opinions.
- AF4 (R): written notes, oral responses and explanations show how far the children understand presentational features.
- AF7 (R): discussion and reference to other texts shows how far the children can relate the story to its contemporary context.

PHASE 2: ANALYSING STRUCTURE AND FEATURES (3 DAYS)

Session 5

We are learning to ...	Resources
• understand the structure of interactive texts • use key questions to develop ideas for a new story (PNS Strands 7.3, 9.1) **Assessment Focuses** AF (R): 2, 7	*Planet Prison* ITP: 2.4 PCM: 2.6

Shared teaching

- Recap the 'Big Picture' and share the learning objectives. Explain that, in this session, the children will identify the main features of the genre in preparation for writing their own stories in Phase 3.
- Show 'Story ingredients' (ITP 2.4). *What genre would you classify* Planet Prison *as?* Click on the heading 'Genre'. *Would you agree this is a Futuristic or Sci-fi adventure?*
- Read the introductory screen of *Planet Prison* (screen 1, Level 1a). *What aspects are typical of this genre?*
- Highlight and discuss details about: the setting (Planet Celba, Planet Earth – space); the characters (Cad, the CLAWs – heroine and dangerous enemies); the themes (brutal CLAW regime, occupation – forces of good and evil); the plot (Cad's mission – plot revolves around a mission, task or quest); the language ('human inhabitants', 'mission' – technical or scientific sounding words 'Celban', 'the CLAWs' – invented names, 'Units' – invented ideas).
- Read screen 2 (Level 1a) of *Planet Prison* and repeat the activity, identifying further details about: the setting (the year 2540); the themes (oppression; supremacy); the plot (back story); and language.
- Show ITP 2.4 again. Click on each heading in turn to reveal a summary of the main features. *Which have we already identified in* Planet Prison*? What about the others, do they relate to* Planet Prison*? Can you give an example of how or where?*
- Discuss a few other examples of sci-fi or futuristic adventures the children are familiar with, e.g. books, comics, TV, film, computer adventure games. *Do they have the same features*?

Independent and Guided

- The children work in groups to share examples of other futuristic or sci-fi texts they are familiar with. They choose one text to focus on and complete 'Story ingredients' (PCM 2.6). (Alternatively, provide a range of sci-fi materials for the children to compare to *Planet Prison.*) Support the children with an identified need. (T+/TA)

Plenary

- A spokesperson for each group summarises their discussion of one text. Compare the features with those listed on ITP 2.4. *What are the similarities and differences?* Add to the Learning Wall.
- Recap the learning objectives.
- Remind the children that they are going to be writing their own sci-fi story. *What key questions do you need to think about in preparation for writing your story?* (E.g. *What is the setting? Who is the hero or heroine and enemy? What is the purpose of the mission or adventure?*) Scribe key questions and add the list to the Learning Wall.

Assessment pointers

- S&L: group work will show how well the children can adopt group roles and express relevant ideas.
- AF2 (R): group discussions show how far the children are able to select relevant examples from the text.
- AF7 (R): group discussions and oral responses show how far they can identify common features in different examples of the genre.

Session 6

We are learning to ...	Resources
• understand the structure of interactive texts (PNS Strands 7.3) **Assessment Focuses** AF (R): 2, 4	*Planet Prison* ITP: 2.5, 2.6 PCM: 2.7

Shared teaching

- Share the learning objective and explain that, in this session, the children will look at how single episodes are built up over a series of screens which will help in planning and writing their stories in Phase 3.
- Recap features of a futuristic or sci-fi plot, e.g. it is based around a mission with many adventures along the way.
- Show 'Story map' (ITP 2.5). *What is unusual about the plot of this story?* (E.g. the choice of reading routes; the divergence of storylines.) *Do the storylines still fit the features of a futuristic or sci-fi plot?* (Yes, all routes lead to the final challenge and involve overcoming problems along the way.)
- Explain that the children will plot out the main stages of *Planet Prison*, breaking it down into separate parts or 'episodes' to see the structure and organisation of the story clearly.
- Return to ITP 2.5 and encourage the children to help you complete the diagram. *Do you remember what the next episode is? What could we call the episode?* Save annotations for use in Session 7.
- Recap one of the chosen routes that was taken through *Planet Prison*, during the shared reading in Phase 1.
- Show 'Story structure' (ITP 2.6) and explain that the children are going to look at the episodes from the shared reading route in more detail. Focus on the first two episodes on Screen 1 and use Modelled Writing to complete the chart. *What can we call this episode? What is the problem and solution? How does this episode move the plot forward?* (E.g. introduces a new character, takes the character closer to the target location, gives the character new information or a key object.)
- Talk Partners discuss the next episode on Screen 2 from the shared teaching route, thinking of a title and details to complete the chart.
- Take feedback and complete the chart on ITP 2.6. Encourage the children to support their ideas with details from *Planet Prison. How are these episodes important in the overall structure? How can we make the route choices stand out?* (E.g. use a different colour.)
- If necessary, reread *Planet Prison* and work through the screens of the shared reading route again, breaking them down into separate episodes.

Independent and Guided

- In groups, the children identify the last three episodes in the shared reading route, completing 'Story structure' (PCM 2.7). When groups are finished, they send out Envoys to share ideas and take feedback to report back to their groups. Support the children with an identified need. (T+/TA)

Plenary

- Show ITP 2.6 and display Screens 2 and 3. Invite groups to help you complete the rest of the story structure.
- Recap the learning objective. *Was it easy to plan the sequence of episodes? What problems did you have?*

Assessment pointers

- S&L: group work will show how well the children can adopt group roles and express relevant ideas.
- AF2 (R): response to questions, completed PCMs and group discussion show how far the children can select details and ideas from the text.
- AF4 (R): plotting the structure of the text shows how far the children understand the structure and organisation of the text.

Session 7

We are learning to ...	Resources
• understand how screens link together to form an episode (PNS Strands 7.3) **Assessment Focuses** AF (R): 4, 5	*Planet Prison* ITP: (2.5) PCM: 2.8

Shared teaching

- Recall annotated 'Story map' (ITP 2.5) and recap that each storyline is built using a series of episodes, each vital to the overall story.
- Discuss the episodes on ITP 2.5. *Could any of the episodes be left out? Why is this episode important? How does it link to what follows?*
- Share the learning objective.
- Recap the episode 'Rogue attack at Zolta Park'. *Where does this come in the story? What happened before it? Why is it important to the plot? How does it take the story forward?*
- Reread *Planet Prison* and go to screen 8 (Level 3a/b). *What does this screen tell us?* Talk Partners summarise key points, e.g. the Rogues launch a surprise attack on the CLAWs.
- Take feedback and scribe responses.
- Show screens 9–10 (Level 3a/b). *Could any of these screens be left out? How does each screen link to the following screen?*
- Show screens 8–10 (Level 3a/b) again. Focus on how the events are told, e.g. the use of description (text), action (text or visual), and dialogue (text or audio). *How is each used?* (E.g. action for pace; dialogue and text to carry the story forward; occasional descriptive detail for effect.)
- Identify examples of sentences describing actions, sentences with descriptive detail and lines of dialogue in screens 8–10 (Level 3a/b).
- Discuss interesting sentence constructions, e.g. short exclamations, the use of dashes to add pauses and contractions for natural speech, e.g. 'Blood as well as life juice – she's part human! Seize her!'; sentences reordered for effect and descriptive detail, e.g. 'With laser bolts whipping through the air, Cad ran.'; and complex action and *–ing* starters, e.g. 'Reaching the Chief CLAW's patrol vehicle, Cad grabbed a speed bike from the hold and sped off.'
- Scribe examples and add them to the Learning Wall.

Independent and Guided

- Groups select and analyse a different episode from *Planet Prison*, completing 'Storyboard' (PCM 2.8). They summarise the content of each screen, identifying when action, dialogue and description are used. Within the group, pairs or individuals are given the additional responsibility of recording examples of useful dialogue, interesting action sentences or sentences with descriptive detail to display on the Learning Wall. Support the children with an identified need. (T+/TA)

Plenary

- Recap the learning objective and take feedback.
- *What have you learnt about the structure of the story? How will this help you plan your story? Can you think of other key questions to consider?* (E.g. *What problems could be faced along the way?*)
- Add key questions to the Learning Wall.

Assessment pointers

- S&L: group work will show how far the children can engage with others, draw ideas together and promote discussion.
- AF4, 5 (R): storyboards and responses to questions show how far the children understand the structural features of the text and can identify and comment on the author's language choices and their effect.

Session 8

We are learning to …	Resources
• use dialogic talk to explore and evaluate possibilities and agree choices • use key questions to develop ideas for a new story (PNS Strand: 1.3, 9.1) **Assessment Focuses** AF (W): 1, 2	ITP: 2.7, 2.8, 2.9 PCM: (2.1), 2.9

Shared teaching

- Share the learning objectives and explain that, in this session, the children are going to explore ideas and agree on the content for group stories.
- Show 'Writer's brief' (ITP 2.7) and discuss the success criteria. Click the headings to reveal more information. *Is there anything you would like to add?*
- Recap the key questions already displayed on the Learning Wall. *What key areas do we need to focus on when planning a story?* (E.g. setting, theme, plot and characters.)
- Talk Partners discuss more key questions that will help them write their stories, focusing on the key areas.
- Show 'Writer's questions' (ITP 2.8). *Are your questions included? Are there any you would like to add?*
- Show 'Story ideas' (ITP 2.9). Lead a class discussion to model exploring and evaluating one or two of the suggestions, e.g. *If I chose 'A race against time', what would be the mission? Why would it be necessary? Is there potential for lots of adventures or alternative storylines? Which of these sounds most appealing or interesting for the audience?*
- Agree on an idea and discuss answers to some of the key questions on ITP 2.8, e.g. ideas for a main hero or heroine, an enemy, a setting with a number of possible locations, etc.
- Show ITP 2.7 and remind the children to refer the story ideas back to the 'Writer's brief', e.g. *Do you think the audience will like that hero or heroine? Do you think the setting is right for people who like computer games?*

Independent and Guided

- In groups, the children discuss and evaluate story ideas, select one and then develop answers to the key questions on ITP 2.8. They record agreed ideas on 'Story ideas' (PCM 2.9). Remind the children to discuss their ideas in relation to the 'Writer's brief' on ITP 2.7. Where necessary, the children use 'Talk to develop thinking' (PCM 2.1) to help structure their discussions. Support the children with an identified need. (T/TA+)

Plenary

- A spokesperson for each group gives an oral summary of their idea, 'selling it' to the rest of the class. *Does this sound like a suitable or attractive idea for the target audience? Would you want to read the text? Can you see any problems or weaknesses*? Take feedback.
- Recap the learning objectives.

Assessment pointers

- S&L: group work will show how far the children can engage with others, draw ideas together and promote discussion.
- AF1, 2 (W): completed PCMs, oral feedback and peer assessment show how far the children can generate interesting ideas that are appropriate to task, reader and purpose, and how far they can select appropriate ideas and sustain appropriate style to engage the reader's interest.

Session 9

We are learning to …	Resources
• plan a story structure with more than one reading route • plot out the sequence of events, making sure everything links together logically (PNS Strands 10.1) **Assessment Focuses** AF (W) 1, 2, 3	ITP: (2.5, 2.7), 2.10 PCM: (2.9), 2.10

Shared teaching

- Share the learning objectives.
- Recall annotated 'Story map' (ITP 2.5) and recap the structure of *Planet Prison*. Discuss the choices made by the reader, the different reading routes and the different endings.
- Explain that the children will work as a group, in pairs and independently to plot the different routes through their story. Remind them that a good plan is essential so everyone knows which part of the story they are writing.
- Show 'Planning frame' (ITP 2.10) and use Modelled Writing to complete it with story ideas from Session 8. *What needs to be included in the opening to introduce the story?* (E.g. introduce the setting, etc.) *What about an opening event?*
- Discuss the first two choices for ITP 2.10, e.g. what to do, where to go, who to call, etc. Explain that the choices must take the storyline in two totally different directions.
- Talk Partners discuss a choice of what to do, where to go, who to call, etc. Take feedback.
- Add both choices to ITP 2.10, e.g. 'go to Earth' or 'go to Planet Zoltan'.
- Choose the first option and continue planning this part of the story. *So we take the first option to go to Earth. Then what happens?*
- Take feedback and add ideas to ITP 2.10. Use Modelled Writing to demonstrate making short notes, e.g. problem: trapped on watch tower; solution: jet pack to escape.
- Use Think Alouds to show how events will link together, e.g. Perhaps she could land in the enemy base; that would take her nearer the command module. I'll call my next episode 'Inside the enemy base'.

Independent and Guided

- The children work in the same groups as in Session 8 to plan a five-episode story on an enlarged copy of 'Planning frame' (PCM 2.10), referring to completed 'Story ideas' (PCM 2.9). Each group decides on their first two choices, then splits into two smaller groups to plan storylines 1 and 2. They then reassemble to agree on the storylines and endings and complete PCM 2.10. Support the children with an identified need. (T/TA)

Plenary

- Recap the learning objectives and pair up groups to explain their stories to each other using the plans on PCM 2.10. *Is everything linked together logically? Is the structure of the story clear?*
- Take feedback. *What did you like about the group's plan? What do you think needs improving?*
- Recap 'Writer's brief' (ITP 2.7) and discuss whether the story plans will appeal to the target audience.

Assessment pointers

- S&L: group work will show how well the children can adopt group roles, drawing ideas together and promoting effective planning.
- AF1, 2 (W): independent and guided tasks show how far the children can develop ideas imaginatively around the task, reader and purpose.
- AF3 (W): plans, group discussion and feedback show how far the children can organise and structure ideas.

Session 10

We are learning to ...	Resources
• write an effective opening that will appeal to the reader • organise our opening into separate screens (PNS Strands 9.2, 10.1) **Assessment Focuses** AF (W): 1, 2, 3, 4, 7	ITP: (2.10), 2.11 PCM: (2.10)

Shared teaching

- Share the learning objectives and explain that the children are going to start writing their stories. Discuss different ways to present these on paper or using computers. *How will you make the different screens clear? How will you make the options for the reader stand out?*
- Show 'Story opening' (ITP 2.11) and discuss the success criteria needed for a good story opening. *Is there anything you would like to add or change?* Remind the children that the purpose of a good opening is to capture the reader's interest and give them the information they need.
- Recall annotated 'Planning frame' (ITP 2.10) and discuss ideas for how to start the story. *How can we capture the reader's interest?*
- Use Modelled Writing to compose the opening sentence for a story, using Think Alouds and giving reasons for your choice, e.g. *I think I'm just going to say what the character does and not who they are. That's intriguing because it makes the reader wonder who they are.*
- Use Modelled Writing to compose the next few sentences of the opening. *What other information can we give?* (E.g. setting and events)
- Model choosing appropriate language to establish the genre or a new focus. *What words can we use to show this is a science fiction text?* (E.g. mega-city, transporter)
- Refer to ITP 2.10 and explain that the children need to start a new screen for each movement in time or place. Draw a diagram of 3–5 screens, plotting the existing opening text onto screen 1. Start a second screen. *How could I introduce some back story here?*

Independent and Guided

- The children work in the same groups as in Sessions 8 and 9 to write a story opening, referring to completed 'Planning frame' (PCM 2.10) and the annotated success criteria on ITP 2.11. One group member writes the story but all group members are responsible for what is written. If possible, allow the children to compose the stories on computers, using software that can map each screen. Alternatively, compose the story on separate sheets of paper to represent the different screens. Support the children with an identified need. (T+/TA+)

Plenary

- Recap the learning objectives. *Do you think your opening will appeal to the reader? How did you try to capture the reader's attention?*
- Pair up groups to share their story ideas, discussing whether they meet the success criteria on ITP 2.11. They write Two Stars and a Wish for use in Session 11.
- Take feedback and ask for examples of their two stars and a wish.

Assessment pointers

- S&L: group work will show how well the children can adopt group roles, drawing ideas together and promoting effective writing.
- AF1, 2 (W): completed drafts demonstrate the children's ability to write imaginative and appropriate text.
- AF3, 4 (W): structuring content on separate screens shows how far the children can sequence and structure ideas and events with cohesion.
- AF7 (W): use of appropriate vocabulary shows how far the children are able to use language effectively.

Session 11

We are learning to ...	Resources
• write an episode for our story using a series of screens • check that the story ideas link together logically (PNS Strands 10.1) **Assessment Focuses** AF (W): 3, 4	ITP: (2.10) PCM: (2.10)

Shared teaching

- Recap the children's work from Session 10.
- Share the learning objectives and explain that, in this session, the children will complete the opening (Episode 1) and write Episode 2 of their stories.
- Show annotated 'Planning frame' (ITP 2.10) and use Modelled Writing to compose the lead-up to the first choice, e.g. *Jo had to make a decision – fast! Should she fly to Planet Zoltan and ... or should she fly to Earth and ... .*
- Model adding the choice for the reader, e.g. *Click on Planet Earth or Planet Zoltan to move on.*
- Discuss the notes for Episode 2 of the chosen storyline on ITP 2.10 and explain that you are going to 'tell' the episode before writing it. Explain that oral rehearsal allows us to rehearse sentences and develop interesting details to include in our writing. It gives us a chance to think through the sequence of events and check that the episode works.
- Refer to the notes on annotated ITP 2.10 and 'tell' the sequence of events for the chosen storyline. Select suitable connecting words and phrases to link events, e.g. *A moment later Jo was ... ; Suddenly ... ; Now ...* ,etc.
- Model making decisions about when to start new screens, e.g. *I think I need a new screen here because I'm now going to introduce the problem.*
- Use Modelled Writing to write the first few screens for Episode 2. Focus on linking screens together to achieve cohesion by using connecting words or phrases and making sure that pronouns are clear.

Independent and Guided

- The children work in the same groups as in Sessions 8–10 to reread their story openings and refer back to their Two Stars and a Wish from Session 10. They make changes to the openings and compose text for the 'choice' screen. Divide each group into two smaller groups to write Episode 2 for the different storylines, referring to completed 'Planning frame' (PCM 2.10). Encourage the use of oral rehearsal to develop detail, plan separate screens and check that ideas link together. Support the children with an identified need. (T+/TA+)

Plenary

- Recap the learning objectives. *How have you written your episode over a series of screens? How have you linked the screens together? Are there any problems you need help with?*

Assessment pointers

- S&L: group work will show how well the children can adopt group roles, drawing ideas together and promoting effective writing.
- AF3, 4 (W): peer and self-assessment, written work and group discussion show how far the children can organise texts logically.

Session 12

We are learning to ...	Resources
• write different kinds of sentences, thinking about the effect on the reader • check that we use commas to separate parts of a sentence (PNS Strands 11.1, 11.2) **Assessment Focuses** AF (W): 1, 2, 5, 6	ITP: (2.10), 2.12, 2.13 PCM: (2.10)

Shared teaching

- Share the learning objectives.
- Recap annotated 'Planning frame' (ITP 2.10). Establish where Episode 3 fits in the story: the main character has another problem to overcome that is vital to the overall story and ends up with another choice.
- Show 'Choose-your-own adventure stories' (ITP 2.12) and discuss the success criteria. *Is there anything you would like to add or change? How might we make events tense or exciting for the reader?*
- Show 'Writing sample' (ITP 2.13). Read the text to the class. *There are lots of exciting events here, so why doesn't it sound lively?*
- Take feedback. Focus on the overuse of simple sentences of a similar length and construction. Explain that effective writing is a mixture of simple, compound and complex sentences.
- Refer to the interesting sentence constructions from Session 7 displayed on the Learning Wall and encourage the children to use these later when they are writing.
- Encourage the children to offer suggestions to improve the text on ITP 2.13. *How can we vary the sentences? How does this change affect the reader?* (E.g. combine the first three sentences into one complex sentence to present information quickly; use 'but' to link the two short sentences and signal that there is a problem, 'Jo froze but it was too late'.) Select a sentence from ITP 2.13 to extend with descriptive detail to create mood or impact, e.g. 'She heard a noise'. Talk Partners discuss how the sentence might be extended.
- Take feedback. Remind the children that sometimes a short sentence can be effective for emphasis or to show significance, e.g. 'The Zoltans had seen her'.
- Use Think Alouds to model moving clauses around on ITP 2.13 and discuss the effect. Reinforce the correct use of commas.
- Focus on the effect created by adding suitable adverbs to the text on ITP 2.13, e.g. 'Painfully, she clambered to her feet.' Use Think Alouds to model placing adverbs in different positions before making the final amendment. Again, reinforce when commas are needed.

Independent and Guided

- The children work in the same groups as in Sessions 8–11 to revise sentences in Episode 2. In smaller groups, they write the two versions of Episode 3, referring to annotated 'Planning frame' (PCM 2.10) and the success criteria on ITP 2.12. They should end each version of Episode 3 with another choice to be made. Encourage oral rehearsal of sentences, using different constructions and focusing on the effect created. Support the children with an identified need. (T+/TA+)

Plenary

- Recap the learning objectives. Focus on the success criteria on ITP 2.12 and ask the smaller groups to review each other's episodes. Encourage the children to use Two Stars and a Wish to give feedback.

Assessment pointers

- S&L: group work will show how well the children can adopt group roles, drawing ideas together and promoting effective writing.
- AF1, 2, 5, 6 (W): completed drafts of Episode 3 and revised sentences show how far the children can vary sentences for effect and use commas when writing imaginative texts appropriate to purpose.

Session 13

We are learning to ...	Resources
• combine action, description and dialogue • use dialogue to move the story forward (PNS Strands 9.2) **Assessment Focuses** AF (W): 1	ITP: (2.10), 2.14, 2.15

Shared teaching

- Share the learning objectives and explain that, in this session, the children will write Episode 4 of their stories.
- Recap annotated 'Planning frame' (ITP 2.10). Establish where Episode 4 fits in the story. (it leads up to the climax)
- Show 'Dialogue' (ITP 2.14) and use the three screens to discuss how dialogue is used within the story. Show Screen 1. *How is the CLAW's line of dialogue significant to what happens next?* (it gives us information about Cad and takes the plot forward)
- Show Screen 2. *What is the purpose of this dialogue?* (E.g. tells us what is happening; what could happen.) *Why is it more effective to show what is happening through dialogue rather than by just telling us?* (E.g. it draws the reader into the situation.)
- Show Screen 3. *How does this dialogue help to bring the story to its climax?* (E.g. it establishes a history between the characters.)
- Discuss how the dialogue is presented on these screens. *How is this different from a conventional text?* Compare speech bubbles with conventional direct speech, e.g. punctuation, reporting clauses. *What are the advantages or disadvantages of using speech bubbles?* (E.g. disadvantages: no reporting clause to show how the words are spoken; pictures are needed to show who is speaking; exchanges are limited by the number of speech bubbles on one screen.)
- Show 'Inventing dialogue' (ITP 2.15). Read the examples. *How could we say the same thing using a line of dialogue?* (E.g. 'It is the escaped human. Seize her!' or 'Merlin! Is that you?')
- Take feedback and add ideas to the each speech bubble on ITP 2.15. Use Modelled Writing to write the same thing using speech marks and a reporting clause. Explain that the children can choose which method to use, but they must use the same method throughout the story.

Independent and Guided

- The children work in the same groups as in Sessions 8–12 and organise smaller groups or individuals (depending on group size) to write the four versions of Episode 4, following the group plan and focusing on combining action, description and dialogue. Work with groups, revising writing from Session 12. Support the children with an identified need. (T+/TA+)

Plenary

- Recap the learning objectives. The four smaller groups or individuals in each group swap around their episodes, giving feedback. *Have they used dialogue effectively? Is there too much or not enough?* Encourage the children to say what works well or what could be done to improve the dialogue.
- Take feedback and add example dialogue to the Learning Wall.

Assessment pointers

- S&L: group work will show how well the children can adopt group roles, drawing ideas together and promoting effective writing.
- AF1 (W): completed drafts of Episode 4 show how far the children can use appropriate action, description and dialogue in writing.

Session 14

We are learning to ...	Resources
• write an effective ending for our story (PNS Strands 9.2)	*Planet Prison*
Assessment Focuses	ITP: (2.10), 2.16
AF (W): 1, 2, 3	PCM: (2.10)

Shared teaching (1)

- Share the learning objective and explain that, in this session, the children will write the ending for their stories.
- Recap annotated 'Planning frame' (ITP 2.10) and establish where Episode 5 fits in the story. (it's the last episode and ending)
- Show 'Story endings' (ITP 2.16) and discuss the success criteria. *Is there anything you would like to add or change?*
- Show screens 7–8 (Level 4f) of *Planet Prison.* Reinforce the terminology for discussing the structure of the ending: the lead-up brings the story to the final scene, e.g. arriving at Zolta Park and meeting Petra; the climax or crisis is where the main character faces the final challenge or comes close to disaster, e.g. the army advancing; the resolution act is the act that defeats the enemy, e.g. throwing the grenade; the resolution result is what happens as a result of the main character's action, e.g. the CLAWs collapse and Cad runs to free the humans; the ending is the final screen or line, e.g. Petra speaking.
- Scribe the terminology and add the list to the Learning Wall.
- Refer to ITP 2.10 and orally rehearse ideas for ending the story, incorporating points from the success criteria on ITP 2.16.

Independent and Guided (1)

- The children work in the same smaller groups to develop the four endings, referring to completed 'Planning frame' (PCM 2.10). Encourage the children to refer to the success criteria to develop their ideas. Remind the children that the four endings should vary in some way, while still achieving the main mission. *Can you use a key object or piece of information introduced earlier?* Support the children with an identified need. (T/TA)

Shared teaching (2)

- Discuss different ways of closing a story, e.g. using a comment from one of the characters; allowing the main character to think aloud; looking to the future; commenting on the significance of the resolution.
- Using the model story, provide examples of some of these ways, e.g. 'Now we have the crystal, the Zoltans will never be able to control us.'

Independent and Guided (2)

- The smaller groups continue to write the story endings, focusing on including different closing lines, referring to PCM 2.10 and ITP 2.16. They then read Episodes 4 and 5 to ensure the events are logically linked, lead up to the climax and all problems are resolved. The children then proofread their texts, checking spellings and punctuation. Support the children with an identified need. (T/TA)

Plenary

- Recap the learning objective. The smaller groups share their endings with the rest of the group. Encourage the children to use the success criteria on ITP 2.16 to offer positive and constructive feedback.
- Encourage groups to share ways in which stories were resolved and closed. *Do you think this ending is particularly effective?*

Assessment pointers

- S&L: group work will show how well the children can adopt group roles, drawing ideas together and promoting effective writing.
- AF1, 2, 3 (W): drafted endings show how far the children can use imaginative details in structuring an ending appropriate to the task.

Session 15

We are learning to ...	Resources
• say how successful our own writing is and say what we have learned from completing a writing task (PNS Strands 9.1)	ITP: (2.7, 2.12)
Assessment Focuses	PCM: 2.11, 2.12
AF (W): 1, 2	

Shared teaching (1)

- Choose one groups' work (preferably work that demonstrates both good points and scope for improvement) and display for the class.
- Share the learning objective and explain that, in this session, the children will evaluate their completed stories against 'Choose-your-own adventure stories' (ITP 2.12) and 'Writer's brief' (ITP 2.7).
- Show 'Marking ladder' (PCM 2.11) and work through some of the points, relating them to the story you have chosen. If a point has not been covered, encourage the class to offer suggestions as to how this could be resolved. Encourage positive and constructive feedback.

Independent and Guided (1)

- The children work in the same groups as in Sessions 8–14 to complete PCM 2.11 for their stories. Areas that have not been covered should be identified and final changes made. Encourage the children to think about the presentation of their text and ways in which illustration (and if using computers, sound effects, clips and animation) could be added. Support the children with an identified need. (T/TA)

Shared teaching (2)

- Take feedback. *What final changes have you made?*
- Give out 'Reader's response' (PCM 2.12) and refer to one group's story. Read one storyline and model making comments as you read, e.g. *That was a good choice to give the reader because it caused lots of discussion, but perhaps this character could be a little more interesting if we created more mystery about them.* Encourage the children to give positive and constructive feedback.
- Focus on PCM 2.12. *Which of these questions could you respond to positively? What worked well?* Talk Partners discuss specific examples.
- Take feedback and summarise the main points the children should look for in evaluating their classmates' work.

Independent and Guided (2)

- Groups read each other's stories, choosing different storylines. They then discuss opinions about the story and complete PCM 2.12 referring to ITP 2.7 and ITP 2.12 when necessary. Join groups together to share their feedback. Hold guided sessions to discuss groups' achievements. Support the children with an identified need. (T+/TA)

Plenary

- Take feedback on the stories that the children have read. *What did you like about the story? What could be done to improve it? How might you share your completed stories with others?* (E.g. on the school website.)
- Recap the learning objective and the unit as a whole. *What have you learnt about structuring or creating a text like this? What else have you learnt from writing a collaborative story? What have you enjoyed most? What do still find difficult?*

Assessment pointers

- S&L: group work will show how far the children can manage discussion and feed back with sensitivity.
- AF1, 2 (W): peer and self-assessment show how far the children can write imaginative, interesting texts appropriate to the task and purpose.

Talk to develop thinking

1. Speak your thoughts.

Say what you think:
It makes ... seem ...
I think it means...

Explain your ideas:
I think ... because ...

Suggest ideas (you don't have to be certain):
Perhaps ...
Maybe ...
I wonder ...

Ask questions:
What if ...?
Can you explain ...?
How do we know ...?
Why ...?

Respond to others:
I agree/disagree because ...
But what about ...?
Have you thought of ...?

2. Listen to others and think about what they say.

Does what they say help you understand more?

Does what they say add to your own ideas?

Do you agree or disagree?

Does what they say make sense?

Does what they say make you think differently about the subject?

Reading strategies

Tick the strategies you have used.

	Date:____	Date:____	Date:____
Using what I already know about this kind of text or theme. *I think Cad is going to have to ...*			
Visualising the story. *I imagine life in a Unit is ...*			
Predicting what might happen. *I think they will ...*			
Summarising what has happened. *In this part of the story, Cad ...*			
Checking I understand. *So does that mean ...?*			
Asking questions. *Is the locket important?*			
Interacting with the text. *I think we should choose that option because ...*			
Thinking about how the characters are feeling. *I think Cad must be feeling ...*			
Relating the text to my own personal experience. *If I were in that situation, I would ...*			
Looking for patterns and links in the text. *The name of the Unit that escaped is the same as ...*			

Story ending

Answer the questions about the ending of *Planet Prison*.

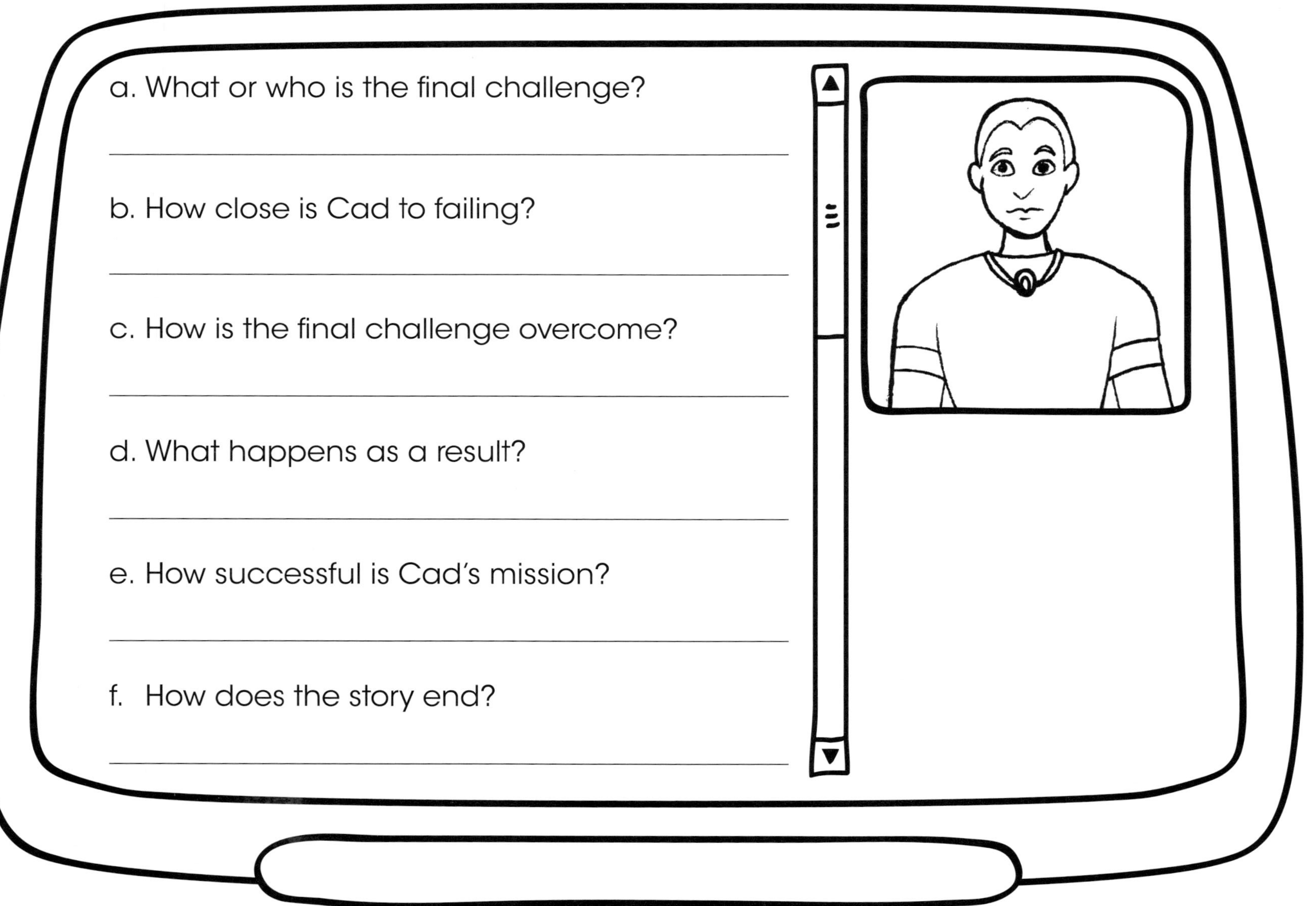

a. What or who is the final challenge?

____

b. How close is Cad to failing?

____

c. How is the final challenge overcome?

____

d. What happens as a result?

____

e. How successful is Cad's mission?

____

f. How does the story end?

____

Multimedia prompts

Look at how these features are used in a sequence from *Planet Prison*.

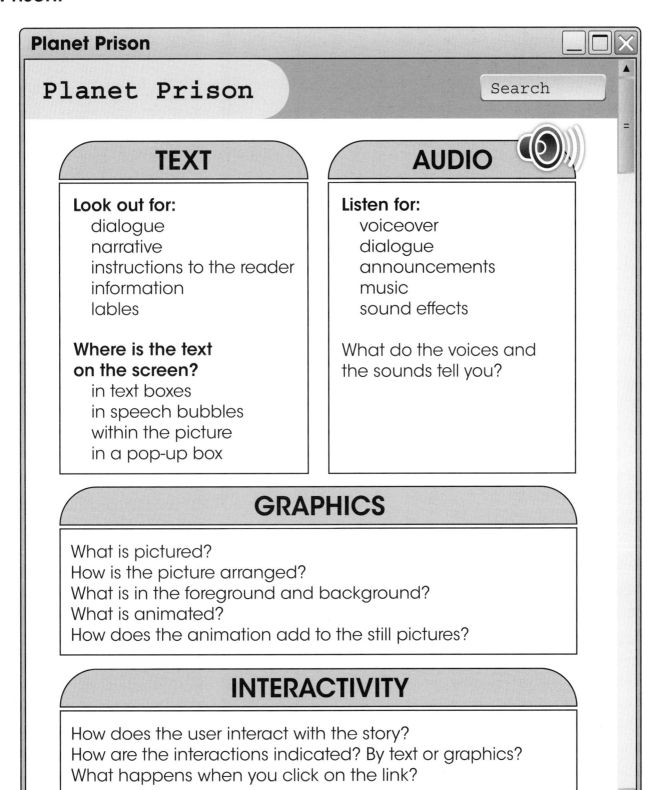

Planet Prison

Planet Prison

Search

TEXT

Look out for:
- dialogue
- narrative
- instructions to the reader
- information
- lables

Where is the text on the screen?
- in text boxes
- in speech bubbles
- within the picture
- in a pop-up box

AUDIO

Listen for:
- voiceover
- dialogue
- announcements
- music
- sound effects

What do the voices and the sounds tell you?

GRAPHICS

What is pictured?
How is the picture arranged?
What is in the foreground and background?
What is animated?
How does the animation add to the still pictures?

INTERACTIVITY

How does the user interact with the story?
How are the interactions indicated? By text or graphics?
What happens when you click on the link?

Multimedia storyboard

Write about the text, audio, graphics and interactivity in a sequence from *Planet Prison*.

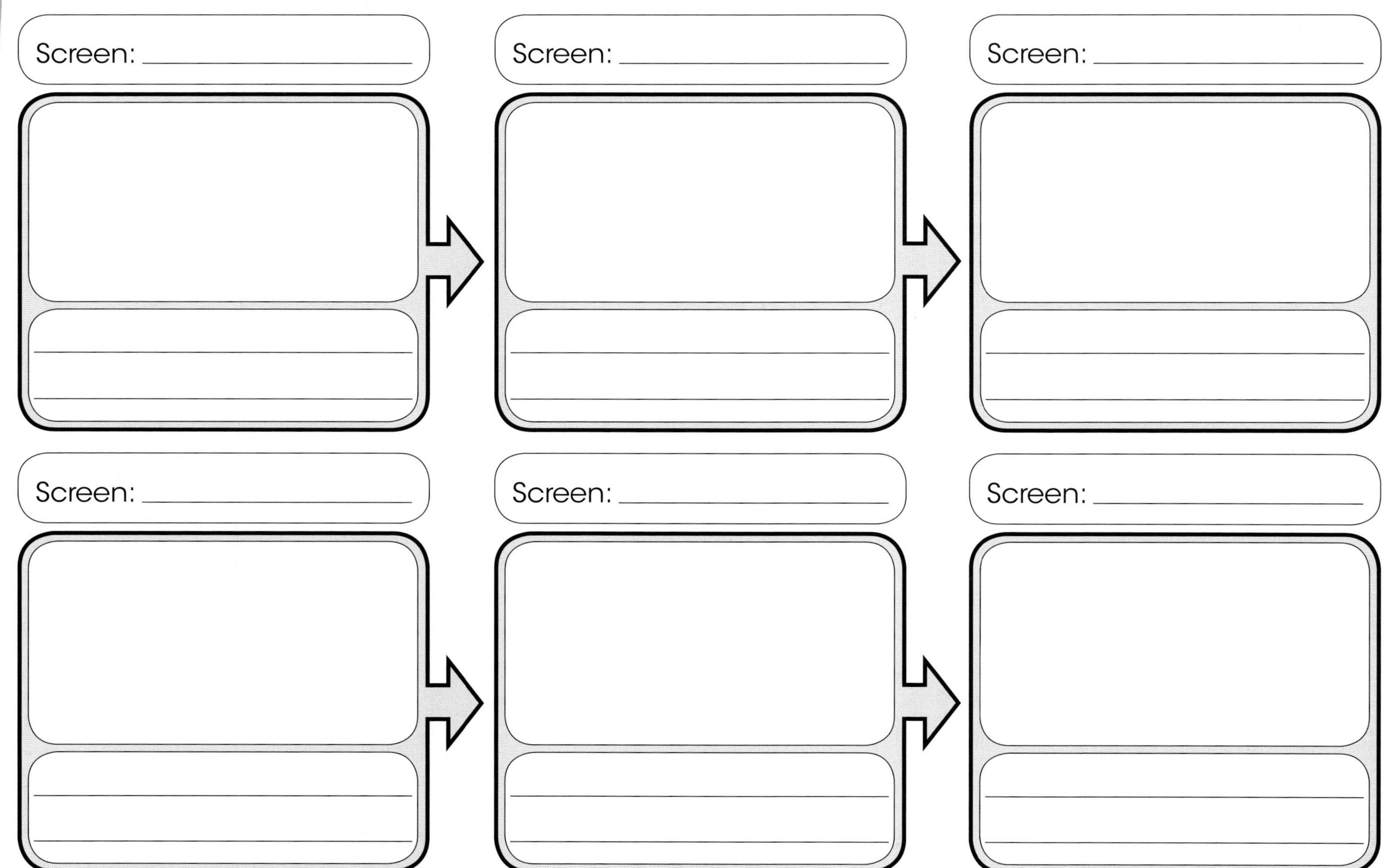

Name: ______________________ Date: ______________ **2.6**

Story ingredients

Complete the mind map about another futuristic or sci-fi adventure.

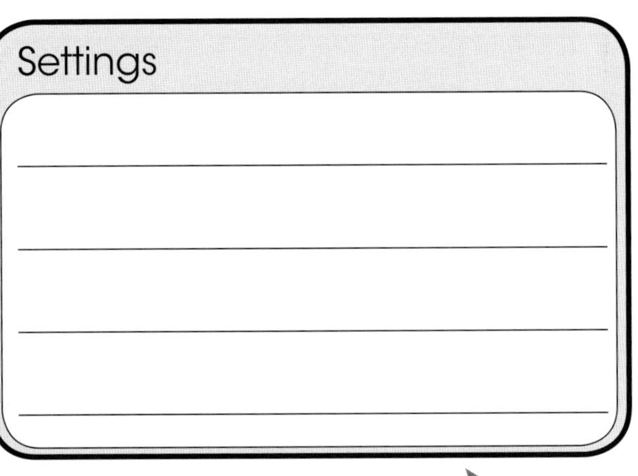

Settings

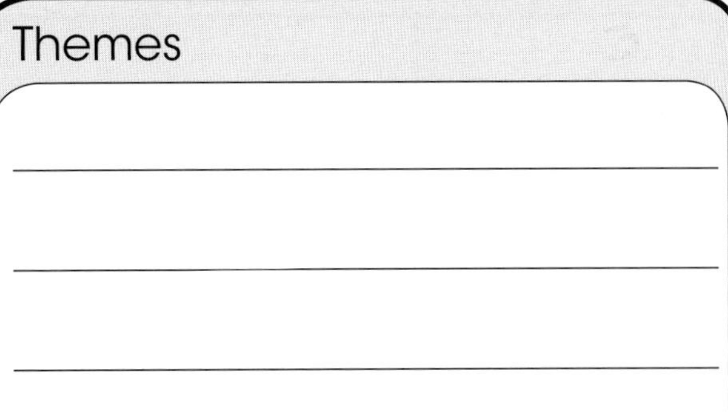

Themes

Characters

Futuristic or sci-fi adventure

Name: ______________________

Language

Plot (opening, events, ending)

Story structure

Plot the last sequence of episodes through *Planet Prison*.

Episode 4: ______________________

Problem(s): ______________________

____

Solution(s): ______________________

____

Purpose:

____

____

____

____

____

Episode 5: ______________________

Problem(s): ______________________

____

Solution(s): ______________________

____

Purpose:

____

____

____

____

____

Episode 6: ______________________

Problem(s): ______________________

____

Solution(s): ______________________

____

Purpose:

____

____

____

____

____

Storyboard

Choose one episode from *Planet Prison* to analyse in detail, summarising each screen. Draw the layout of each screen.

Episode: ____

Screen: ________

Key events: ________________________

____

____

Dialogue, action, description: ________________________

____

____

Screen: ________

Key events: ________________________

____

____

Dialogue, action, description: ________________________

____

____

Screen: ________

Key events: ________________________

____

____

Dialogue, action, description: ________________________

____

____

Story ideas

Plan ideas for your story.

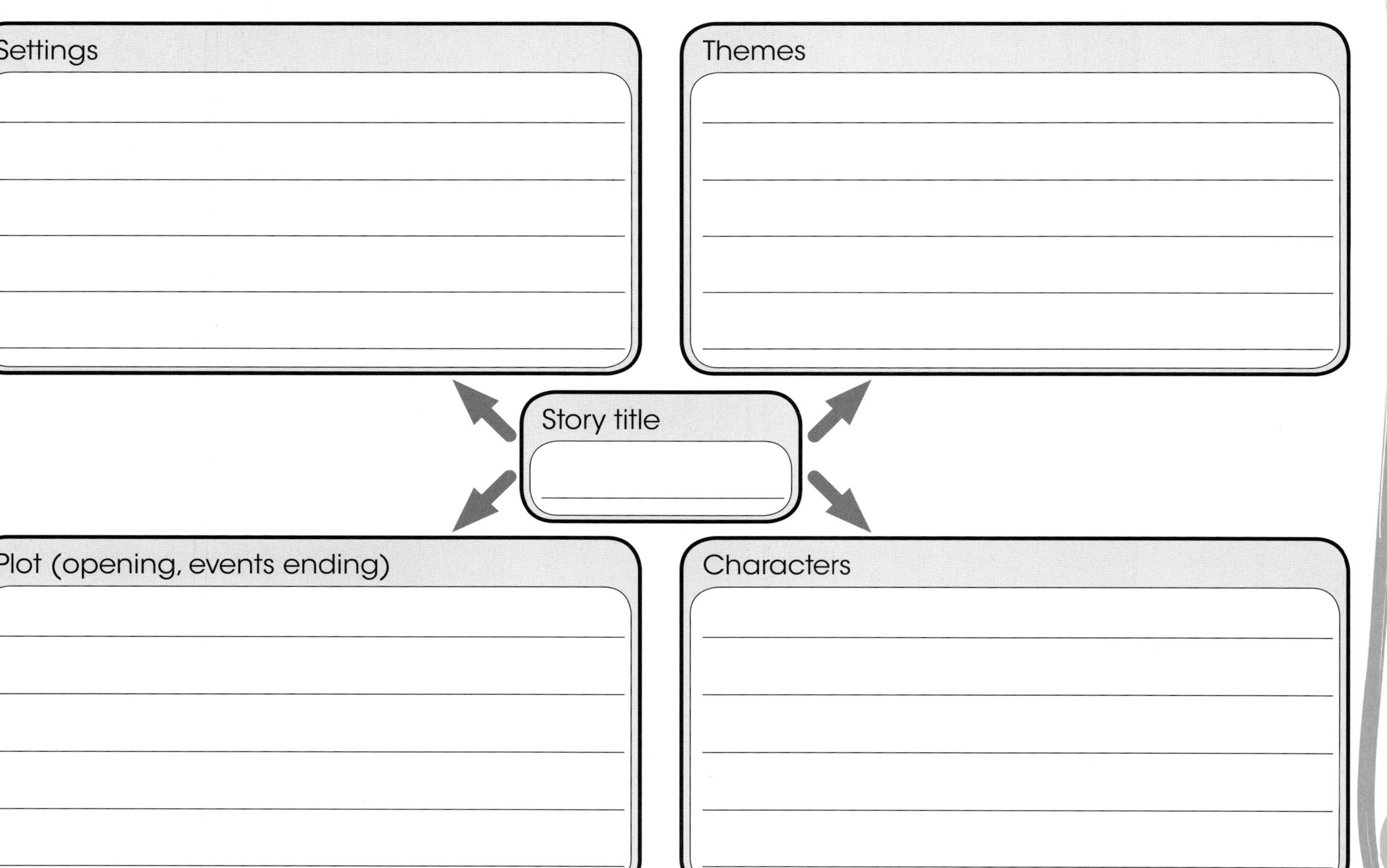

Planning frame

Add notes to plan the storylines.

Episode 1

Episode 2a

Episode 2b

Episode 3a

Episode 3b

Episode 4a

Episode 4b

Episode 4c

Episode 4d

Episode 5a

Episode 5b

Episode 5c

Episode 5d

Marking ladder

Use the marking ladder to check your work.

My comments		My teacher's comments
	Our story has an interesting 'story world'.	
	It introduces appealing characters that fit the story genre.	
	It has a series of episodes where the main character overcomes a range of problems.	
	It has several routes for the reader to choose from.	
	It has plenty of dramatic moments with action, description and dialogue to develop the events.	
	It has an interesting way of closing, perhaps words from a character.	

Reader's response

1. Read another group's story. Discuss and answer the questions.

a. How are you involved in the story?

____

b. Are there several routes through the story? Do the events link together?

____

c. Does the story have a clear structure?

____

d. How is the 'story world' created? Is it an interesting setting?

____

e. How are the characters introduced? Are they interesting?

____

____

f. Are there dramatic moments? Where and how are these developed?

____

____

g. Is the story well told? How does it keep you interested?

____

____

2. What else made the story exciting for you?

____

____

____

____

Narrative Unit 3

MILLIONS – novel (Author study)

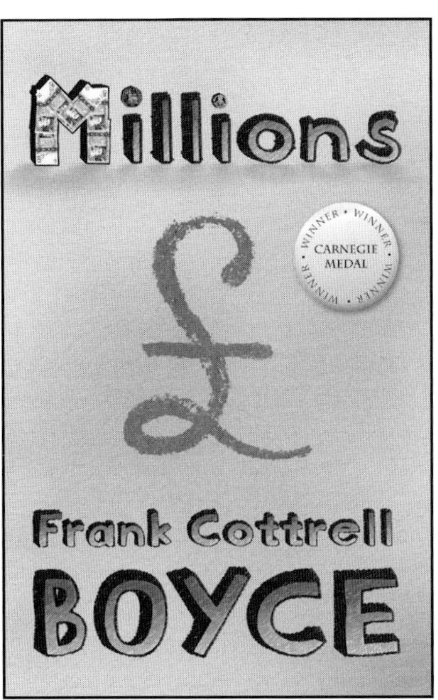

Medium term plan (3 weeks)	
Phase	**Learning Outcomes**
Phase 1: Recording responses to reading (5 days)	• Children can use a reading journal in a variety of ways to record, explore and extend their thinking about a story.
Phase 2: Drama, speaking and listening (5 days)	• Children can use a range of drama and other oral techniques to explore characters, dilemmas, themes, moods and points of view.
Phase 3: Writing to explore and respond (5 days)	• Children can use a range of writing activities to help them explore and respond to the story. • Children can say how they use a reading journal to help them reflect on a text.

Narrative Unit 3

MILLIONS

Big picture

The children read and explore the novel *Millions*. They contribute to a class reading journal and write a personal reading journal to record their responses to the story. They use a range of oral techniques, particularly drama and role play, to investigate the characters and themes in more detail. They also explore the story further through a range of writing experiences, including transformation writing and analytical writing, to develop empathy with the characters, consider different viewpoints and extend their thinking about the themes.
Note: *Millions* contains strong emotional content and bereavement.

Prior learning

This unit assumes that the children can already:
- discuss their responses to stories in reading groups
- work in role to explore characters and different points of view
- make notes and gather evidence to explain or support ideas
- use techniques such as visualisation and prediction to explore texts
- adapt sentence constructions.

Key aspects of learning

Communication: Discuss ideas and response; work collaboratively in groups; communicate ideas and response through writing and drama.
Creative thinking: Write a poem in response to a story theme.
Information processing: Select and present information and ideas from the story in different forms.
Evaluation: Share responses orally and in writing and judge the effectiveness of their own and others' work.
Empathy: Write and speak in role.
Reasoning: Give reasons for their response to the story; construct reasoned arguments to explain their inferences and opinions.
Self-awareness: Reflect on their personal response to the text.

Progression in narrative

In this unit the children will:
- make judgements in response to story endings
- identify common elements of an author's style
- respond to a narrator's point of view; express opinions about characters; compare and contrast different responses to the same character; revise responses to a character as insights develop.

Cross-curricular links

Citizenship: Discuss the value of money, economic choices, world poverty/wealth and the role of charities such as Water Aid.
ICT: Explore ways of discussing books, e.g. online discussion forums, website reviews, creating blogs or podcasts.

Reading time

4 hours

PHASE 1: RECORDING RESPONSES TO READING (5 DAYS)

Session 1

We are learning to …	Resources
• use a reading journal to make notes about a book (PNS Strands 8.2) **Assessment Focuses** AF (R): 2, 3	*Millions* ITP: 3.1 PCM: 3.1, 3.2

Shared teaching

- Introduce the 'Big Picture'. Explain that in this session, the children will be using a reading journal to record thoughts, ideas and responses while reading a story. Shared responses will be recorded in a class journal. They will also keep their own reading journal to record their responses to the story.
- Share the learning objective. Give out 'Reading journal tips' (PCM 3.1).
- Show 'First thoughts' (ITP 3.1). Talk Partners discuss their thoughts about the book based on the cover. *What do you think the book might be about? Do you know any other books by this author?*
- Click on each category on ITP 3.1. Take feedback and model taking brief notes.
- Give out copies of *Millions* by Frank Cottrell Boyce. Talk Partners find further clues about the book from the back cover blurb.
- Take feedback and record the children's ideas on ITP 3.1. Save these for use in Session 15.
- Read Chapter 1 with the children following in their own books. The children Think-Pair-Share first impressions. *Was it what you expected? Was anything surprising? What do you particularly like? Was there anything you didn't like or that puzzled you?*
- Model making additional notes on the class journal page, recording more definite observations, e.g. *It is told in the first person,* and clues from the text, e.g. 'it all sort of started with a robbery' (page 2).
- Discuss initial impressions of the main character. *What do you think about Damian? What would you make of him if he arrived in our class? How would you describe him?* Allow the children Think Time to note a few words and phrases in their personal reading journals. Talk Partners discuss what details created these impressions.
- Read Chapter 2. *Think about the characters of Damian and Anthony.*

Independent and Guided

- The children record their initial thoughts about the characters of Damian and Anthony, using evidence from Chapters 1 and 2 to support their ideas.

(ooo) Add notes to personal reading journals about the characters, using PCM 3.1 as a prompt. (T+)

(oo) Complete 'Character table' (PCM 3.2).

(o) As above. (TA+)

Plenary

- Take feedback and record these ideas by creating a Role on the Wall for each character. *What have you learnt about Damian and Anthony? What do they look like? How do they behave? What evidence is there in the text to make you say that?*
- Recap the learning objective. *How have you used reading journals in this session?* (E.g. predictions, response to characters, noting evidence)

Assessment pointers

- AF2, 3 (R): reading journal entries, discussion and oral responses show how far the children can support opinions by referring to different parts of the text and make inferences about characters and the story based on evidence.

Session 2

We are learning to …	Resources
• discuss themes, motives and feelings in stories • understand how the viewpoint influences how we see events (PNS Strands 7.2) **Assessment Focuses** AF (R): 2, 3, 6	*Millions* ITP: 3.2 PCM: 3.3, 3.4

Shared teaching

- Recap the children's reading journal entries from Session 1 and share the learning objectives.
- Show 'Quotes' (ITP 3.2). *Reading journals can be used to collect important quotations from the text.* Use the quotations from Chapters 1 and 2 to encourage discussion about the characters, story and themes, e.g. *I wonder what it means? What could it be referring to? What does it make you think about?* Allow the children Think Time.
- Take feedback. Encourage tentative ideas, using appropriate language, e.g. *I wonder if … , perhaps … , it might be referring to … .* Record the children's ideas on the Learning Wall for future reference.
- Give out 'Reading bookmark' (PCM 3.3). Read Chapter 3 of *Millions. Note anything interesting or puzzling on your reading bookmark.*
- Take feedback. *What have you noted? What did you find interesting or surprising? Was there anything you didn't understand?* Encourage others to respond. *What do you think? Can you help explain this?*
- Clarify the meaning of words such as 'hermitage'. Record any new vocabulary on the Learning Wall and encourage the children to begin a glossary in their reading journals.
- The children share their notes from PCM 3.3 in small groups. Encourage them to discuss interesting, surprising or puzzling details and clarify things they didn't understand. Record unanswered queries on sticky notes.
- Take feedback. Add unanswered queries to the Learning Wall.
- Refer to the Chapter 3 quotation on ITP 3.2. *This is interesting because Damian is always trying to be good. But do others see his actions as 'good'?* Talk Partners discuss, using their reading journals to note examples of where others view his actions differently. The children then Think-Pair-Share ideas.

Independent and Guided

- The children use various strategies to explore the themes and characters that have been introduced in the book so far.

●●● Choose a format to show Mr Quinn's view of Damian, e.g. a letter home, a scripted telephone conversation or a comic strip. (TA)

●● Explore ideas about the hermitage. (T+)

● Write notes in the thought bubbles to show Anthony and Damian's contrasting views about Cromarty on 'Cromarty Close' (PCM 3.4).

Plenary

- Recap the learning objectives. Share reading journal entries and ideas about the themes and characters so far.
- *Damian's ideas are rather different from those of other people. The story is told in the first person from his point of view. Do you think this is a good thing or not?* (E.g. *Yes, it's interesting; but on the other hand we have to be aware that Damian often misses the point.*)

Assessment pointers

- AF2, 3, 6 (R): reading journal entries, group discussion and responses will show how far the children can retrieve and use information from the text, make inferences and deductions and comment on the effect of narrative viewpoint on the reader.

Session 3

We are learning to …	Resources
• express personal responses, saying why and how a text affects us • use a reading journal to make notes about a book (PNS Strands 8.1, 8.2) **Assessment Focuses** AF (R): 2, 3, 6	*Millions* ITP: 3.3, 3.4 PCM: 3.5

Shared teaching

- Share the learning objectives.
- Show 'Objects and ideas'(ITP 3.3). Click on each item except for the 'Money' hotspot. *Which parts of the story does this remind you of? What does it make you think about?* Record ideas on ITP 3.3.
- Encourage the children to be reading detectives and look out for hidden links and connections to these themes. Read Chapter 4.
- The children Think-Pair-Share responses to Chapter 4. *What are your thoughts and feelings at the end of this chapter? Did you find anything surprising or puzzling? Are you left wondering?*
- Take feedback from one group. Encourage others to respond and build on what they say, e.g. *What do you make of the visitation? Do you think it really happened?*
- Add the children's ideas to ITP 3.3.
- Reread the 'takeaway scene' (pages 34–35). Show 'Emotions register' (ITP 3.4). *What emotions does Damian show in this scene? What has brought about this sudden change? How do the rest of the family react? How are these feelings shown?* Talk Partners discuss ideas.
- Take feedback. The children drag the words onto the target on ITP 3.4, to show how well they describe the characters' feelings. *How are the family coping with the death, based on the evidence in this scene?*
- Talk Partners reread the last paragraph of Chapter 4 (page 37). *What are Damian's emotions now? Why do you think this is? Does this visitation help him?*
- Take feedback from one or two pairs. Encourage others to comment and build on what they say, e.g. *Do you think the visitation helped him?*
- Read Chapter 5. Allow the children Think Time. Encourage them to reflect on how this chapter makes them feel and think. They then make notes in their reading journals in preparation for discussion.

Independent and Guided

- The children respond to Chapter 5 in pairs or small groups.

●●● Perform a close analysis of Chapter 5. (T+)

●● Discuss and respond to Chapter 5 in reading groups, using 'Discussion prompts' (PCM 3.5).

● As above. (TA+)

Plenary

- Recap the learning objectives.
- Model ideas for updating journal entries, e.g add more character details to the 'inner view' on the Role on the Wall from Session 1, or add ideas from Chapter 5 to annotated ITP 3.3 (focusing on the 'Saints', 'Memories' and 'Being good' hotspots).
- The children look at the notes about character that they made in their personal reading journal in Session 1. *Has your view of Damian changed?* The children then update their entries accordingly.

Assessment pointers

- AF2, 3, 6 (R): the children's notes, discussion and oral responses show how far they are able to select ideas and information from different parts of the text, make inferences and deductions based on these and comment on the overall effect on the reader.

Session 4

We are learning to …	Resources
• make and record predictions based on clues in the story • construct sentences using 'If … , then …' (PNS Strands 8.2, 11.1) **Assessment Focuses** AF (R): 2, 3; AF (W): 5	*Millions* PCM: 3.6

Shared teaching

- Read Chapter 6 of *Millions*.
- Encourage responses to the turn of events at the end of Chapter 6. *What does Damian think has happened? What do you think has happened? How do you think Damian felt when he saw the money? How would you have felt if this had happened to you?*
- Share the learning objectives. Think-Pair-Share predictions for the next chapter. *What might happen next? How will Damian react? What will he do? If this were you, what would you do?*
- Take feedback. Encourage discussion of different courses of action and exploration of possible consequences, e.g. *So if he tells his Dad, then what do you think might happen? What if he hides the money? What might happen then?*
- List the possibilities using conditional sentences to show possible consequences of actions. Discuss the 'If … , then …' structure of these sentences, e.g. *If Damian decides to tell his dad, then he might … .*
- Discuss and rate suggestions as most and least likely, based on knowledge of the character and clues given in the text.
- Read Chapter 7. Allow Think Time. *Compare the predictions with what actually happens.*
- Take feedback. *Were you right? Were the outcomes and consequences as you predicted? Was there anything surprising?*
- Talk Partners reflect on Damian's decision and the consequences. *Was it a good idea to tell Anthony? What makes you say that? What happens as a result? Is this good or bad?*
- Discuss how a different decision could have affected the story. *Were they right not to tell Dad? What if he had told Dad? How might Chapter 7 have been different?*
- Think-Pair-Share ideas and encourage predictions. *I wonder what Damian and Anthony will do with the money? What would you predict? Will the money be a good or a bad thing? How do you think they will cope with situations that might come up?*

Independent and Guided

- The children discuss possible courses of action, their consequences and outcomes.

(ooo) Record predictions in reading journals using conditional sentences. In groups, judge which is most and least likely to happen, based on clues in the story so far.

(oo) As above, using 'Making predictions' (PCM 3.6). (TA+)

(o) As above. (T+)

Plenary

- Recap the learning objectives. Add the children's 'most likely' predictions to the Learning Wall, reinforcing conditional forms. *What clues led to you make these predictions?*

Assessment pointers

- S&L: group work will show how far the children can engage with others, draw ideas together and promote discussion.
- AF2, 3 (R): oral responses, discussion and predictions show how far the children can make inferences and deductions from the text.
- AF5 (W): reading journal entries show how well the children can use conditional sentences.

Session 5

We are learning to …	Resources
• write a commentary on the story so far • use complex sentences to express ideas (PNS Strands 8.2, 11.1) **Assessment Focuses** AF (R): 2, 3, 6; AF (W): 3, 4, 5	*Millions* *Author reading* (film) ITP: 3.5, 3.6 PCM: 3.7

Shared teaching

- Recap the children's predictions from Session 4. *Which clues in the text hinted that everything might not turn out well?* (E.g. 'I'm not sure now that it was the best idea' (page 52).)
- Read Chapter 8. The children look for evidence that supports or undermines their predictions. Additionally, watch Frank Cottrell Boyce read an extract from the unit in *Author reading*.
- Share the learning objectives. Talk Partners discuss the boys' actions and their consequences and make lists in their reading journal of actions (how they spend the money); consequences (good and bad); and hints that suggest problems ahead.
- Take feedback. *Do you think they use the money well? How might things go wrong?* Encourage others to respond. *Do you agree?*
- Read Chapter 9. Talk Partners make notes in their reading journals. *What are the different ways Damian and Anthony spend the money?* The children list the problems that are becoming apparent, e.g. limited time to spend the money; having to lie to their dad, etc.
- Share and discuss ideas in groups. *What can we tell about Damian and Anthony's characters, motives and interests from how they spend the money? What other problems are appearing? What implications are there for future events?*
- Take feedback from one group. *Do you agree with what has been said? Do you want to read on? What questions do you want answering?*
- Explain to the children that they are going to write a more formal reading journal entry: a commentary on the story so far.
- Show 'Writing commentaries' (ITP 3.5) and discuss the success criteria. Encourage the children to suggest more criteria, and add the list to the Learning Wall.
- Show 'Model commentary' (ITP 3.6). Use Modelled Writing to create the first two sentences. Compose complex sentences that link ideas succinctly, e.g. *Damian finds a bag of money, which he believes has been sent to him by God. Unfortunately, he tells his brother who … .*

Independent and Guided

- The children write a commentary on the story so far in their reading journals using 'Commentary tips' (PCM 3.7) as a guide. Support the children with an identified need. (T+/TA+)

Plenary

- Recap the learning objectives. Read the children's complex sentences that comment on the characters or story.
- *How have you used your reading journals so far? What sort of entries have you made?*

Assessment pointers

- S&L: group work will show how well the children can adopt group roles and express relevant ideas.
- AF2, 3, 6 (R): writing, discussion and oral responses show how far the children can refer to the text, make inferences and deductions about characters and events, and comment on the overall effect.
- AF3, 4, 5 (W): written commentaries show how well the children can organise ideas, structure paragraphs and use complex sentences.

Session 6

We are learning to ...	Resources
• use freeze frames to explore the story • use drama to explore decisions and dilemmas (PNS Strands 4.1) **Assessment Focuses** AF (R): 2, 3	*Millions*

Shared teaching (1)

- Read Chapter 10 of *Millions*.
- Share the learning objectives.
- Recap events of the story so far and Damian and Anthony's different ideas about using the money. Talk Partners discuss the characters' reactions to events so far.
- Take feedback. *Which character has had good ideas about what to do with the money and which character's ideas are bad? What makes you say that? How would you rate the ideas yourself?*
- Use Freeze Frames to explore incidents from Chapter 10. *Damian thought it would be easy to give the money to the poor, but what went wrong? Why don't his efforts at doing good always have the desired outcome? What do you think Damian means when he says 'it would have worked too, if it hadn't been for people'?*

Independent and Guided

- In groups, the children are assigned different scenes from Chapter 10. They then prepare Freeze Frames of key moments. The children focus on facial expressions and gestures to show the characters' thoughts and feelings. They prepare to speak the characters' thoughts. Support the children with an identified need. (T+/TA+)

Shared teaching (2)

- Groups show their freeze frames to the rest of the class. *How have they portrayed the differences between the characters, the tension and the problems? How do Damian's hopes contrast with other people's attitudes?*
- Recap the central dilemma: whether to give the money to the poor or spend it on themselves. *After his experiences in this chapter, will Damian change his mind?*
- Talk Partners list reasons for both options, including ideas from the text and any of their own. *What good reasons are there for giving the money to the poor? What might Anthony say after the events in Chapter 10?*
- Use Conscience Alley to explore the dilemma. The children form two lines, one that will argue for giving money to the poor, the other will argue for spending it on themselves. Choose a child to play Damian.
- Ask the child that is playing Damian whether he or she has changed their mind. *Was it an easy decision? Have the rest of you changed your mind too? What do you think Damian should do?*

Plenary

- Recap the learning objectives. *How have the drama activities helped you to think about the issues?* (E.g. exploring different viewpoints; highlighting negative attitudes, etc.)

Assessment pointers

- S&L: drama activities will show how well the children can explore issues through sustaining roles.
- AF2, 3 (R): observation of drama activities will show how far the children can refer closely to the text and respond to the implied meaning.

Session 7

We are learning to ...	Resources
• present a persuasive argument to a character • use dialogic talk to explore issues, themes, motives and feelings in stories (PNS Strands 1.1, 1.3) **Assessment Focuses** AF (R): 2, 3	*Millions* ITP: (3.3, 3.4)

Shared teaching

- Share the learning objectives.
- Recall annotated 'Objects and ideas' (ITP 3.3). Click on 'Money'. Discuss quotations from the story so far that relate to money. *Which character said or believes this? Is it true based on events so far? Has money bought them happiness? What effect has it had on people? Is the money proving to be a good or a bad thing?* Add notes to ITP 3.3.
- Read Chapter 11. The children note references about the effect the money has on people on bookmarks or sticky notes. They then Think-Pair-Share ideas.
- Take feedback from one or two groups. Encourage others to respond and build on what is said. *Do you agree about that effect?*
- Recall 'Emotions register' (ITP 3.4). Discuss the effect of the money on Damian. *When Damian first found the money he was very excited. How about now?* Think-Pair-Share ideas for Damian's emotions at key points in Chapter 11, e.g. in the school playground; arriving at the hermitage; the saint's visitation; after talking to Anthony.
- Take feedback. *Why is Damian disheartened by events at school and confused after talking to Anthony?* Encourage close reference to the text. The children drag relevant words onto the target on ITP 3.4, to show how well they describe how Damian is feeling.
- Discuss the conversation about giving money to charity (pages 109–111). *Why does Damian seem to change his mind? What do you think Anthony's motives might be?*
- *Can money have a positive effect? Can giving money to charity make a difference or are there so many problems in the world that it's a waste of time trying?* Allow the children Think Time to consider the questions.
- Take feedback. *How could you convince Anthony that giving money to a charity is a good idea? You'd need to be more persuasive in your argument than Damian. How can you present ideas persuasively*? (E.g. give reasons; use persuasive and emotive words and phrases; use their knowledge of what might appeal to Anthony; anticipate conflicting views and be ready with responses; use a persuasive voice and body language.)

Independent and Guided

- Pairs discuss and note arguments for giving the money to a charity. and anticipate arguments for and against. Then Role Play the scene. One child presents the argument and the other plays Anthony, challenging the ideas. Encourage the use of persuasive voice and body language. Support the children with an identified need. (T/TA)

Plenary

- Recap the learning objectives. *Do you think you could have persuaded Anthony? What have you found out about presenting a persuasive argument? How have these activities helped you to think about the theme of money in the story?*

Assessment pointers

- S&L: role plays show how well the children can respond to issues and empathise with characters.
- AF2, 3 (R): discussion and oral responses show how well the children can refer to the text and comment on implied feelings and themes.

Session 8

We are learning to ...	Resources
• use drama to understand characters • write in role to empathise with characters and explore situations • write a reading journal entry based on a drama activity (PNS Strands 4.1, 8.2, 9.2) **Assessment Focuses** AF (R): 2, 3	*Millions* ITP: 3.7

Shared teaching

- Read the first part of Chapter 12 with the children (as far as '"Just think about that."' page 126).
- Share the learning objectives.
- Show 'Thought tracking' (ITP 3.7). Select two confident children to read dialogue from pages 125–126, with appropriate expression. Freeze Frame the action at key points and Thought Track the characters. *What do you think the characters are thinking at this point? Where does it show you this in the text?* Then model noting ideas on ITP 3.7, e.g. *I was trying to protect you.*
- Use Modelled Writing to create a short journal entry about one of the characters, using the notes on ITP 3.7, e.g. *Anthony has known the truth about the money all along but was trying to protect Damian.*
- Read the rest of Chapter 12, with the children focusing on the inner concerns of the characters. *What are they worried about?*
- Take feedback. *How do these events make you feel? How would you feel if it were you? What do you think was the worst moment for Damian and Anthony?*
- Take feedback. Identify a key moment from Chapter 12 to practise Hot-Seating, e.g. the headmaster's office; the Latter Day Saints; the toy shop.
- Talk Partners refer to the text and think of questions they would like to ask the characters in this scene, e.g. about the money, their concerns, their reactions to the events or their thoughts on other characters.
- One child takes the role of Anthony, Damian or one of the other characters. Other children question the character in the hot-seat about their thoughts, feelings and motives at this point in the story.

Independent and Guided

- The children continue to use Hot-Seating to explore the characters of Damian and Anthony at this point in the story.

(ooo) Take it in turns to role-play Anthony or Damian in the hot-seat, answering questions from the rest of the group. Then write a journal entry about one of the characters, based on notes.

(oo) As above. (T)

(o) As above. (TA)

Plenary

- Recap the learning objectives.
- *How have the drama activities helped you to understand the characters' motives, thoughts and feelings?* (E.g. exploring Anthony's thoughts as well as Damian's; making inferences from the text.)

Assessment pointers

- S&L: hot-seating will show how well the children can sustain roles to explore characters.
- AF2, 3 (R): observation of drama activities, notes and journal entries show how well the children can refer to textual evidence and make inferences and deductions.

Session 9

We are learning to ...	Resources
• use drama to act out a scene from a story • use drama to explore emotions at key moments in a story (PNS Strands 4.1) **Assessment Focuses** AF (R): 2, 3	*Millions* ITP: (3.7), 3.8

Shared teaching

- Recap the situation at the end of Chapter 12. Encourage predictions about the next chapter. *If the bin is there, who else is there?* (the woman, Dorothy) *Why do you think she is there? What might happen?*
- Read Chapter 13. *Do you trust Dorothy? Do you agree with Damian about this or Anthony? What makes you say that?*
- Take feedback. Recall 'Thought tracking' (ITP 3.7) and use it to compare Damian and Anthony's impressions of Dorothy. *What do they think about her? How do you know?* Divide the class into two and then into Talk Partners. One half focuses on Damian and the other on Anthony. Encourage the children to refer to the text to find what their character says about Dorothy and how he behaves towards her. They make notes in their reading journals.
- Take feedback. Add ideas to ITP 3.7, e.g. for Damian: her 'unique' wave (page 143); cooking together was fun; she made Dad laugh; we felt like a family again.
- *Why is Anthony so suspicious of Dorothy? Could there be more than one reason?* (E.g. in terms of the money and the family.)
- The children reread their initial impressions of Anthony in their first reading journal entry. *Is your view of Anthony changing? How do we see a different Anthony at the end of Chapter 13?* Think-Pair-Share ideas.
- Show '*Millions*' (ITP 3.8). Read through the extract on ITP 3.8. Model highlighting actions in one colour and dialogue in a different colour. *Is a narrator needed or are the events clear without one?*
- One group performs the text while the rest of the class make suggestions. *How should the lines be spoken? What facial expression or body language should be used? What might the characters be thinking when they speak or react?*

Independent and Guided

- The children use sticky notes to mark up action and dialogue on various scenes in the book. They then perform the scene as a readers' theatre activity.

(ooo) Work on the carol singers scene (pages 147, 158–160).

(oo) Work on the scene where Dorothy leaves (pages 156–158). (TA+)

(o) Work on the scene in Anthony's bedroom (pages 157–160, 163–165). (T+)

Plenary

- Recap the learning objectives.
- Watch a performance. *Do you agree with this interpretation of the scene? Have they portrayed the conflicting views of the characters effectively through their body language and voice? How?*

Assessment pointers

- S&L: drama pieces will show how far the children can sustain roles and scenarios to explore the text.
- AF2, 3 (R): journal notes will show how well the children can refer to the text for relevant details, and drama activities and discussion will show how far they are able to respond to implied meaning.

Session 10

We are learning to ...	Resources
• analyse how authors use language and other techniques to create suspense, tension and excitement • explore dramatic ways of creating suspense and tension (PNS Strands 4.1, 8.3) **Assessment Focuses** AF (R): 2, 3, 5, 6	*Millions* ITP: 3.9 PCM: 3.8

Shared teaching

- Read Chapter 14 with the children. Recap key events. *Do you think Saint Peter's visitation will help Damian? What do you think will happen at the nativity?*
- Read Chapter 15 without interruption to enjoy the exciting build-up. *Which part did you like best? Were there any surprises? Which were the most exciting or tense moments?*
- Share the learning objectives.
- Reread the paragraph where Damian enters the old house, beginning 'Obviously I knew ...' (page 187). *What mood or emotions are conveyed here? How is this created?* (E.g. repetition of 'empty'.)
- Set up a Forum Theatre. One child role-plays Damian entering the house. Other children suggest body shapes, facial expressions and movements to convey his feelings and use ideas from the text to question Damian. *What can you see? How does it make you feel?*
- Repeat the activity for another moment, e.g. hearing the front door open. Convey dramatically the tension and emotion in the text.
- Show '*Millions*' (ITP 3.9). Read with suitable expression and intonation. Think-Pair-Share how the author creates tension/suspense.
- Take feedback. Annotate ITP 3.9, highlighting different techniques used, e.g. delay; character's reactions; empty words ('someone'); short sentences; fragments of sentences; powerful verbs ('punched', 'clattered'); repetition, etc.
- Repeat Forum Theatre for the suspense scene on ITP 3.9. Focus on conveying suspense and emotions through reactions, movements, body shape, facial expression and sound. *How could this be improved?*

Independent and Guided

- In pairs, the children select, read and annotate another tense moment from Chapter 15 using 'Creating suspense' (PCM 3.8) to help them. The children then act out the scene, focusing on showing tension and the emotions of the characters.

●●● Work on any scene from Chapter 15.

●● As above, focusing on any part of the nativity play. (T+)

● Work on the scene on pages 180–181. (TA)

Plenary

- Recap the learning objectives. *What writer's techniques did you discover? How did you convey the tension dramatically?* Record the techniques used and add to the Learning Wall.

Assessment pointers

- S&L: drama pieces will show how far the children can sustrain roles and scenarios to explore the text.
- AF2, 5, 6 (R): text annotations, oral responses and reading journal entries show how far the children can make textual references and quotations, comment on the effect of language and sentence choices and the overall effect on the reader.
- AF3 (R): discussion and drama activities show how far the children can make inferences about mood, feelings and emotions.

PHASE 3: WRITING TO EXPLORE AND RESPOND (5 DAYS)

Session 11

We are learning to ...	Resources
• write in role to empathise with characters and explore situations • use knowledge of different texts to make decisions about form and style (PNS Strands 8.2, 9.1) **Assessment Focuses** AF (R): 3; AF (W): 1, 2, 3, 4	*Millions* ITP: (3.7), 3.10

Shared teaching

- Recap how Chapter 15 ended. *What would have been Damian's 'big, happy ending'? But this is not the end, so what do you think will happen? What might go wrong? How will the story end?* Think-Pair-Share predictions. Add suggestions to the Learning Wall.
- Read Chapter 16. Encourage the children to comment on the turn of events. *This certainly doesn't seem like a happy ending. What do you think? How do you feel about these events – about Dad, about Dorothy? What would you do if you were Damian?*
- Share the learning objectives.
- Recall 'Thought tracking' (ITP 3.7) to focus on the characters' worries and problems at this point. Talk Partners discuss suggestions.
- Take feedback. Record examples on ITP 3.7, e.g. Damian: I am worried about the change in Dad; Glass Eye; Dorothy leaving.
- *Who could Damian ask for advice? Who would you ask?* Discuss a range of possibilities both real, e.g. a friend, teacher, agony aunt or helpline and imaginary ones, e.g. a saint or guardian angel.
- Show 'Agony aunt email' (ITP 3.10). *Imagine Damian writes to an agony aunt, asking for advice. Which bits sound like Damian could have written it?*
- Use Modelled Writing to complete the email, writing in the role of Damian, summarising the situation, outlining his concerns and feelings and asking for help.
- Use Think Alouds to make decisions about paragraphing, e.g. *That paragraph introduces the problem so let's have a new paragraph to summarise the situation.*
- Model maintaining a style appropriate for the character and the purpose. *What might Damian say here? How might he put this?*
- Recap other problems Damian or Anthony might write about, e.g. the money; Glass Eye; Dorothy.

Independent and Guided

- The children write about a different problem at this point in the story.

●●● Choose a form of text that provokes empathy with Damian or Anthony. Also choose the audience and purpose of the text. (T+)

●● Write either a letter or an email in the role of Damian or Anthony, and decide who to write it to. Explain a different problem and ask for advice.

● As above, using the Modelled Writing example on ITP 3.10. (TA+)

Plenary

- Recap the learning objectives and encourage pairs to share their writing. *Which bits sound the most convincing? Have they used the right features and style? Is it organised in paragraphs?*

Assessment pointers

- AF3 (R): writing in role shows how far the children can make inferences about a character's thoughts and feelings.
- AF1, 2, 3, 4 (W): the finished writing shows how far the children can write interesting and imaginative texts using appropriate features and style, organising ideas and constructing paragraphs.

Session 12

We are learning to ...	Resources
• use knowledge of different texts to make decisions about form and style • write in role to empathise with characters and explore situations (PNS Strands 9.1, 9.2) **Assessment Focuses** AF (R): 2, 3; AF (W): 1, 2, 3	*Millions* PCM: 3.9

Shared teaching

- Recap the end of Chapter 16. *What do you think about Dorothy now? Has she been telling the truth? What will happen next?* Think-Pair-Share predictions.
- Read Chapter 17. *How do you feel at the end of this chapter? How do you feel about Damian? What about Anthony? Why has this chapter been a roller coaster of emotions for everyone?*
- Share the learning objectives. Explain that because it is Damian's story, we see events from his point of view. *But what about the other characters? If we read between the lines we can learn a lot about their feelings, thoughts and motives as well.*
- *If you could ask anyone a question about events in this chapter, who and what would you ask?* (E.g. *I'd like to ask Dorothy: Were you really going to leave with the money? If so, why did you change your mind?*)
- The children Think-Pair-Share questions for the characters, recording them on sticky notes. Take feedback. Sort questions by character and add to the Learning Wall.
- Assign small groups one character each: Damian, Anthony, Dorothy, Dad. Each group answers questions on behalf of its character, referring back to Chapter 17. They discuss events from their character's point of view and decide how they might answer possible questions.
- Use Hot-Seating. Each group takes the 'hot-seat' in turn. When a question is asked, allow Think Time before a spokesperson answers.
- Introduce the independent task of writing in role to give a character's version of events, their thoughts and feelings. *What different forms could this take?* (E.g. a diary entry, a thought monologue, a personal letter, a story extract from a different point of view.)
- Remind the children that when choosing the format for their writing, it should be interesting and challenging, but it must also be a format that they are familiar with. The children should be aware of the features, organisation and style needed.

Independent and Guided

- The children write an event from Chapter 17 as one of the characters (Dad, Dorothy or Anthony).

●●● Complete 'Writing in role' (PCM 3.9) in pairs, then write independently.

●● As above. (T+)

● As above, choosing either the diary entry or letter format. (TA+)

Plenary

- Recap the learning objectives. *Did you find the activity interesting and challenging? Have you used appropriate features, structure and style?*

Assessment pointers

- S&L: hot-seating will show how well the children can sustain roles to explore characters.
- AF2, 3 (R): hot-seating and writing in role show how far the children can select relevant ideas and events from the text and make inferences and deductions.
- AF1, 2, 3 (W): completed writing shows how well the children can write from a clear viewpoint with relevant ideas and detail and also use appropriate features and style in organising and structuring ideas.

Session 13

We are learning to ...	Resources
• write a poem in response to an idea, mood or feeling in the story • choose an appropriate poetic form to express the idea or feeling (PNS Strands 8.2, 10.1) **Assessment Focuses** AF (R): 3, 6; AF (W): 1, 2, 3, 7	*Millions* ITP: 3.11, 3.12

Shared teaching

- Recap the story so far. *Damian thought the money was a gift from God. He thought it would be a good thing, but what has he found? What would be his greatest wish, hope, dread or fear now?*
- Read Chapter 18. Talk Partners discuss their response. *How does this make you feel? What does it make you think about the money? Which parts of the text make you feel or think that?*
- Take feedback. Discuss the effect of words and phrases, e.g. 'money was crawling up the walls' (page 239).
- Share the learning objectives. *The money is at the centre of the story. What is the book's message about money and its effect on people? What is the author trying to tell us?*
- Show 'Money sayings' (ITP 3.11). Talk Partners discuss each of the quotes. *What does each saying mean? Which ones remind you of the events in* Millions*?*
- Take feedback. Explore the meanings of the quotes and link to *Millions*.
- Read the scene where Damian is inundated with appeals for money (pages 234–237). *How does Damian feel at this point?* Explain to the children that they will be presenting this scene as a performance poem with a number of voices circling round Damian.
- Show 'Performance poem' (ITP 3.12). Read the ideas listed. Ask the children to suggest other lines, thinking about rhythm and language patterns, e.g. short punchy lines; repeating phrases such as 'Needing money to …'.
- Use Modelled Writing to create a list poem with a repeating chorus on ITP 3.12. *We want to convey the sense of being overwhelmed by needs.* Use Think Alouds to explain choices in terms of the effect you want to achieve, e.g. *I'll shorten that line to fit the rhythm better.*
- Model reading the poem aloud to see how it is working. *Is there a sense of being overwhelmed? Does the rhythm and patterning work?*
- Encourage the children to choose an idea for their poem, referring to the suggestions on ITP 3.11

Independent and Guided

- In pairs, the children write poems, responding to the money theme.

●●● Choose the form of poem to write, e.g. a performance poem, a cinquain, blank verse, etc.

●● As above. (TA)

● Write a list poem. (T+)

Plenary

- Recap the learning objectives and encourage pairs to share their poems. *Does it convey an idea or mood?*

Assessment pointers

- AF3, 6 (R): discussion and oral response show how well the children can make inferences and comment on the author's purpose.
- AF1, 2, 3, 7 (W): poems show how well the children can write imaginative and thoughtful texts, using features of the selected form, organising and structuring ideas and make vocabulary choices.

Session 14

We are learning to …	Resources
• express personal response, saying why and how a text affects us (PNS Strands 8.1)	*Interview with Frank Cottrell Boyce* (film)
Assessment Focuses	*Millions*
AF (R): 6	ITP: 3.13
	PCM: 3.10, 3.11

Shared teaching

- Recap events from Chapter 18. Update predictions about how the story will end. *What will Damian do? Will there be a happy ending?*
- Read from Chapter 19 to the end of the story. Take feedback. *Did you like the ending?*
- Share the learning objective. Show 'Discussion prompts' (ITP 3.13). Allow Think Time and ask the children to note personal responses in their reading journal. Talk Partners discuss their thoughts and opinions.
- Take feedback. *Was anyone disappointed with the ending?*
- Discuss alternative endings suggested by the group. *Would that have been a better ending?* Discuss any puzzles or loose ends identified. *Are there any hints or is it left entirely open? Why might the author have chosen to do this?*
- Encourage the children to comment on the overall effect of the ending. *Do you find it sad, happy, amusing or thought provoking? Which parts make you think or feel that?* The children explain their ideas, referring to events such as Damian's choices and the language and imagery in the final paragraph. Make a note of key points.
- Focus on the author's intentions. *What questions would you ask the author about* Millions*? What would you ask the author about the ending*? Model an example, e.g. *Why did you have Damian burn the money rather than give it to the police*? Talk Partners discuss and record another question for the author.
- Select a group to take on the collective role of the author. *Respond to some of these questions. Explain and justify the chosen ending.*
- Watch *Interview with Frank Cottrell Boyce Part 1*. Encourage the children to make notes in their reading journal of what he says about the ending. *Does this confirm or disprove our thinking?*
- Use Modelled Writing to create a few sentences about the author's intentions using ideas noted during the session, e.g. *When Damian chooses to … it makes us think … . In the final paragraph the author creates a feeling of … by … .*

Independent and Guided

- The children write reading journal entries in response to the ending.

(ooo) Choose one of the writing tasks on 'Ending responses' (PCM 3.10).

(oo) Write a commentary on the ending, using 'Sentence starters' (PCM 3.11). (T+)

(o) Write up notes from the session into complete sentences. (TA)

Plenary

- Recap the learning objective.
- Share different types of response. If there is time available, watch *Interview with Frank Cottrell Boyce: Part 2* where he talks more generally about writing.

Assessment pointers

- AF6 (R): discussion, oral response and reading journal entries show how far the children are able to comment on the effect on the reader and the author's intention.

Session 15

We are learning to …	Resources
• reflect on how we have used our reading journal	*Millions*
• use complex sentences to express ideas (PNS Strands 8.1, 11.1)	ITP: (3.1), 3.14
Assessment Focuses	PCM: (3.11), 3.12
AF (R): 6 ; AF (W): 1, 2, 3, 4, 5	

Shared teaching

- Share the learning objectives.
- Recall annotated 'First thoughts' (ITP 3.1). *Now that you have read* Millions*, was it what you expected? What would you say now about the genre, themes, characters and story?*
- Show 'Discussion forum' (ITP 3.14). *Have you ever joined a discussion forum? What is their purpose? Do you find them useful?*
- Read the thread about *Millions* on ITP 3.14. *Do you think it might appeal to this reader or not? How would you respond?* Remind the children that comments such as 'good', 'boring' or 'okay' are not very useful as they don't tell the reader anything. *What would you say that would be useful?* Talk Partners discuss their ideas.
- Take feedback. Add a response to the thread on ITP 3.14.
- Explain that in this session, the children are going to write more detailed reviews of the book. Encourage them to decide on a specific purpose and audience for their review, e.g. for other pupils via the school website or library, for general readers on a book website or to help the Carnegie Medal judges make their decision.
- Show 'Review' (PCM 3.12). Discuss the elements required in a review, such as story summary; informative details (e.g. about characters); comments on effectiveness or weaknesses; personal response or opinions supported by reference to the text; a quotation to give a flavour of the story.
- Use Modelled Writing to compose one section of the review, e.g. *Is the story a page-turner?* Form complex sentences to explain the impact of key story features on the reader, e.g. *The story is written as if Damian is looking back on the events, which means … .*

Independent and Guided

- The children compose reviews to be presented on screen or on paper.

(ooo) Decide on the form and audience. Adapt the prompts on PCM 3.12 accordingly.

(oo) Use PCM 3.12 and 'Sentence starters' (PCM 3.11) to write reviews for 11-year-old readers. (TA+)

(o) As above. (T+)

Plenary

- Recap the learning objectives. *What examples do you have for the 'Your opinion?' section? Would this review be helpful?*
- Talk Partners discuss the different ways they have used their reading journals to respond to *Millions*. Encourage the children to select one response to refine and present as part of a whole-class reading journal.
- Recap the unit as a whole. *What did you enjoy the most? What do you still find difficult? Would you like to read any more of the author's work?*

Assessment pointers

- S&L: pair work will show how far the children can listen and respond to others.
- AF6 (R): discussion, oral responses and written reviews show how well the children can comment on the overall effect of the story.
- AF1, 2, 3, 4, 5 (W): reviews show how far they can write imaginative texts appropriate to task, reader and purpose using complex sentences.

Reading journal tips

Use the tips to help you to record your thoughts and ideas about *Millions* in your reading journal.

Notes – *things you have noticed*

Personal responses – *your ideas; impressions; thoughts; feelings*

Grids and charts – *comparing characters, settings etc.*

Lists – *interesting words; significant objects; events; themes*

Questions – *for the characters or the author; things you want answered in the book*

Predictions – *predict what might happen before you start; in the middle; and towards the end of the book*

Drawings – *of characters and settings; diagrams; story maps*

Character gallery – *a list of characters to keep track of who's who*

Glossary – *a list of new or interesting words*

Quotations – *direct quotes from the text to show interesting language; what characters say; parts you really like*

Writing in role – *a character's diary; letters, etc.*

Review – *for different purposes: for a newsletter; website; book-buyer etc.*

Summaries – *of chapters or the whole book*

Character table

Use the table to make notes about the characters in *Millions*.

	Damian	Anthony
First impressions		
How he is described		
His behaviour		
Things he says		
What others say about him		

Reading bookmark

Use the bookmark to make notes on things to discuss from Chapter 3 of *Millions*.

Reading bookmark

Name: ____________________

Title: ____________________

Chapter: ____________________

That's interesting!

page ___: ____________________

____

____

page ___: ____________________

____

____

That's surprising!

page ___: ____________________

____

____

page ___: ____________________

____

____

That's puzzling!

page ___: ____________________

____

____

page ___: ____________________

____

____

I like that!

page ___: ____________________

____

____

page ___: ____________________

____

____

I don't understand that!

page ___: ____________________

____

____

page ___: ____________________

____

____

Fold

Cromarty Close

Add labels to the diagram to show what Damian and Anthony think about Cromarty Close.

Discussion prompts

Use the questions to help you discuss Chapter 5 of *Millions*.

How does Chapter 5 make you feel? Why?

How do you feel about Damian at this moment? Why?

Can you empathise with Damian? What makes you say that?

How would you describe the mood of this chapter? How is this created?

What memories does Damian have of his mother?

Why do you think Damian likes saints? How do you know?

How do you think different characters have dealt with the death?

'She's completely dead, isn't she?' (page 33). Why is Damian so upset by this remark?

Making predictions

Use clues from the story to write different predictions about what might happen.

If they do this …

… then this might happen.

… or this might happen.

Or if they do this …

… then this might happen.

… or this might happen.

If someone else does this …

… then this might happen.

… or this might happen.

Commentary tips

Use these tips to write your commentary about *Millions*.

Interest

Has the writer made you want to read on?

The author has made me want to find out …

I want to read on because …

Summary of events

What has happened in the story so far?

At the start of the story …

Then …

Meanwhile …

In the end …

Comment on the problems

What problems have come up?

Whether to report the money …

How to convert it …

Comment on the characters

What do you think about the characters?

Damian seems …

Who do you empathise with?

I can understand how Anthony is feeling because …

Give your predictions

How might the story continue?

Based on what i know so far, I think that … might happen because …

Give evidence

Refer to specific details in the story.

In Chapter 7 it says that …

"It was all a bit unenlightening." (page 65)

Creating suspense

Use the tips to annotate your chosen text from Chapter 15 to show how the author created suspense.

Say what effect was created.

In Chapter 15 the author creates …
In this scene there is a sense of …

Say how the author created this effect.

One of the ways he does this is by …

He also uses …

Use short quotations to give evidence.

For example, when he says …

Use technical vocabulary.

similes
powerful verbs
use the first person

Use complex sentences.

The words that the author uses are very powerful because …

Use connectives to explain and show effects.

… which creates …
… in order to …

Writing in role

Connect the different parts with arrows to show what you are going to write and how.

Dad | Dorothy | Anthony

Diary | Letter | Story | Other

Damian, Anthony and their father discover that Dorothy has stolen the money.

Dorothy has bought a car. They all plan to sell it for euros.

Dorothy and Damian change half the money. They spend half and use the rest as wallpaper.

Anthony is angry. He blames Damian for everything.

12th June
I was ...
I felt ...

Dear ...
Yours faithfully ...

Damian was ...

Informal | formal

first person | third person

Ending responses

Read the different responses to the ending of *Millions*. Choose one and continue it.

An alternative ending

If our Anthony was telling the story, it would be the happiest ending ever. He would put, 'And so they got some money after all. Despite Damian's meddling!'

Dad decided to split the money between us all. Anthony put his in a high-interest savings account, while he waited for the right investment opportunity to come along. Dad and Dorothy spent the money on a holiday. As for me, I

A story update

Well, it's been three years since I found all that money. It only seems like yesterday! I still don't regret giving it away, oh, and burning it! I think it was rather saintly of me. I did try to help a lot of people, after all.

Anthony has finally got over it. He's studying hard at secondary school now. Surprise, surprise – he wants to be an investment banker!

Dad and Dorothy are still together, in fact

A letter to the author

19th August 2012

Dear Mr. Cottrell Boyce,

I really enjoyed reading your book *Millions*. I thought it was great! The ending was quite good too, but I wished it could have been happier. It would have been nice if they could have all kept the money and gone on a big holiday together. Why did you decide to

Damian's blog

It's finally all over. The man with the glass eye has been caught and the money we had left is now on its way to Nigeria. I know it will help out a lot of people. Anthony is not very happy about it. He says we've blown a big investment opportunity. But Dad is

Sentence starters

Use the sentence starters to help you to write about *Millions*.

Summarising

Frank Cottrell Boyce has chosen to …

The author uses/creates/shows …

The author makes this seem/makes us think …

Damian tells us …

The effect

This creates/suggests …

The reader sees/feels …

We are told/made to wonder …

The effect of this is …

My view on this

I think this gives …

This makes me think/feel …

This reminded me of …

I thought this was …

because …

The ending

In the final paragraph …

In Chapter …

At the end of the story …

Useful connectives

for example
also
furthermore
as a result
because of this
in order to
which means
as if
such as
by

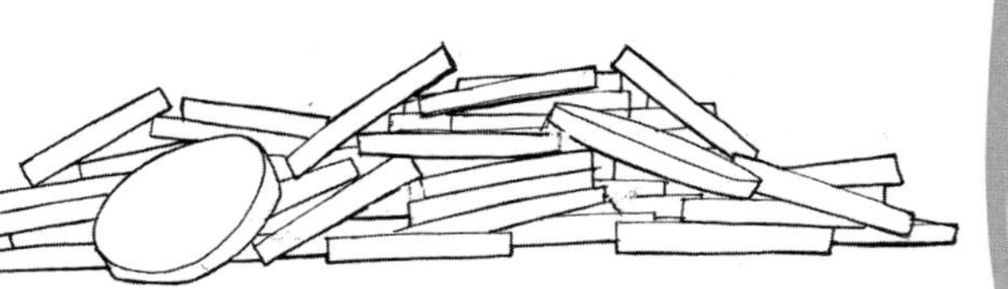

Review

Complete the review of *Millions*.

Book title: ____________

Author: ____________

Story summary: ____________

Main characters: ____________

My opinion: ____________

Highlights: ____________

Weaknesses: ____________

Favourite quotation: ____________

Star rating

☆ ☆ ☆ ☆ ☆

Narrative Unit 4

EYE OF THE WOLF – novel (Narrative technique)

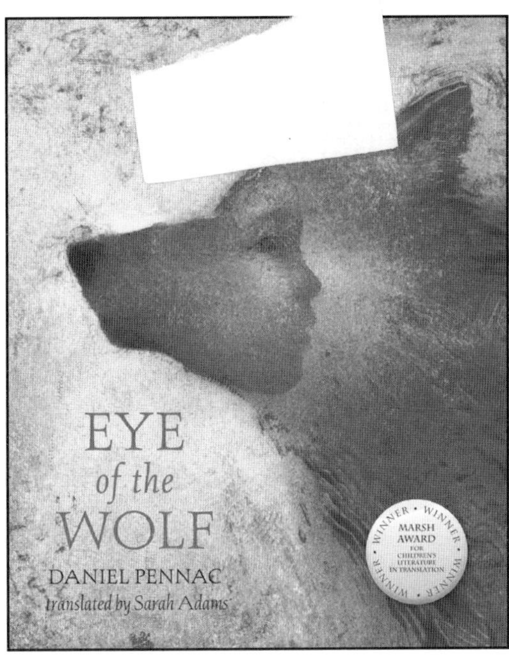

Medium term plan (3 weeks)	
Phase	**Learning Outcomes**
Phase 1: Reading, exploring and analysing the text (8 days)	• Children can comment and express views on moods, themes and ideas conveyed in a story. • Children can make sense of changes in time and narrator in a story with a complex structure. • Children can identify a range of techniques used by an author to reveal events in an intriguing way.
Phase 2: Storytelling (3 days)	• Children can use a range of storytelling and performance techniques to tell an engaging narrative.
Phase 3: Writing (4 days)	• Children can write a story with a flashback, clearly indicating the passage of time between events. • Children can use paragraphs to structure their writing. • Children can use elements of the author's style in their own story.

Narrative Unit 4

EYE OF THE WOLF

Big picture

The children read and respond to *Eye of the Wolf*, a story that uses flashbacks as part of the narrative structure. They use a variety of techniques to explore characters, themes, moods and ideas conveyed in the story and examine the unusual structure of the text. The children analyse features of storytelling style and then plan and rehearse their own oral story inspired by another character/creature from the novel. The children then produce a written version of their oral story.

Prior learning

This unit assumes that the children can already:
- find evidence in a text to support responses
- identify different narrative perspectives
- tell a story using voice effectively
- use paragraphs to structure a narrative; form complex sentences.

Key aspects of learning

Communication: Work collaboratively; communicate outcomes orally and in writing.
Creative thinking: Develop their own narrative in response to a story.
Empathy: Empathise with characters; recognise emotions.
Enquiry: Ask questions; locate evidence to answer them.
Evaluation: Justify their views; evaluate their own and others' work.
Information processing: Combine and present information.
Reasoning: Give opinions; make inferences; express reasoned views.

Progression in narrative

In this unit the children will:
- recognise different narrative structures; analyse paragraph structures and how links are made; evaluate story endings
- recognise that the narrator can change and be manipulated
- recognise how authors use language to influence the reader
- plan and tell engaging stories with different narrative styles
- plan the plot, characters and structure for own storiest
- use expressive or figurative language to create a setting.

Cross-curricular links

Art: Create illustrations, focusing on mood, for a book or on-screen story.
Global dimension: Global citizenship, diversity, social justice, sustainable development; similarities and differences between people.
ICT: Use edits and fades to move between the present and the past.
Geography: Investigate the book locations.
Music: Discuss music to accompany an oral or on-screen story.
PSHE: Debate topical issues; the impact of choices on others; the environment; the lives of people in other places.

Reading time

1 hour 10 minutes

PHASE 1: READING, EXPLORING AND ANALYSING THE TEXT (8 DAYS)

Session 1

We are learning to …	Resources
• identify who is telling the story and explain how this affects how we see things • empathise with a characters and make inferences (PNS Strands 7.2, 8.2) **Assessment Focuses** AF (R): 2, 6	*Eye of the Wolf* ITP: 4.1, 4.2 PCM: 4.1

Shared teaching

- Show the front cover of *Eye of the Wolf. What might it be about?*
- Read 'How they met' (pages 7–14) with the children following in their own books. Encourage them to try to visualise the scene as you read.
- Discuss the story so far. *Was it what you expected? Did it surprise you? What did you like or find effective? How did it make you feel?*
- The children Think-Pair-Share questions raised by the opening. Add the questions to the Learning Wall.
- Share the learning objectives.
- Show 'Story opening' (ITP 4.1). *Who are the main characters?* (The boy and the wolf.) *How is the boy's behaviour strange or intriguing?*
- Focus on the narrative viewpoint. *Who is telling this story? How do we know?* (It is told in the third person as if the narrator is watching the events; it says: 'the boy', 'the wolf'.) *Whose viewpoint is presented? How do we know?* (The wolf's viewpoint; we hear his thoughts; we see the boy through his eyes.)
- *How does this affect our view of the story and how we feel about the characters?* Allow Think Time before taking responses, e.g. it puts us on the wolf's side; we share his curiosity about the boy; we find out quite a lot about the wolf but nothing about the boy.
- Talk Partners discuss what it would be like to be a wolf. *What would you see, hear, feel, think, remember?*
- Take feedback and show 'The wolf' (ITP 4.2), focusing on impressions of the wolf. The children drag one or two words onto the target to show how well they describe the wolf, giving evidence to support their responses.

Independent and Guided

- The children work in pairs to explore the wolf's thoughts and feelings, finding evidence to support their ideas and responses.

(ooo) Use 'Interior monologues' (PCM 4.1) to record the wolf's thoughts and attitudes. (TA+)

(oo) Create a Role on the Wall showing emotions and sense of the character on the inside; add quotes to support views on the outside.

(o) Create a Role on the Wall for the wolf, showing memories on the outside and feelings and emotions on the inside. (T+)

Plenary

- Show ITP 4.2 and encourage the children to suggest additional words to describe the wolf, giving evidence to support their ideas. Add examples of work to the Learning Wall.
- Recap the learning objectives. *How did the point of view help you to empathise with the character?*

Assessment pointers

- S&L: pair work will show how well the children can recount ideas and listen and respond to others.
- AF 2 (R): completed activities will show how far the children are able to select relevant points from the text.
- AF 6 (R): contributions to discussion will show how far the children understand viewpoint and the overall effect of this.

Session 2

We are learning to ...	Resources
• explain how and why authors might use flashbacks in a story • use visualisation and drama to respond to the story (PNS Strands 7.3, 8.2) **Assessment Focuses** AF (R): 2, 3, 4, 5	*Eye of the Wolf* ITP: 4.3, 4.4 PCM: 4.2, 4.3

Shared teaching

- Share the learning objectives.
- Introduce the term 'flashback'. *What do you think a flashback is? Have you read other novels that use this technique?*
- Read pages 17–23 with the class. Encourage the children to visualise what you are reading. *What has happened? Did anything puzzle or surprise you? What did you notice about how the story is told?* (E.g. shifting viewpoint, flashback to wolf's early life; figurative language.)
- Show 'Wolf's eye' (ITP 4.3) and read the extract from the text. *Visualise the story as if it were a film. What details did you see most vividly? Why do you think the author used the wolf's eye as a way into his story?* (E.g. seeing into his mind's eye.)
- Show '*Eye of the Wolf*' (ITP 4.4). *When exactly does the flashback take place?* Highlight the sentence starting 'When everything has become pitch black ... '. *What does this phrase suggest?* (E.g. 'Everything has become pitch black' – like the blank screen at the start of a film; 'the pupil is alive' – the wolf's memories come to life.)
- Highlight the next sentence starting 'There, staring and growling at the boy ... '. *How is the change made clear to the reader?* (E.g. change of scene, different characters.)

Independent and Guided

- The children work in pairs to explore the sequence of key events in *Eye of the Wolf* so far.

ooo Read through the story so far and make links between key events in the present and the flashback, e.g. the black pupil links to Black Flame; the wolf's blue fur links to the description of him as a cub and his name, Blue Wolf; the cage label (Alaskan Wolf, Barren Lands) links to the setting of snow in Alaska, the Far North. (T+)

oo Complete 'Storyboard' (PCM 4.2) to show how the key events of pages 17–23 might look as a scene in a film.

o Use 'Time jigsaw' (PCM 4.3) to sequence events in the story so far. (TA+)

Plenary

- Take feedback from different pairs.
- Recap the learning objectives. *Why do you think the author chose to use a flashback?* (E.g.to hide things; to show how the past explains the present; so we find things out bit by bit, as the characters do.)
- Add work to the Learning Wall.

Assessment pointers

- S&L: pair work will show how well the children can express and explain relevant ideas.
- AF2, 3 (R): discussion of the flashback technique will show how far the children can refer closely to relevant pieces of the text and comment on structure.
- AF4, 5 (R): discussion of hidden links and figurative language will show how far the children can infer and deduce information from the text and comment on the use of language and literary features.

Session 3

We are learning to ...	Resources
• understand how the viewpoint influences how we see events • recognise when the narrative viewpoint changes (PNS Strands 7.2) **Assessment Focuses** AF (R): 2, 3, 6	*Eye of the Wolf* ITP: 4.5

Shared teaching

- Share the learning objectives.
- Read pages 24–37. Talk Partners discuss the relationship between the wolves and the humans. The children use sticky notes to mark things they find interesting.
- *The story is told from the wolves' point of view. How does this influence our view of events?* (E.g. their only experience of humans is of hunters so all humans are hunters.)
- The children Think-Pair-Share responses. *How do you feel about the hunters – sympathetic, neutral or hostile? Did anything surprise you or remind you of something else?*
- Show 'Talking heads' (ITP 4.5). Talk Partners choose one character to focus on. *What does your character think about humans?* Encourage the children to look for evidence in the text to work out their character's thoughts and attitudes.
- Take feedback. Encourage the children to explain which parts of the text they referred to. *What do you infer from what Black Flame and Grey Cousin say?* (E.g. 'A human being is a collector.' or 'Humans? Two legs and a gun'.) *What is Blue Wolf's experience of humans?* (A childhood spent always moving to escape from hunters.) Click the image of each wolf on ITP 4.5 and write the children's ideas in the thought bubbles.
- *How are Shiny Straw's thoughts different from the others?* (E.g. inquisitive, fascinated, excited.) *How do we know? What makes her different?*
- *What does the last paragraph on page 32 say about Shiny Straw? Whose viewpoint is being given?* (Black Flame's) *What about the last paragraph on page 33?* (Blue Wolf's) *I wonder why we are given these different viewpoints?*

Independent and Guided

- The children work in pairs or small groups to explore events in the story from different viewpoints.

ooo Write from Shiny Straw's point of view, about her opinion of her life, family, human beings, etc.

oo Imagine a meeting between humans and wolves from a human perspective. (T+)

o Write about the hunters from Blue Wolf's point of view. (TA+)

Plenary

- Take feedback. Invite different groups or pairs to give examples of their character's viewpoints.
- Recap the learning objectives. *How does a character's point of view influence our view of events? Does the author of the story always stick to the same point of view?*

Assessment pointers

- S&L: pair and group work will show how well the children can adopt group roles and express and respond to opinions.
- AF2, 3 (R): group work will show how far the children can refer closely to the text, making inferences and deductions.
- AF6 (R): response to questioning and group work will show how far the children are able to identify and comment on different viewpoints.

Session 4

We are learning to ...	Resources
• empathise with characters and make inferences • create visual representations of events and time in stories (PNS Strands 7.2, 8.2) **Assessment Focuses** AF (R): 4	*Eye of the Wolf* ITP: 4.6

Shared teaching

- Recap how Chapter V ends. Encourage predictions based on what is already known.
- Read Chapters VI–VIII (pages 38–50). Encourage the children to visualise the events as they read.
- Think-Pair-Share responses to the wolf's story. *What are your thoughts/feelings? What would you ask the wolf about his experiences?* Collect questions and see if they can be answered later.
- Share the learning objectives. *Look back over the wolf's memories and see how the events have affected him.*
- Show 'Memory chart' (ITP 4.6) to summarise the wolf's main memories. Talk Partners identify the remaining memories from pages 38–50.
- Take feedback, adding short titles to Screens 1 and 2 of ITP 4.6, e.g. 'Rescuing Shiny Straw', 'Captured by humans'; 'Waking up in a cage'; 'Meeting Perdrix'; 'Alone again'; 'Meeting the boy'.
- Talk Partners discuss the significance of the memories on ITP 4.6. *Which do you think are the happiest/saddest memories?*
- Talk Partners focus on one memory from ITP 4.6. *Imagine you are the wolf. Think about your experience of humans within that memory. How do you feel?*
- Take feedback. *How do these feelings fit with the attitude, behaviour and feelings we noticed at the start of the story?*
- Add Perdrix's memory to Screen 3 of ITP 4.6. The children Think-Pair-Share this 'story within a story'. *What does it add? Why is this memory part of Blue Wolf's story too?*
- Talk Partners discuss the 'last memory' (page 49). *What has happened between the boy and the wolf? Why is this significant?* (A connection has formed; the wolf appreciated the boy's act of kindness; he had sworn to have nothing to do with humans but is intrigued by the boy.)
- Use ITP 4.6 to focus on time in the story. *Which events are told in detail? Which memories represent long periods of time? How do you know?* Discuss time-lapse markers and sentences that move the story along, e.g. 'he was falling, falling ...', 'over the next ten years', etc.

Independent and Guided

- In pairs the children create visual representations of time in the story.

(ooo) Produce a parallel flowchart and timeline for Blue Wolf's family based on Perdrix's story. (T+)

(oo) Use time-lapse markers from the text to create a timeline of Blue Wolf's memories, annotated with his thoughts and feelings.

(o) Create a flowchart of memories with phrases and sentences indicating the passing of time. (TA+)

Plenary

- Take feedback. Display time link markers and visual representations on the Learning Wall.
- Recap the learning objectives. *Why are time link markers important? Why are some events passed over briefly and some told in detail?*

Assessment pointers

- S&L: pair work will show how far the children can listen and respond to others.
- AF4 (R): independent work and discussion will show how far the children understand organisational features and their significance.

Session 5

We are learning to ...	Resources
• use visualisation and drama to respond to the story • use drama to explore emotions at key moments in a story • recognise recurring themes and ideas within the story (PNS Strands 4.1, 7.2, 8.2) **Assessment Focuses** AF (R): 2, 3	*Eye of the Wolf* ITP: 4.7, 4.8 PCM: 4.4, 4.5

Shared teaching

- Show 'Role on the wall' (ITP 4.7). *We now know the wolf's story but what about the boy?* Talk Partners discuss questions about the boy's story. *What do you want to ask the boy?* Add suggestions to ITP 4.7.
- Focus on page 51 ('The Human Eye'). *What do you think might happen in this section of the book, based on what you know so far about its structure?* (E.g. flashback; story told through memories.)
- Share the learning objectives. Read 'The Human Eye' (pages 53–63). *Look out for hidden links to the wolf's story or recurring ideas.*
- Think-Pair-Share personal responses to the boy's story. *What have we learned about the boy's early life? What do you think about this? What did you find most powerful?*
- Discuss any hidden links the children have noticed, e.g. characters separated from family; man as a destructive force; storytelling.
- Show 'The boy's first memory' (ITP 4.8). Point out the direct link with the night when Blue Wolf was captured. *Why do you think the author has done this?* Encourage the children to visualise this scene. *What do you picture? What mood is created? Which words and phrases help us to imagine the place and create the mood?* Highlight these on ITP 4.8.
- Organise a Forum Theatre with a group creating a tableau of the scene, expressing mood, actions and feelings through positioning, facial expression and body language. The other children advise, some circulating, whispering highlighted phrases from the text to create atmosphere. Invite questions to those in role about how events make them feel. Photographs could be taken to add to the Learning Wall.
- Ask two children to enter the tableau as the woman and Toa the trader. Ask the children to question and explore the thoughts of these characters. *Who do you think the woman is?*
- Discuss the overall impact of the scene. The children quick-fire words and phrases (descriptive words or words relating to feelings), e.g. devastation, desperation, fear. Record these around the extract on ITP 4.8.

Independent and Guided

- The children explore themes and hidden links from what they have read of the story so far.

(ooo) Answer questions and record quotations relating to the theme of stories and storytelling on 'Storytelling' (PCM 4.4).

(oo) Explore links between the wolf's story and the boy's story. (T+)

(o) Use 'Character ratings' (PCM 4.5) to explore the positive and negative images of human beings. (TA)

Plenary

- Take feedback from different groups.
- Recap the learning objectives. *What themes have you been investigating? What does this tell you about the story?*
- Add work to the Learning Wall. Remind the children to look out for these themes as they continue reading.

Assessment pointers

- AF2, 3 (R): drama and independent activities will show how far the children can refer to text and make inferences.

Session 6

We are learning to …	Resources
• empathise with characters and make inferences • identify scene change and time-lapse markers to help keep track of events as we read (PNS Strands 7.2, 8.2) **Assessment Focuses** AF (R): 2, 3, 4	*Eye of the Wolf* ITP: (4.7), 4.9

Shared teaching

- Recall annotated 'Role on the Wall' (ITP 4.7) from Session 5. *Which questions have been answered? Do you have any questions to add?*
- Remind the children of the first part of the boy's story in 'The Human Eye' (pages 53–63). *What images come to mind?* (E.g. the night of destruction; travelling through the desert.)
- Continue to read 'The Human Eye' (pages 64–79). Talk Partners discuss key images and scenes, using sticky notes to mark changes in scene.
- Take feedback and discuss responses to Africa's story. *What images have stayed in your mind? How would you feel if you were Africa? Would you like to be Africa? Have you noticed other recurring themes?* Refer the children to the Learning Wall if necessary.
- Share the learning objectives. Show 'Africa's story' (ITP 4.9). Two memories have been completed with scene change and time-lapse markers from the text. *Why are these important?* (E.g. they show where and when the scene takes place; they move the story along, they structure the narrative.)
- The children Think-Pair-Share other scenes to record, referring to their sticky notes to locate markers. Take feedback, agreeing titles for the memories, e.g. 'Telling stories to the Bedouins'; 'Sold'; 'Working as a shepherd'. Record the scene change and time-lapse markers on ITP 4.9. *Why are these markers important?*
- Encourage the children to visualise various scenes. *Who would be there? What is happening?* Ask a group to Freeze Frame the scene. Invite the class to question the characters in role about feelings, motives, thoughts, attitudes and the character's life. Those in role answer from their character's point of view.
- Take feedback about the freeze frame. *Did this help you to understand the characters better? What sort of character is Africa? What would other characters say about him? What would he say about himself?*

Independent and Guided

- The children work in pairs or small groups to orally tell Africa's story from different first person perspectives.

ooo Tell memories or anecdotes about Africa from other character's perspective, e.g. Toa, Saucepans, the nomads, etc.

oo Tell the story of Africa, including thoughts and feelings. (TA+)

o Tell the story from Africa's point of view. (T+)

Plenary

- Recap the learning objectives.
- Take feedback to create a Role on the Wall for Africa. List his own feelings within his outline. Write comments made by other characters on the outside. *Was it easy to empathise with Africa?*

Assessment pointers

- S&L: freeze frames and oral retellings will show how well the children can explore different viewpoints.
- AF2, 3 (R): response to questions in the role of characters will show how far the children can infer, deduce and use ideas from the text.
- AF4 (R): responses to questions will show how far the children can identify and comment on the structure of the text.

Session 7

We are learning to …	Resources
• use drama to understand characters • discuss themes, motives and feelings in stories (PNS Strands 4.1, 7.2) **Assessment Focuses** AF (R): 2, 3, 6	*Eye of the Wolf* ITP: 4.10 PCM: 4.6

Shared teaching

- Share the learning objectives.
- Show 'Feelings graph' (ITP 4.10). Reflect on Africa's changing experiences so far. *Which are his happiest and saddest times?*
- Continue to read 'The Human Eye' (pages 80–93). Take feedback about the text. *Where would you put Africa on the feelings graph now?*
- Talk Partners discuss changes in Africa's life. *How does his life in Green Africa compare with his life in Yellow Africa and Grey Africa?*
- In groups, the children Freeze Frame the story at this point showing Pa and Ma Bia and Africa. Allow the children Think Time about their character in role. *How do you feel about your life and your family? What are your hopes? Do you have any fears, concerns or worries?* (E.g. Ma Bia might be optimistic; Pa Bia might have worries about the future.) *Use clues in the text to help you.*
- Take feedback and predictions about how the story might continue.
- Read 'The Human Eye' (pages 94–97). *Why has the mood suddenly changed again? What is happening to Green Africa?* Encourage the children to draw on details in the text and prior knowledge to explain what is happening to the forest. *How is it affecting the animals and people who live there? What do you think they mean by 'the Other World'?*
- Encourage the children to explore the theme of human relationships with the natural world and its creatures. *How is this represented in the story? Does this remind you of any other parts of the story? Can you see any connection with the wolf's story? Do you think the author has a message about human beings?* The children Think-Pair-Share ideas, mind mapping ideas to add to the Learning Wall.

Independent and Guided

- In pairs or small groups the children explore the theme of human relationships with the natural world and its creatures.

ooo Use 'Human beings' (PCM 4.6) to give examples of the positive and negative views of human beings presented in the book.

oo Compose a 'Message to Mankind' as if from the wolf, the gorilla, the crocodile, Ma Bia or Pa Bia, explaining how their life is affected by human activity. (T)

o Give character ratings for Ma Bia, Pa Bia and Africa according to whether the children like or dislike them, giving reasons for their ratings. (TA)

Plenary

- Take feedback and recap the learning objectives. *What message does the writer have about human beings? Is it all negative? Why are Ma and Pa Bia important characters in the story?*

Assessment pointers

- S&L: freeze frames will show how well the children can convey ideas about characters.
- AF2, 3 (R): drama activities will show how far the children can refer to the text, making deductions and inferences.
- AF6 (R): response to questions and group work will show how far the children understand the author's viewpoint.

Session 8

We are learning to ...	Resources
• reflect on how an ending contributes to the overall mood, message and themes (PNS Strands 7.2)	*Eye of the Wolf*
	ITP: (4.2), 4.11
	PCM: 4.7
Assessment Focuses	
AF (R): 2, 3, 4, 6	

Shared teaching (1)

- Refer back to questions added to the Learning Wall in Session 1. *Which questions have been answered? Are there any new puzzles?*
- Look at the title page of 'The Other World' (page 99). *I wonder what this refers to?* Invite predictions about the story's ending.
- Share the learning objectives.
- Read 'The Other World' (pages 101–112). At the end of the story, allow Think Time before inviting responses. *Did you like the ending?*

Independent and Guided (1)

- The children work in groups to discuss the questions on 'Group discussion' (PCM 4.7). Encourage the children to discuss each point thoroughly before the group secretary makes notes. Support the children with an identified need. (T/TA)

Shared teaching (2)

- Take feedback from the groups. *Did you notice any links to themes we have already identified? How and why has the relationship between the wolf and the boy changed? How is the change shown at the end?*
- Recall 'The wolf' (ITP 4.2) and look at the opening of the story again. *Would you choose the same words to describe the wolf now? How has the wolf changed?* Add new suggestions to ITP 4.2.
- Reread pages 109–111. Talk Partners discuss why the wolf opening his eye is significant. *Have his eyes been opened in more ways than one?* (E.g. opening our eyes to the wider world, seeing others and their experiences.)

Independent and Guided (2)

- The children work in pairs or groups to explore themes and how the different strands of the story are brought together.

ooo Explore the symbolism of the eye. (T+)

oo Write thought monologues showing the wolf's thoughts on the boy at the start and at the end of the story.

o Identify how a given character came to be in the zoo. The group collect responses on a group diagram. (TA+)

Plenary

- Show 'Book cover' (ITP 4.11). Discuss the illustration. *Having read the ending, what ideas do you think it represents? How does it link to the themes and structure of the story? Why is it called* Eye of the Wolf*?*
- Recap the learning objectives.

Assessment pointers

- S&L: pair and group work will show how well the children can adopt group roles and express and respond to opinions.
- AF2, 3, 4, 6 (R): response to questions and group work will show how far the children can refer to the text, making inferences and deductions, and comment on structural choices at the end of the story and also comment on the overall effect of the story on the reader.

PHASE 2: STORYTELLING (3 DAYS)

Session 9

We are learning to ...	Resources
• identify a range of storytelling techniques (PNS Strands 7.3)	*Eye of the Wolf*
	ITP: (4.8), 4.12
	PCM: 4.8
Assessment Focuses	
AF (R): 2, 5	

Shared teaching

- Refer back to the Learning Wall to remind the children of the storytelling theme in *Eye of the Wolf. How is this theme developed? Who tells the stories? What is the effect on listeners?*
- Introduce 'The Big Picture' for Phases 2 and 3. Explain that the children are going to tell the story of one of the animals in *Eye of the Wolf*, first orally (in Phase 2) and then in writing (Phase 3).
- Share the learning objective. *People say Africa is a good storyteller. What makes a good storyteller?* Discuss examples of storytelling the children might recall, identifying points about how the story is told and the performance given.
- Discuss the differences between oral and written storytelling, e.g. use of expression and gestures in oral storytelling, use of language features in written storytelling. *Do you think the narrator's voice in* Eye of the Wolf *has features of good storytelling? What are they?*
- Recall 'The boy's first memory' (ITP 4.8). Read the extract, using the expression, intonation and gestures of a storyteller. *What is the storyteller trying to do?* (E.g. create an image and mood; bring the story to life for the reader/audience) *How does he do this?* (E.g. details; sensory description, putting the reader there, 'Everywhere you look ...'; the present tense to suggest immediacy.)
- Discuss and highlight sentence and language features on ITP 4.8. *What do you notice about the sentence structures?* (E.g. short sentences such as 'It's a terrifying night'; broken sentences 'A moonless African night'; ellipsis; list of three sentences for pace, etc.)
- Identify examples of effective vocabulary on ITP 4.8, e.g. expressive adjectives, powerful verbs, etc. Highlight these in different colours.
- Show 'Storytelling techniques' (ITP 4.12). Click each category and identify which features have already been discussed. *Is there anything else to add?* Encourage the children to offer suggestions and add to ITP 4.12.

Independent and Guided

- The children work in pairs to find and record examples of good storytelling techniques or effective language in *Eye of the Wolf.*

ooo Choose an extract and make notes to help read it effectively. Then perform with a partner. (T+)

oo Choose an extract and complete 'Storytelling techniques' (PCM 4.8).

o As above. (TA)

Plenary

- Take feedback and encourage the children to suggest new examples of storytelling techniques and effective language to add to ITP 4.12, e.g. use of repetition, alliteration, etc.
- Recap the learning objective.

Assessment pointers

- S&L: pair work will show how well the children can express and explain relevant ideas.
- AF2, 5 (R): shared and group discussions will show how well the children are able to identify, comment on and explain a range of language and literary features.

Session 10

We are learning to …	Resources
• use storyboards to help us picture the story (PNS Strands 8.2)	*Eye of the Wolf*
Assessment Focuses	ITP: 4.13, 4.14
AF(R): 2, 3	PCM: 4.9, 4.10

Shared teaching (1)

- Share the learning objective and explain that the children are going to plan stories in the same style as *Eye of the Wolf. What are the key features of this style?* (E.g. third person, from an animal's viewpoint – showing its thoughts and feelings through a series of memories.)
- Explain that today, the children are going to plan out the scenes of the animal's story so they have a clear idea of the sequence of events.
- Show 'Animal pictures' (ITP 4.13). Focus on the animals in the zoo. *What might they be feeling and thinking? Is this a happy memory?*
- Focus on the picture of the black gorilla on ITP 4.13. *What do we know about the black gorilla from the story? What kind of memories might he have?* (E.g. growing up in the rainforest, helping Ma and Pa Bia, seeing the landscape change, being captured, arriving at the zoo.) Click the picture to record ideas in the thought bubble.

Independent and Guided (1)

- Pairs choose one of the animals from ITP 4.13 and record ideas on 'Animal memories' (PCM 4.9). Encourage the children to use ideas from the text and their own ideas. Support the children with an identified need. (T/TA)

Shared teaching (2)

- Take feedback. *Which animal did you choose? What memories might they have? What ideas did you get from the story? What ideas were your own?* Add suggestions for each animal on ITP 4.13.
- Show 'Story planner' (ITP 4.14). Recap the flashback structure of *Eye of the Wolf.* Explain that the planner sets out a similar structure, starting with the animal in the zoo, then using flashbacks to reveal events from their past, returning to the present and providing a surprise ending.
- The children suggest ideas about the black gorilla's memories, referring back to ITP 4.13. Model organising these on ITP 4.14 to form a linked sequence of events, e.g. *I think I'll follow that really happy memory of collecting fruit with Ma Bia with the sad memory of seeing the rainforest being destroyed.*
- Remind the children of time-lapse and scene change markers from Sessions 4 and 6. Model how to use these appropriately to link the gorilla's memories and note these on ITP 4.14.

Independent and Guided (2)

- Pairs complete 'Story planner' (PCM 4.10), selecting and sequencing memories from completed PCM 4.9, noting or drawing scenes and adding time-lapse and scene change markers. Support the children with an identified need. (T/TA)

Plenary

- Take feedback. *What memories did you put in your story planner?*
- Recap the learning objective. *Do you think the story planner will help you to tell the story effectively?*

Assessment pointers

- S&L: pair work will show how far the children can listen and respond to others.
- AF2, 3 (R): group discussion and independent work will show how far the children can select ideas from the text and make deductions.

Session 11

We are learning to …	Resources
• use a range of storytelling and performance techniques (PNS Strands 1.1)	ITP: (4.12, 4.14)
Assessment Focuses	PCM: (4.10), 4.11
AF (R): 4	

Shared teaching

- Share the learning objective and explain that, in this session, the children are going to rehearse telling their stories.
- Remind the children of good storytelling techniques discussed in Session 9, referring to annotated 'Storytelling techniques' (ITP 4.12).
- Show annotated 'Story planner' (ITP 4.14). Demonstrate how to use ITP 4.14 to tell the beginning of the story explaining that it's important to have an effective story opening to get the listener's attention, e.g. *The gorilla sits in his cage … still, motionless. He sits and he stares. Children make silly faces in front of his cage but the gorilla still sits and he stares.* Use words and gestures to create vivid images for the audience. Discuss the techniques you have used.
- Talk Partners discuss ideas for the opening of their stories referring to completed 'Story planner' (PCM 4.10).
- Take feedback and discuss good ideas.
- Discuss the next scene on the story planner on ITP 4.14. *How did the author lead into the flashback in* Eye of the Wolf? (E.g. using the eye, fade to black, time-markers, clear change of scene.) Model this next stage of the story. (E.g. *But if you look deep, deep into the darkness of Gorilla's eyes, the zoo, the cage, the bars all disappear. Time and memories flash by, until the darkness becomes tinged with green and there staring right back at you, wide eyed, is a baby gorilla clinging to its mother.*) Continue, using words and gestures to create the scene in the rainforest.
- Discuss the features you used that made the story come to life. *How might I continue this story?* Encourage the children to offer suggestions and ideas for language you could use.

Independent and Guided

- Pairs take it in turns to tell their stories, starting with the first two scenes then as far as they can get.
  - ●●● Refer to PCM 4.10 to tell as much of the story as possible.
  - ●● As above. (T)
  - ● Use PCM 4.10 and 'Story frame' (PCM 4.11). (TA+)

Plenary

- Take feedback. *Did you enjoy your partner's story? What techniques did they use?*
- Recap the learning objective.
- Ask a confident pair to tell part of their story and invite comments. Introduce new points, e.g. expressing different moods or reinforcing performance techniques such as intonation, gesture, pauses, etc.
- Encourage the children to keep practising telling their story. e.g. on the way home. At the end of Phase 3 the stories will be presented to an audience.

Assessment pointers

- S&L: oral readings will show how far the children can interpret their stories through speech, gesture and movement.
- AF4 (R): responses to questions and pair work will show how far the children can identify and comment on the structure of their own texts.

Session 12

We are learning to ...	Resources
• use paragraphs to help pace the story • try out different versions of sentences (PNS Strands 10.2, 11.1) **Assessment Focuses** AF (W): 3, 4, 5, 6	ITP: (4.14) PCM: (4.10, 4.11)

Shared teaching

- Recap 'The Big Picture' for Phase 3 and explain that the children are now going to write the animals' stories. Agree a format for the finished work, e.g. a collection of short stories, a picture book, an on-screen story (combining images, music or voiceover). The stories will be drafted over the next two sessions.
- Share the learning objectives.
- Talk Partners discuss how writing a story is different from telling one, e.g. the reader can't see the storyteller's facial expression and gestures or hear his intonation.
- Take feedback. *How can we get around not seeing and hearing the storyteller when writing?* (E.g. structuring writing into paragraphs; constructing sentences; using punctuation to replace intonation.)
- Recall annotated 'Story planner' (ITP 4.14). *The boxes will now become paragraph planners. How can this clarify the story structure for the reader?* (E.g. clearly showing each memory.)
- Use Modelled Writing to create an opening for the story planned on ITP 4.14. Focus on how to use structure and punctuation to write in a storytelling style, e.g. *I wonder if I should make that one sentence, or three separate short sentences ... perhaps I should join those two sentences together. I could use a semi-colon or a dash.*
- Explain that you want the children to write a sentence about the children jumping around in the story and contrast it with the gorilla sitting and staring. *Can you do that in one sentence?* Talk Partners write and display their sentences.
- Take feedback. Encourage the children to discuss the differences in formation, conjunctions and punctuation and give reasons for their choice of sentence.
- Use Modelled Writing to create the first memory flashback. Emphasise the importance of signposting this clearly for the reader, e.g. using linking sentences and connecting ideas that show something unusual is happening.

Independent and Guided

- The children work independently to write their stories using completed 'Story planner' (PCM 4.10), and 'Story frame' (PCM 4.11), if needed. Work with groups on setting an appropriate level of targets or success criteria. Support the children with an identified need. (T+/TA)

Plenary

- Recap the learning objectives.
- Talk Partners check paragraphing and that time-lapse or scene change markers have been used. *Is the flashback and story structure clear to the reader? Could any sentences be improved?*

Assessment pointers

- AF3, 4, 5, 6 (W): drafted narratives will show how far the children can use paragraphs to structure ideas and maintain cohesion, vary sentences and punctuation for clarity and effect.

Session 13

We are learning to ...	Resources
• use a range of narrative techniques to engage the reader • use carefully chosen words and figurative language (PNS Strands 9.2, 9.4) **Assessment Focuses** AF (W): 1, 2, 7	ITP: (4.12), 4.15, 4.16

Shared teaching

- Share the learning objectives and explain that, in this session, the children will complete the first drafts of their stories. *What is characteristic of the author's style in* Eye of the Wolf? (E.g. the storytelling style, distinctive narrative viewpoint, rich descriptive language.)
- Show 'Stories with flashbacks' (ITP 4.15) and discuss the success criteria for writing a story in a similar style to *Eye of the Wolf*. Add the children's suggestions to ITP 4.15.
- Recall annotated 'Storytelling techniques' (ITP 4.12) to recap storytelling techniques, e.g. details and sensory description; commenting on the action; repetition and echoes; thoughts of characters; language, e.g. expressive adjectives, powerful verbs, similes, figurative language; patterns of sound.
- Show 'Writing sample' (ITP 4.16) and read the extract. It describes one of the gorilla's memories. *Does this extract use the storyteller's style? Does it convey a mood?* The children Think-Pair-Share their suggestions for improvement.
- Use Think Alouds to model revising the sample text on ITP 4.16, e.g. *I want to make the first sentence appear to be from the gorilla's point of view. I don't want to mention people; I want to keep the focus on the gorilla and the forest. It's better to suggest rather than tell.*
- The children rework sentences from ITP 4.16. *Try to create a sense of destruction and bring the scene alive.* Discuss the pros and cons of the suggestions, giving reasons for choices and encouraging the children to explain the effect they wanted, e.g. *I like the word 'tremble' because it suggests fear as well as the shaking movement.* Make changes to ITP 4.16 , then display the example text for comparison.
- Highlight language effects on the example text, such as alliteration (E.g. slashing, slicing, smashing, etc.) which can sound violent; similes (E.g. dry earth – as dry and cracked as the elephant's skin) which help us picture the scene; and metaphors (E.g. The Other World was creeping closer) which can give a sense of menace.
- Discuss ways of showing, rather than telling, that the gorilla is sad, through actions, thoughts or dialogue. (E.g. 'Soon there will be nothing left', he thought.)

Independent and Guided

- The children work independently to revise their writing from Session 12 and to complete their story. Support the children with an identified need. (T+/TA+)

Plenary

- Take feedback and recap the learning objectives. *What techniques did you use?*
- The children share a paragraph with a partner. *Do you like your partner's paragraph? What language have they used effectively? What mood is created?*

Assessment pointers

- AF1, 2, 7 (W): completed drafts will show how far the children are able to choose vocabulary for effect and maintain an appropriate style and overall effect.

Session 14

We are learning to ...	Resources
• write different kinds of sentences, thinking about the effect on the reader • improve sentences, thinking about the sound and effect (PNS Strands 11.1, 11.2) **Assessment Focuses** AF (W): 5, 6	ITP: 4.17 PCM: 4.12

Shared teaching

- Share the learning objectives and explain that, in this session, the children will focus on using a range of sentences to make their writing flow and convey the story effectively.
- Distribute 'Sentence checklist' (PCM 4.12) and review ideas.
- Show 'Sentence surgery' (ITP 4.17) and read the sentence about the dromedary.
- Model commenting on the dromedary sentence, e.g. *This is quite a long compound sentence. It is repetitive with the use of 'and, and, and'. How could we contract it into a neater complex sentence?)* Talk Partners discuss their ideas.
- Take feedback and comment on the children's suggestions.
- Use Modelled Writing to create a more concise, complex sentence on ITP 4.17. (E.g. *Chewing thoughtfully, the dromedary stood and gazed at the trader.)*
- Repeat for the sentence about the cheetah on ITP 4.17. *How could we strengthen or change the focus of this sentence?* Take feedback. Talk Partners experiment with different conjunctions and/or rearranging the order of the cheetah sentence.
- Take feedback and discuss ideas for improvement. Use Modelled Writing to improve the cheetah sentence on ITP 4.17. (E.g. *Although he was very tired, never once did the cheetah take his eyes off the Abyssinian dove.)*
- Read the sentence about the hyena on ITP 4.17. *How could you shorten this sentence to make it more effective?*
- Talk Partners write revised versions of the hyena sentence. Take feedback, then use Modelled Writing to create an improved version, e.g. *Fresh meat. How could a hyena resist?*
- Read the final sentence on ITP 4.17. *How can we make it more interesting by adding more information?* Take feedback. Talk Partners write a revised version of the sentence, referring to the gorilla.
- Take feedback and comment on ideas. Add the children's suggestions to ITP 4.17, e.g. *The boy told him stories about Yellow Africa where ... ; The boy, who was a great storyteller, told him ... .*

Independent and Guided

- The children work independently revising sentences in their own writing, using PCM 4.12 for ideas. Pairs swap feedback and ideas. Support the children with an identified need. (T+/TA)

Plenary

- Hold a whole-class sentence surgery to discuss a sentence one of the children has been having difficulty with. Take suggestions for improvement.
- Recap the learning objectives. Remind the children that constructing sentences in varied ways can improve the effect.

Assessment pointers

- S&L: pair work will show how sensitively the children can give and respond to opinions.
- AF5, 6 (W): redrafted sentences and revised stories will show how far the children are able to vary sentences for effect and use punctuation effectively.

Session 15

We are learning to ...	Resources
• make changes to improve our stories • present our work for an audience using handwriting • present our work for an audience using ICT (PNS Strands 9.1, 12.1, 12.2) **Assessment Focuses** AF (W): 1, 2	ITP: (4.15)

Shared teaching

- Explain that, in this session, the children will evaluate their written stories to see if they are ready for presentation.
- Share the learning objectives. *How will you decide if your story is ready to be presented?* Take feedback.
- Recall annotated 'Stories with flashbacks' (ITP 4.15). The children discuss success criteria for their stories. *Does your story cover all of these points?* Choose one child's story and read it to the class.
- Talk Partners discuss how intriguing the child's story is, giving examples of how it keeps the reader's interest. *Which parts sound best?*
- Take feedback. Relate comments to the success criteria on ITP 4.15, e.g. *Yes, that repetition was a really good use of the storyteller style.*
- Invite discussion about the child's story. Emphasise the positives in the story encouraging the children to offer suggestions of what works well.
- Refer to ITP 4.15 and invite discussion of any parts that could be improved. *Has the author left anything out? Could the author improve the storyteller style, show the character's changing mood and feelings or improve the ending?*
- The children suggest two or three things that the author could do to improve the story before they begin revising it for final presentation.

Independent and Guided

- Pairs share their stories and identify Two Stars and a Wish, referring to the success criteria on ITP 4.15. The children work independently to make the improvement suggested. Support the children with an identified need. (T+/TA+)

Plenary

- Take feedback on the changes made. *What feedback did your partner give? How have you improved your story? Are you pleased with your story now?*
- Recap the learning objectives and the agreed final presentation format, e.g. a book of short stories, a picture book, an on-screen presentation, etc. Discuss what needs to be done to bring the final drafts to presentational standard in this format, e.g. proofreading, producing a polished copy, preparing artwork. Make a schedule for these activities.
- Recap the unit as a whole. *What did you enjoy most? What do you still find difficult? Would you like to read any of the author's other books?*
- If possible, organise a special session to present the final written and oral versions of the story. Make a display of the written narratives alongside other work from the unit. Invite the children from another class to listen to the oral stories.

Assessment pointers

- S&L: pair work will show how sensitively the children can give and respond to opinions.
- AF1 (W): the final stories will show how far the children can write imaginative and interesting texts.
- AF2 (W): feedback and peer and self-assessment will show how well the children can produce appropriate texts and evaluate those produced by others.

Interior monologues

Continue writing the wolf's thoughts.

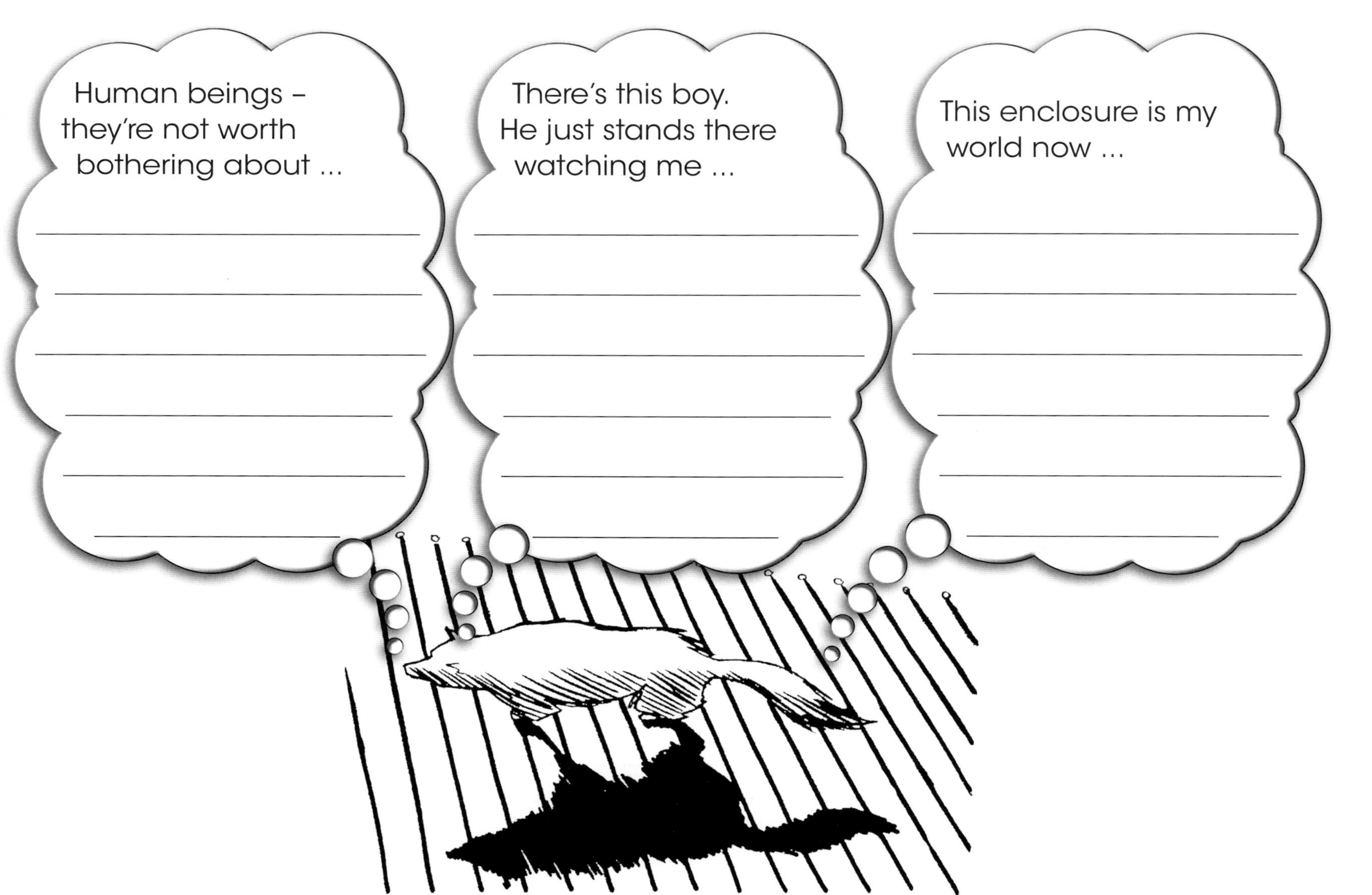

Human beings –
they're not worth
bothering about …
There's this boy.
He just stands there
watching me …
This enclosure is my
world now …

Storyboard

Show what the flashback might look like as a scene in a film.

Type of shot: *Long shot*
Action: *They look into each other's eyes in a zoo that's silent and empty*

Type of shot: ____________
Action: ____________

Type of shot: ____________
Action: ____________

Type of shot: ____________
Action: ____________

Type of shot: ____________
Action: ____________

Type of shot: ____________
Action: ____________

Time jigsaw

Cut up the sentences and put the events in the order described in the book. Then put them in the order in which they actually happened.

The boy looks deep into the wolf's eye and sees his first memory.

Black Flame tells stories to her cubs.

The wolf loses his eye in a fight against humans.

The wolf is captured by humans.

The she-wolf dies.

The wolf swears not to have anything more to do with humans.

The wolf and the she-wolf sit staring straight through the visitors.

The boy stands watching the wolf pace up and down.

A band of hunters are tracking down the wolves.

Storytelling

1. Answer the questions about storytelling in *Eye of the Wolf*.

What stories are told?

Why are they told?

How are they told?

What are the similarities/differences?

2. Discuss what the quotes from *Eye of the Wolf* mean.

'... a name doesn't mean anything without the story that goes with it.' (page 54)

'... he's just another animal until you get to know his life story.' (page 54)

Character ratings

Mark the line to rate each character. Give your reasons.

Toa the trader

dislike ⟺ like

Reasons: ______________________

____

____

____

The woman

dislike ⟺ like

Reasons: ______________________

____

____

____

The hunters

dislike ⟺ like

Reasons: ______________________

____

____

____

Human beings

1. Fill in the boxes to show examples of positive and negative views of human beings from the story. Add your own categories.

Human beings

Negative

A destroyer

A collector

A money maker

A taker consumer

Positive

A storyteller

Africa tells stories that everyone wants to hear: p.92 'everybody gathered around him'

A wise thinker

A healer/sharer

A protector

2. Discuss what message you think the author is trying to tell you.

Group discussion

Discuss and then answer the questions.

a. At the end of the story how do you feel? What is the mood?

b. Does the ending tie up loose ends and solve the puzzles? How?

c. What surprises and revelations are there?

d. What does the ending tell you about the following themes:

- The relationship between the boy and the wolf
- Our view of the world
- Storytelling

Name: ______________________ Date: ______________

Storytelling techniques

Choose an extract from *Eye of the Wolf* and make notes about effective storytelling techniques.

What is the storyteller trying to do?

What do you notice about the sentence structures?

What storytelling techniques are used?

What language is used for effect?

Animal memories

Choose an animal from the zoo and write its memories.

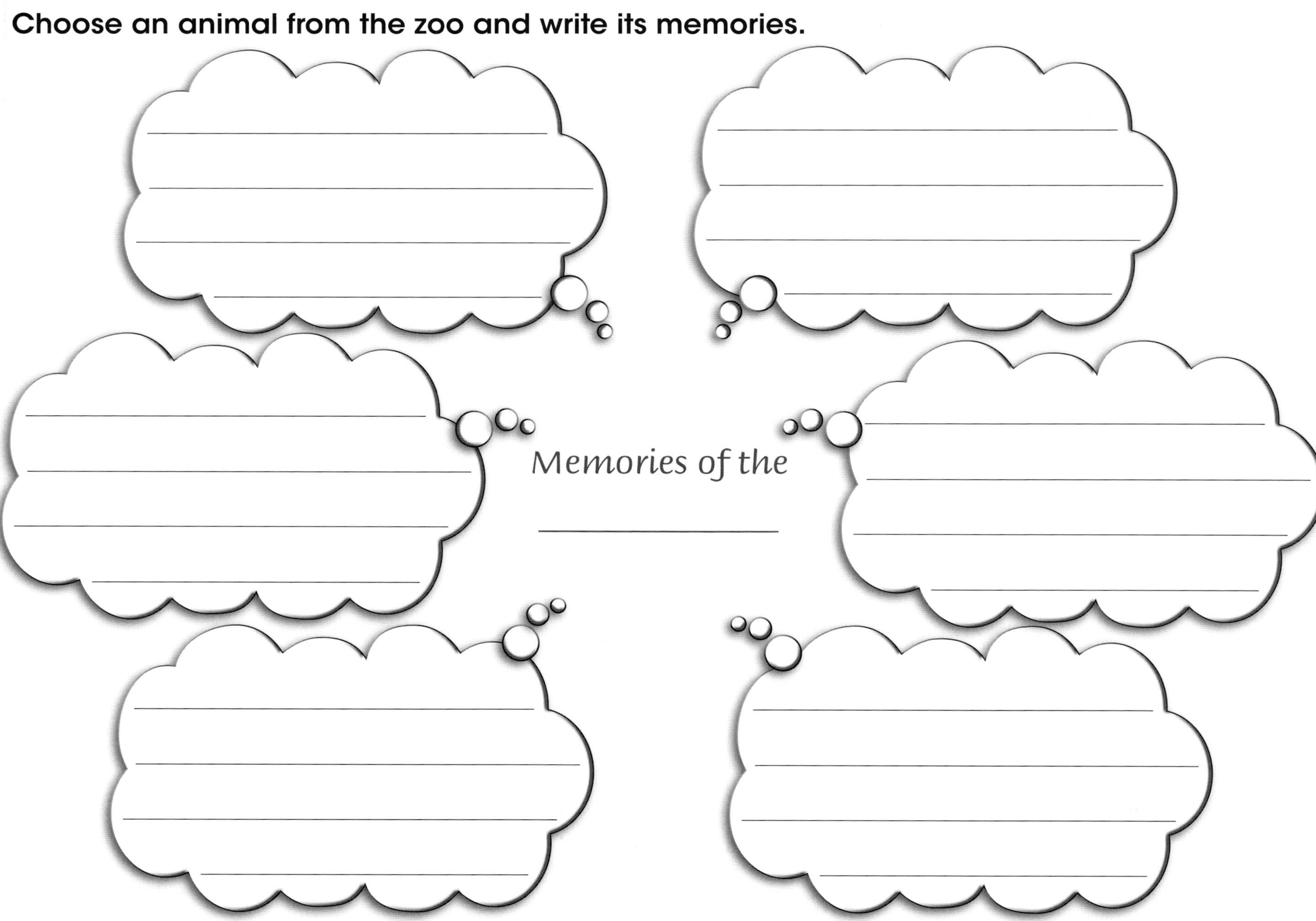

Story planner

Add notes to the storyboard to plan your story.

Type of shot: ____________
Action: ____________

Type of shot: ____________
Action: ____________

Type of shot: ____________
Action: ____________

Type of shot: ____________
Action: ____________

Type of shot: ____________
Action: ____________

Type of shot: ____________
Action: ____________

Story frame

Use these sentence starters to help you to tell your animal's story.

Trapped inside a cage, a ...

Seasons passed by ...

The ... remembers a time many years before when ...

As the years went by ...

Then one day ...

The days turned to months ...

... which brings us right up to date.

But it is a new day now ...

Sentence checklist

Use the list to check your sentences sound right when you read them aloud.

- Use a variety of simple and complex sentences to vary the pace and avoid repetition.
- Use a conjunction to join two ideas, *e.g. although, since, while.*
- Use a different sentence type, e.g. a question.
- Use a short sentence for emphasis or impact.
- Use a 'list of three' sentence for pace.
- Use a different sentence opening, e.g. an adverb, an *-ing* starter.
- Change the order of the clauses in a complex sentence for effect.
- Drop in a clause to give the reader more information.
- Add adverbials to give detail about when, where or how something happens.

Remember:

- check your punctuation
- use commas to mark boundaries between words, phrases or clauses
- a semi-colon can be used to link two ideas in one sentence

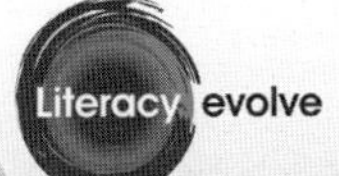

Narrative Unit 5

FANTASTIC, FUNNY, FRIGHTENING! – stories (Revision)

Medium term plan (2 weeks)	
Phase	**Learning Outcomes**
Phase 1: Enjoying authors (4 days)	• Children can identify and answer different types of questions about stories and plays. • Children can make up their own questions about a text.
Phase 2: Learning from authors (3 days)	• Children can identify how paragraphs are used to structure stories. • Children can use a range of connectives in their writing. • Children can write complex sentences and vary the sentence structure in their writing. • Children can identify features of a play script and how words are chosen for effect.
Phase 3: Planning and writing a story (3 days)	• Children can plan and write their own story, using features of their chosen genre. • Children can review, edit and improve their own work and respond to a partner's work.

Narrative Unit 5

FANTASTIC, FUNNY, FRIGHTENING!

Big picture

This unit is designed to provide a series of revision sessions based around narrative writing. The children read a selection of stories and a play and explore them through answering questions and discussion. In doing so, they revise and practise different reading comprehension techniques. They also reinforce this through writing their own questions. The children also look more closely at the authors' techniques and revise paragraphing, sentence structure and punctuation in order to practise applying this in their own writing. They then plan and write their own stories, considering genre and what makes a good story, practising proofreading techniques and to improve their own writing.

Prior learning

This unit assumes that the children can already:

- identify features of different story genres
- answer questions on a range of texts
- use complex sentences and paragraphs in their writing
- write complete short stories in a chosen genre.

Key aspects of learning

Creative thinking: Generate ideas to use in their own stories; use interesting and varied language to develop character, setting and mood.
Enquiry: Answer questions about the texts and make up their own questions to ask.
Empathy: Identify with the feelings of different characters in the texts they read; imagine how characters they write about feel.
Evaluation: Evaluate and improve their own and each other's answers to reading comprehension questions; give feedback on other's stories.
Reasoning: Construct arguments based on the text to answer more complex reading comprehension questions.

Progression in narrative

In this unit the children will:

- identify story structures typical to particular fiction genres
- identify differences and similarities between stories and plays
- look at elements of an author's style in stories and plays
- recognise that authors use language carefully to influence the reader's view of a place, situation or character
- plan and write stories which use different styles of narrative
- plan the plot, characters and structure of own narrative writing
- use paragraphs and sentence length to achieve a particular effect; develop characterisation; use dialogue
- create a setting by using expressive or figurative language.

Cross-curricular links

Art: The children could create their own posters to remind them about aspects of story- and script-writing.
ICT: The children produce word processed final versions of their stories.

PHASE 1: ENJOYING AUTHORS (4 DAYS)

Session 1

We are learning to ...	Resources
• use dialogic talk to explore issues, themes, motives and feelings in stories • discuss themes, motives and feelings in stories (PNS Strands 1.3, 7.2) **Assessment Focuses** AF (R): 2, 3	*Fantastic, Funny, Frightening!* ITP: 5.1 PCM: 5.1

Shared teaching

- Share the learning objectives.
- Recap some of the texts covered in Year 6. *What stories have we read this year? What were they about? What did you like about them? What other types of texts are there?* (E.g. films, play scripts, etc.)
- Remind the children that throughout the year, they have been exploring and developing their understanding of texts. *How is reading like being a detective?* (E.g. looking for hidden meaning from the clues in the text; making deductions and inferences.) Draw out the idea that some information is openly stated whereas other things are implied and have to be deduced.
- Show 'Reading detective tips' (ITP 5.1). *What makes a good reading detective? What skills do you need?* Discuss the tips and encourage the children to add to the list.
- Explain that they are going to revisit *Nule*. Talk Partners discuss what they can remember about *Nule*. *What type of story was this?* (mystery) *What happened in the story?*
- Take feedback and then reread Nule, as the children follow in their books (pages 73–92 in *Fantastic, Funny, Frightening!*). Ask the children to visualise the events and to see what they notice this time.
- Talk Partners discuss what they have noticed from the rereading. *Did you enjoy it? Was reading it this time different? What stood out?*
- Take feedback. Model posing and answering a question about *Nule*, e.g. *How do we know that Libby is frightened of Nule?* Demonstrate the process of finding the answer, identifying strategies needed, e.g. finding the right part of the story by skimming/scanning; close reading to look for the evidence; continuing to read to find further evidence. Point out the part saying 'Libby preferred not to ...'. *What does this refer to? What can we infer from it?*
- Reinforce the idea that answering questions requires close reading around the relevant part of the text, sometimes needing inferences and deductions from the evidence.

Independent and Guided

- In pairs, the children answer the questions about *Nule* on 'Reading detective' (PCM 5.1). When they have finished, groups Jigsaw in order to compare answers.

(ooo) Answer questions a and b on PCM 5.1.

(oo) Answer questions c and d on PCM 5.1. (TA+)

(o) Answer questions e and f on PCM 5.1. (T+)

Plenary

- Take feedback. *How did you find the answers to the questions? Which part of the text did you use?*
- Recap the learning objectives and what it means to be a reading detective. *What skills do reading detectives need?* Make a list and add this to the Learning Wall.

Assessment pointers

- S&L: pair work will show how well the children can express and explain relevant ideas.
- AF2, 3 (R): pair work will show how well the children can select relevant information and make deductions and inferences from the text.

Session 2

We are learning to …	Resources
• explore story structure, presentation and language • say how authors create certain effects and explore the impact on the reader (PNS Strands 7.3, 8.3) **Assessment Focuses** AF (R): 2, 3, 4, 5, 6	*Fantastic, Funny, Frightening!* ITP: (5.1), 5.2 PCM: 5.2

Shared teaching

- Explain that throughout the year, the children have been learning to appreciate authors' skills, e.g. how they shape stories, how they achieve particular effects, etc.
- Share the learning objectives.
- Read *Moving House* (pages 69–72) from *Fantastic, Funny, Frightening!*
- Discuss the story. *What did you like? Were there any surprises or puzzles? Why does the narrator like the house? How does he get into the cellar? Why can't he get back upstairs? How do you know he has been there a long time?* Encourage the children to support their ideas with references from the text.
- Show '*Moving House*' (ITP 5.2). *How has the author organised the story? Can we divide the story into different parts? What does each part focus on?* (E.g. four main parts: 'curiosity', 'realisation of the situation', 'true horror' and 'moral of the story'.) Allow Think Time before taking responses.
- Focus on the first page of *Moving House* on ITP 5.2. *Why do you think the author chose to start the story like this?* Encourage the children to give precise reasons for their answers rather than general comments. *Why does it make us want to read on?* (it's created a sense of mystery)
- Now look at the use of language. *How does the author draw attention to the cellar?* (E.g. using the word 'especially', repeating the word 'cellar'.)
- Show 'Reading detective tips' (ITP 5.1) and remind the children of the skills that they used to answer questions in Session 1.

Independent and Guided

- In groups, the children answer questions about *Moving House* on 'Author techniques' (PCM 5.2). When they have finished, they use Envoys to share responses with other groups.

ooo Answer all of the questions on PCM 5.2.

oo Choose four of the questions to answer on PCM 5.2. (TA+)

o Choose two of the questions to answer on PCM 5.2. (T+)

Plenary

- Take feedback. *What techniques did the author use? What effect did they have on the reader? Which do you think was the most effective?*
- Recap the learning objectives. Discuss the techniques that the children used to answer questions about how the text was written, e.g. identifying words and phrases, looking at how sentence lengths vary and explaining the effects. *What clues did you use to find your answers?* Annotate the evidence on ITP 5.2.

Assessment pointers

- S&L: pair and group work will show how well the children can adopt group roles and express and respond to opinions.
- AF2, 3 (R): written answers show how well the children can refer to and make inferences from the text.
- AF4, 5, 6 (R): oral and written answers show how far the children are able to recognise and comment on structural and presentational features, authors' language choices and their effect on the reader.

Session 3

We are learning to …	Resources
• explore themes in stories and poems • say how authors create certain effects and explore the impact on the reader (PNS Strands 7.2, 8.3) **Assessment Focuses** AF (R): 2, 6, 7	ITP: 5.3, 5.4, 5.5 PCM: 5.3

Shared teaching

- Share the learning objectives. Explain to the children that they are now going to use their reading detective skills to answer questions on a play script.
- Recap the features of a play script. *What does a play script have that a story doesn't?* (E.g. stage directions, cast list, scenes) *How is dialogue set out in a play script?*
- Read Scene 1 of '*Excalibur*' (ITP 5.3). Discuss the meaning of any unfamiliar vocabulary. *What do you think the different characters are like? How do we know this? What do you think is going to happen next?*
- Explain that the children will be writing three-star answers. These are answers that require us to comment on stories, giving opinions and explaining our thinking. They require longer, more detailed, answers referring to the text to back up ideas, and are worth a greater number of marks in tests.
- Show 'Three-star answers' (ITP 5.4). Read the success criteria and encourage the children to add to the list.
- Show 'Model answers' (ITP 5.5). Read the question on the left and click to see the answer. *Is this a three-star answer?* Discuss the strengths of this answer and reinforce the success criteria on ITP 5.4. Highlight words and phrases used to develop ideas within the answer. (E.g. *For example … , Also … , particularly when … , But I think … , because …)*
- Read the question on the right and click to see the answer. *Do you think this is a three-star answer?* Point out that it is a general comment that does not explain or refer to specific aspects of the story. Talk Partners discuss how to improve this answer to make it a three-star answer.
- Take suggestions and model how to improve the answer by referring to the text, e.g. *For example the part when … ; I liked the way the …)*

Independent and Guided

- The children complete 'Three-star answers' (PCM 5.3) using the success criteria on ITP 5.4 to help them.

ooo Complete PCM 5.3 individually. (T)

oo Complete PCM 5.3 in pairs.

o Complete PCM 5.3 as a group. (TA)

Plenary

- Recap the learning objectives.
- The children share examples of 'three-star answers'. Take feedback, referring to the success criteria on ITP 5.4. *Have they given an opinion? Have they supported their opinion by referring to the text? How could they improve their answer?*
- Read the rest of ITP 5.3 to the children.

Assessment pointers

- AF2, 6, 7 (R): oral and written answers to questions show how far the children are able to comment on the overall effect of the text, similarities and differences between texts and reference to the texts.

Session 4

We are learning to ...	Resources
• use active reading stategies to explore the text • write a range of questions about a story (PNS Strands 8.2) **Assessment Focuses** AF (R): 2, 3, 4, 5, 6	*Eye of the Wolf* ITP: (ITP 5.4), 5.6 PCM: 5.4

Shared teaching

- Share the learning objectives and explain that the children will write their own questions for an extract from a story read during the year.
- Focus on the start of *Eye of the Wolf.* Reread 'How they met' (Part I), as the children follow in their own books. Talk Partners discuss responses. *How did it make you feel? What did you picture? What makes it so effective? What stood out to you?*
- Show 'Questions for the reader' (ITP 5.6). Show and discuss the different types of questions, referring back to examples from Sessions 1–3. Record an example of each question type on ITP 5.6.
- Talk Partners devise a 'find the information question', referring back to Part 1of *Eye of the Wolf,* e.g. *How did the wolf feel when he first saw the boy?* Take feedback. Add good examples to the Learning Wall, e.g. questions where the answer isn't too obvious and needs information from more than one sentence.
- Talk Partners repeat the process for a 'deduce and infer' question. *Can you write a question about the feelings or motives of the wolf?*
- Take feedback. Select good examples, e.g. questions where the answer is not something we are 'told', and add to the Learning Wall.
- Remind the children of the success criteria on 'Three-star answers' (ITP 5.4). Then ask the children to answer the questions.
- Share and discuss good answers, reinforcing strategies, e.g. rereading, using clues, thinking what is implied, making links. *Has anyone written a three-star answer?* Reinforce key points, e.g. using examples or quotations, making a number of relevant points, explaining ideas.
- Repeat the process focusing on author techniques.

Independent and Guided

- The children write questions and example answers for *Eye of the Wolf* using 'Ask another' (PCM 5.4). They fold the paper so their partner can only read the questions. They then swap and answer questions. Pairs then unfold the paper and compare and rate each other's answers.

ooo Complete PCM 5.4 using a range of different question types. Swap with a partner and answer their questions. In pairs, compare and rate each other's answers.

oo Write 'find the information' and 'deduce and infer' questions. (TA)

o As above. (T)

Plenary

- Share questions. *Can you tell which type of question this is? Have you used a range of question types?*
- Share answers. *What was good about your answer? Did you refer to the text? How did your answer compare with your partner's answer?*
- Recap the learning objectives. Discuss what the children have learnt about writing questions for other readers.

Assessment pointers

- AF2, 3 (R): written answers show how well the children can refer to and make inferences from the text.
- AF4, 5, 6 (R): oral and written answers show how far the children are able to recognise and comment on structural and presentational features, authors language choices and their effect on the reader.

PHASE 2: LEARNING FROM AUTHORS (3 DAYS)

Session 5

We are learning to ...	Resources
• explain how and why an author uses paragraphs in a story • identify and use conjunctions and connectives to link paragraphs (PNS Strands 7.3, 10.2) **Assessment Focuses** AF (R): 4; AF (W): 3, 4	*Fantastic, Funny, Frightening!* ITP: 5.7, 5.8 PCM: 5.5

Shared teaching

- Share the learning objectives, explaining that, in this session, the children will see how good authors structure their stories and use paragraphs to develop their ideas.
- Recap *The Balaclava Story* from *Fantastic, Funny, Frightening!* (pages 31–46). Show 'Story plan' (ITP 5.7). *What are the main events in* The Balaclava Story*? Where would these go on the story peak plan?* Use the children's suggestions to complete ITP 5.7, demonstrating how the story is organised into parts.
- Focus on the build-up and the climax of *The Balaclava Story.* Talk Partners discuss why this part of the story is so effective? *How does it build up drama/suspense?*
- Take feedback. Identify where this part of the story fits on ITP 5.7.
- Begin identifying what each paragraph is about. *Can you suggest a short sentence to summarise each paragraph*? Discuss the first two or three as a class. Talk Partners then continue to summarise paragraphs.
- Take feedback, reinforcing that each paragraph has a main idea or event, which is developed within it, e.g. stealing the balaclava then regretting having done this.
- Focus on the paragraph divisions. *Why does the author start a new paragraph each time?* Talk Partners identify when new paragraphs are used to indicate changes in time/place/event.
- Take feedback. *Why has the author used a new paragraph here? What effect does this have?* Explain that occasionally paragraph divisions are used for impact.
- Remind the children that conjunctions and connectives are important as they connect paragraphs and make links between the ideas.

Independent and Guided

- In pairs, the children use 'Paragraph jumble' (PCM 5.5) to reorder the paragraphs in a new story. They then underline the phrases that establish links between and within paragraphs. The children compare results with another pair. Support the children with an identified need. (T+/TA+)

Plenary

- Take feedback. *How have you sequenced your story? Why did you put the paragraphs in this order? Which connecting words did you find?*
- Show 'Paragraphs' (ITP 5.8) and encourage the children to add to the list. Add the list to the Learning Wall.
- Recap the learning objectives. Record a list of connectives and conjunctions and add this to the Learning Wall to support the children's own writing later on.

Assessment pointers

- S&L: pair work will show how well the children can express and explain relevant ideas.
- AF4 (R): group work will show how far the children can organise paragraphs.
- AF3, 4 (W): peer and self-assessment will show how far the children are able to organise a story into meaningful and cohesive paragraphs.

Session 6

We are learning to ...	Resources
• write different kinds of sentences, thinking about the effect on the reader • check that we have used punctuation to help the reader (PNS Strands 11.1, 11.2) **Assessment Focuses** AF (W): 5, 6	ITP: 5.9 PCM: 5.6

Shared teaching (1)

- Share the learning objectives and explain that the children are going to be looking at how authors vary sentences to achieve effects.
- Show '*Virtually True*' (ITP 5.9). Recap different sentence structures and how they achieve particular effects. *What effect is created?* (E.g. action, excitement.) *How do the sentence structures help achieve this effect?*
- Highlight examples of longer sentences, recapping the use of connectives, commas and ordering of clauses. *What effect does the sentence order have? Are the connectives always where we expect them?* (E.g. the author sometimes begins clauses with 'As' and 'But'.)
- Discuss other examples where sentence structures create different moods or effects.

Independent and Guided (1)

- The children work in pairs to complete question 1 of 'Combining sentences' (PCM 5.6). They compare the two versions of the extract, annotating the author's version, noting the use of varied sentences compared to the 'simple version'. Support the children with an identified need. (T/TA)

Shared teaching (2)

- Take feedback. Focus on the notes made about the two versions of text. *What were the differences between the texts? Which did you prefer? What features did you make a note of?* (E.g. complex sentences, exclamation mark, variations in openings, word order and punctuation.) *What effect did they have?* (E.g. leading the reader on, delaying the surprise.)
- Focus on the simple version of the text and use Modelled Writing to restructure the first few sentences. *How could we change the focus of this text? Are there any adverbs we can add? Are there any other connectives we could use? How could we vary the sentence structures? Could we make them more complex/shorter?* Explore altering the text and the position of adverbs for effect.

Independent and Guided (2)

- The children work in the same pairs to complete question 2 of PCM 5.6. They write their own version of the text, combining the simple sentences in a different way to the author's version to achieve a different focus or effect, e.g. to focus more on the narrator's feelings. Support the children with an identified need. (T/TA)

Plenary

- Encourage pairs to share sentences from their own versions of the text and create a whole-class story.
- Recap the learning objectives. Pairs share their version of the text, explaining and giving reasons for the alterations they have made. *Which sentence structures add to the effectiveness? What should we remember about varying sentences next time we write a story?*

Assessment pointers

- S&L: pair work will show how well the children can express and explain relevant ideas.
- AF5, 6 (W): completed PCMs will show how far the children can vary sentence type and length and punctuate sentences accurately.

Session 7

We are learning to ...	Resources
• use drama to explore emotions, responses and character conflicts • identify the features of an effective play script (PNS Strands 4.1, 7.3) **Assessment Focuses** AF (R): 5; AF (W): 7	ITP: (5.3) 5.10

Shared teaching

- Share the learning objectives. *What makes a play script interesting?* (E.g. events that engage or amuse the reader/audience, interesting or appealing characters, a clear layout that performers can follow, etc.)
- Remind the children that in earlier sessions they have looked at the techniques authors use to create interesting stories. *Does a play script use the same techniques? How are they similar? How are they different?*
- View 'Play script analysis' (ITP 5.10) and discuss the layout features.
- Focus on the difference between the dialogue and the stage directions. *What type of language is used in the stage directions and dialogue?* (E.g. stage directions: direct, incomplete sentences, often adverbs; dialogue: short sentences, exclamations, vocabulary that varies with the characters.)
- Remind the children that stage directions give information and clues as to characters' feelings, and dialogue helps create characters, show character relationships and progress the story.
- Explain that in play scripts the dialogue is important so the author has to choose the words carefully because they convey so much information.
- Recall '*Excalibur*' (ITP 5.3). *What effect does the first word have?* (E.g. draws the reader in; intrigues them; also sets the context.) *Is this how you would speak? What does the language tell us?* (E.g. it shows the genre – a traditional, courtly tale.) *What is the difference between how Arthur and Gryflet speak?* (E.g. shows the different status of the two people; describes their character.)
- Go to screen 5 on ITP 5.3 and read the introduction of the second scene, stopping at the end of '... three robbers.' Discuss ideas for what might happen next. *How many characters are involved? Do you think they will act and speak in the same way?*

Independent and Guided

- The children work in groups to Role Play the beginning of Scene 2 when Arthur encounters the robbers. Encourage the children to think about how the different characters would speak. When they have agreed and practised their role play, the children make a note of the dialogue. Support the children with an identified need. (T/TA)

Plenary

- Recap the learning objectives.
- Ask groups to read their dialogue. At the end of each reading, ask the groups to explain their choice of dialogue.
- Take feedback. *What did you like about their role play? What dialogue really stood out?*

Assessment pointers

- S&L: role plays will show how well the children can convey ideas about characters through speech and gesture.
- AF5 (R): response to questions will show how far the children can explain and comment on an author's use of language.
- AF7 (W): role play and written dialogue will show how far the children can choose vocabulary for effect.

Session 8

We are learning to ...	Resources
• explain how authors use story structures to create interest and impact • plan the shape and structure of our own stories (PNS Strands 7:3, 9:1) **Assessment Focuses** AF(R): 4; AF (W): 2, 3	ITP: (5.7) PCM: 5.7, 5.8

Shared teaching (1)

- Share the learning objectives and explain that, in this phase, the children are going to plan and write a story of their choice.
- Discuss the idea of how an audience and genre shape a text. *What audience were the books we have read this year written for? Do you think a different audience could read and enjoy these books? What genres were they? How do you think this shaped the stories?*
- Talk Partners discuss their ideas. Take feedback.
- Explain that when the children are writing their story it is important that they think about their audience and the genre.

Independent and Guided (1)

- The children choose a story from 'Story task' (PCM 5.7). They then form Expert Groups, working together to write success criteria for their tasks, taking into consideration the audience and the genre. Support the children with an identified need. (T/TA)

Shared teaching (2)

- Take feedback and ask groups to share their success criteria. Add these to the Learning Wall.
- Remind the children that throughout the year they have been analysing how authors adapt story structure for impact and have planned and structured their own stories.
- Recall 'Story plan' (ITP 5.7). *Do all stories fit within this model? What about* Planet Prison *or* Eye of the Wolf*? What is interesting about the structure of these stories?* (E.g. branching storylines; sequence of episodes, each with problems; flashbacks; surprise revelations.)
- Explain that they are going to complete a story plan to help plan their own stories. Choose a task from PCM 5.7 and use Modelled Writing to plan the stages in the story on ITP 5.7.
- Reinforce points about planning: writing in complete sentences; using the past tense, including a few words to describe characters or setting details (to help build up suspense); adding time/place markers.
- Once the main planning stages are complete, show how to adapt the story structure for impact, e.g. opening with the most exciting event.

Independent and Guided (2)

- The children complete 'Story plan' (PCM 5.8), referring to PCM 5.7 and the success criteria. Support the children with an identified need. (T+/TA+)

Plenary

- Pairs discuss their plans. *What works well / not so well?* Take feedback.
- Recap the learning objectives.

Assessment pointers

- S&L: group work will show how well the children can organise and sustain collaboration and discussion.
- AF4 (R): response to questions will show how well the children can comment on structural choices and effect.
- AF2,3 (W): success criteria and completed plans will show how far the children can produce appropriate and well organised texts.

Session 9

We are learning to ...	Resources
• use a range of narrative techniques to engage the reader • select style and language features suitable for the genre and purpose (PNS Strands 9.2, 9.4) **Assessment Focuses** AF (W): 1, 2, 7	*Fantastic, Funny, Frightening!* ITP: 5.11 PCM: (5.7, 5.8)

Shared teaching

- Share the learning objectives and explain that, in this session, the children will write their stories. Remind them that the focus is on writing an entertaining and effective story, but in order to achieve this they should also feed in their learning about structure, paragraphs and sentences from Phase 2.
- Talk Partners choose a story they enjoyed from *Fantastic, Funny and Frightening!* and discuss what made it engaging and entertaining.
- Display 'Story ingredients' (ITP 5.11) and take feedback. *What ingredients go into making a good story?* Identify key elements and features of effective stories. Use further questioning to develop any short comments such as 'good characters', 'interesting style'. (E.g. *What makes a good character? Different types of story can have different styles. Give me some examples of styles you have found effective.*)
- Click on each category on the screen to display the tips, linking these back to the discussion.
- Focus particularly on the 'Characters', 'Style' and 'Language' pointers.
- Remind the children that they have some more choices to make before they start writing. *What style will you use? Will you write in the first or the third person? Will you use a chatty style or a descriptive style? Remember your choice must fit with the genre you are writing in.* Allow individual Think Time for the children to think about the style they will use.
- The children review their plans in light of the discussion. Allow them more Think Time, deciding whether to add or change anything.

Independent and Guided

- The children work independently to write their story, using completed 'Story task' (PCM 5.7) and 'Story plan' (PCM 5.8),and the success criteria on the Learning Wall. Hold short sessions to identify particular features/techniques to focus on. Support the children with an identified need. (T+/TA+)

Plenary

- Recap the learning objectives and ask pairs, to check their stories against the statements you have identified. Discuss common problems or points arising.

Assessment pointers

- AF1, 2, 7 (W): peer and self-assessment shows how far the children can develop interesting stories, maintaining purpose, form and style, and selecting effective vocabulary.

Session 10

We are learning to …	Resources
• make changes to improve our stories • check that we have used punctuation to help the reader (PNS Strands 9.1, 11.2) **Assessment Focuses** AF (W): 1, 2, 5, 6, 7	ITP: (5.11), 5.12

Shared teaching

- Share the learning objectives and explain that, in this session, the children will evaluate their stories and decide how they could be improved. *We're not making major changes – we are going to see how little changes can make a big difference to the overall effectiveness.*
- Recall 'Story ingredients' (ITP 5.11) to remind the children of features of effective stories. Focus particularly on points relating to 'Style' and 'Language'.
- Show Screen 1 of 'Sample text for revision' (ITP 5.12) and read the extract with the children following. Ask them for positive points, focusing on the ingredients of effective stories identified earlier. (E.g. taking the reader straight into the story.)
- Talk Partners discuss and identify small changes to improve the text. (E.g. changing words, adding phrases, varying sentence openings or structures, etc.) Remind them to offer constructive criticism rather than negative, e.g. *It would be better if … , Perhaps you could … .*
- Take feedback, encouraging the children to explain how each suggestion would improve the effectiveness.
- Show Screen 2 of ITP 5.12 with the improved first paragraph and discuss why this is better, identifying improvements in vocabulary choices and how sentences have been varied, changed or developed. *How do these changes add to the overall effectiveness of the story?*
- Use Think Alouds to demonstrate improving the second paragraph. Focus on improving words choices, adding descriptive phrases, using appropriate language features to maintain style and varying sentence structures. Encourage the children to make suggestions and try out improvements to sentences orally. Add suggested changes to the second paragraph on ITP 5.12.
- Use Think Alouds to model the importance of rereading to check punctuation and identifying when commas are needed within sentences. (E.g. *Let's read that back. Raise your hand when we come to the end of a sentence. Do we need a comma within that sentence?*)
- Reread the two revised paragraphs to focus on how small changes have improved the overall effectiveness of the story.

Independent and Guided

- In pairs, the children read through their stories from Session 9, making improvements.

●●● Read through each other's stories, suggesting and making improvements to the text. (T+)

●● As above. (TA+)

● As above, working on sentences identified by the teacher.

Plenary

- Recap the learning objectives. Encourage the children to explain the changes they have made. *How have the changes improved the overall effectiveness of your story? Why is it important to read through your story once it is written?*
- Discuss the unit as a whole. *What have you enjoyed most? What techniques will help you in the future? What will you remember next time you write a story?* The children decide on two key points/targets that will help them to write a better story next time.

Assessment pointers

- S&L: pair work will show how sensitively the children can express and respond to opinions.
- AF1, 2 (W): revisions to writing will show how far the children can use imaginative detail and appropriate style.
- AF5, 6, 7 (W): revisions to writing and completed stories will show how far the children can use sentence variation, accurate punctuation and select effective vocabulary.

Reading detective

Answer the questions about *Nule.*

a *'Martin turned and fled back to the bedroom, and dived under the bedclothes … '*

Which **two** words in this sentence show Martin's feelings when he went back to bed?

____

b *'"Were you reading in bed last night?" said Mum, prodding him awake the next morning.'*

How do the mood and the house itself seem different **before** and **after** this point in the story?

____

____

c How did Martin **first** know that everything must be back to normal next morning?

____

d When Martin looked down into the hall in the morning, how was the scene different from the night before? Write down **three** ways.

____

____

____

e Where did Martin place Nule's feet and how had this moved in the morning?

____

____

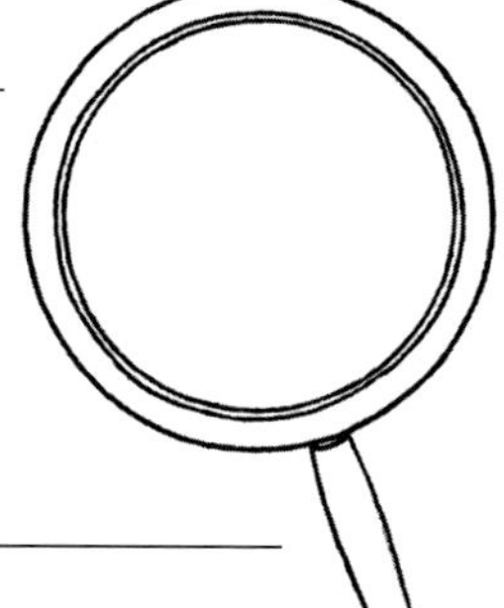

f What problem does Martin have at the end of the story?

____

____

Name: ______________________ Date: ____________ **5.2**

Author techniques

Read and answer the questions about *Moving House* using examples from the text.

a What interesting words and phrases do you notice? What effect do they have?

b Why has the writer italicised some of the words?

c Are there any short sentences in the story? What effect do they have?

d How many people speak in the story? Why do you think this is?

e What different punctuation do you notice? What effect does this have?

f How does the author draw you in and make you want to read more?

Name: ____________________ Date: ____________

Three-star answers

Re-read Scene 1 from *Excalibur*, then answer the questions using evidence from the text. Ask your partner to rate your answers.

a Why does Gryflet want vengeance? Why do you think he was so eager to fight Sir Pellinore?

☆☆☆

b What kind of person do you think King Arthur is? Support your answer with evidence from the text.

☆☆☆

c What do you think will happen when King Arthur fights Sir Pellinore? Refer to other legends you know to support your answer.

☆☆☆

d What similarities did you notice between *Excalibur* and any other legends or fairy tales you have read?

☆☆☆

Ask another

Write three-star questions on *Eye of the Wolf* to ask your partner. Then write what you think the answers should be.

Q: ______________________ ______________________ ______________________	Answer: ______________________ ______________________ ______________________ ______________________ ☆☆☆
Q: ______________________ ______________________ ______________________	Answer: ______________________ ______________________ ______________________ ______________________ ☆☆☆
Q: ______________________ ______________________ ______________________	Answer: ______________________ ______________________ ______________________ ______________________ ☆☆☆
Q: ______________________ ______________________ ______________________	Answer: ______________________ ______________________ ______________________ ______________________ ☆☆☆

Fold

Paragraph jumble

Cut up the story and put the paragraphs in order. Underline any phrases that show links between and within the paragraphs. Then write your own ending for the story.

That's when I decided I would go. Mum did the shopping on her way home on a Friday so she wouldn't be back for an hour at least. I could go and be back before 5 o'clock. She'd never know.

Then one Friday after school all the other lads were going off to the old factory as usual, leaving me standing forlornly at the school gate.

"Are you coming or not?" called Nathan, following the others down the path.

"I can't," I moaned.

"Suit yourself," he replied with a shrug and ran after the others.

It was just so unfair.

I was just about to climb back through the gap when I heard a sound. A sort of soft whimper. It was coming from close by. There it was again. Cautiously, I took a few steps away from the doorway into the wide open space of the factory. I saw a hole in the floor. Peering over the edge, I could just make out a small, black dog looking back at me with sad, pained eyes. It must have fallen down there and now it was trapped. I tried to reach it but I couldn't. It was much too far down. Maybe it was injured. What could I do?

I shouldn't have gone there. I know I shouldn't. Mum was always going on at me.

"I don't want you playing in that old factory. It's dangerous," she warned me every time I mentioned it.

"But it's not fair. Nathan's allowed and he's …"

"I don't care what Nathan's allowed to do. I'm not his mother. But I am yours, so that's that," she said, closing the fridge in a way that suggested the conversation was over.

When I reached the hole in the wire fence I fought my way through it, raced across the deserted yard and made for the corrugated sheeting which lay across the doorway. I pulled the sheet of metal and just like the others had told me, a little gap appeared. I squeezed through, calling out Nathan's name excitedly. Only when I got inside there was no one there.

Combining sentences

1. Compare the author's version with the simple version. Write which one is the most effective and why.

An extract from *Moving House*

As soon as I turned the key it creaked open, and behind it … Yes! There was a flight of steps vanishing into darkness. Of course, I went down them. Down and down. They seemed to go on forever. And they kept turning, and twisting, until I was … Lost.

Simple version

I turned the key. The door creaked open. There was a flight of steps behind it. They vanished into the darkness. I went down. They seemed to go on forever. They kept turning and twisting. Then I was lost.

2. Write your own version of the story remembering to use longer, more interesting sentences.

My version

Story task

Choose one of the tasks below and plan the story.

Task 1

Slowly the mist began to clear ...

Write a story that includes this event. You must decide:

- what the story is about
- where the event happens
- how this event came about
- who the main character/s is/are.

Task 2

Uncle Jack is an inventor. While away on holiday, he has left his nephew and niece in charge of his latest invention – a robot.

Write a story about what happens when his nephew and niece have to take the robot to school. Think about how other characters might react.

Task 3

There was once a poor man who lived in a tiny cottage on the edge of a village. One day the poor man visited a powerful wizard, for he had heard that the wizard had many special powers and incredible potions.

'I would like to be the richest man in the whole wide world,' said the poor man.

The wizard peered at the man for a long time before handing him a small blue bottle containing a special potion ...

Continue this story. You will need to think about:

- what the main character is like
- what is special about the potion
- what the man does and what happens as a result.

Story plan

Add notes to plan your own story.

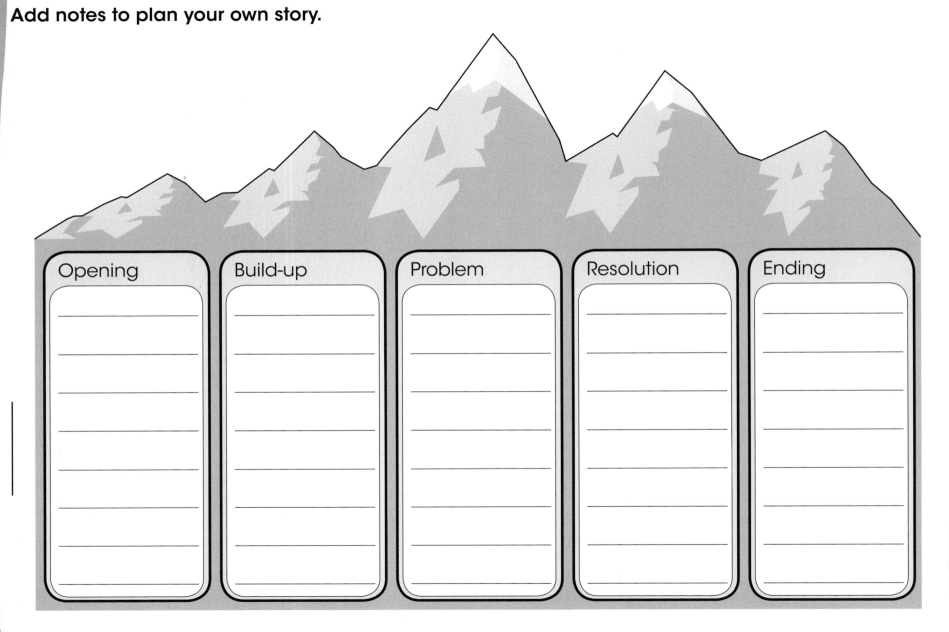

Opening

Build-up

Problem

Resolution

Ending

Poetry Unit 1

BENJAMIN ZEPHANIAH / TED HUGHES (Imagery)

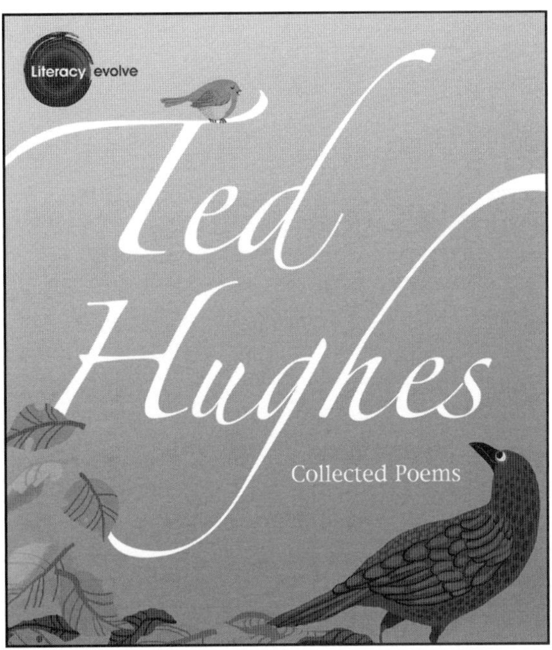

Medium term plan (2 weeks)	
Phase	**Learning Outcomes**
Phase 1: Reading poems that use powerful imagery (3 days)	• Children can identify the ways in which poets construct images. • Children can use talk to explore a poem's meaning and style.
Phase 2: Writing and evaluating poems using powerful imagery (2 days)	• Children can create poems that use powerful words and imagery.
Phase 3: Reading poems that use surprising and amusing imagery (3 days)	• Children can discuss a performance of a poem, noting its key features. • Children can identify how poets use surprising and humorous images.
Phase 4: Writing poems using surprising and amusing imagery (2 days)	• Children can write poems that use surprising and humorous images. • Children can edit and refine their own poems.

Poetry Unit 1

BENJAMIN ZEPHANIAH/TED HUGHES

Big picture

The children are immersed in the poems of two poets with contrasting styles: Ted Hughes and Benjamin Zephaniah. For the first five sessions, the children explore Hughes' use of language in a variety of his poems, responding to the images he uses with close reference to the text. With support, they use stimuli to generate their own images and shape these into a class poem. They go on to write their own poems, drawing on this experience. The children then look in detail at poems and a performance by Benjamin Zephaniah, exploring his use of surprising images and presentational style to provoke a reaction in the reader. They experiment with writing images of their own, first as a class, then individually, picking up on the theme of 'seasons' from earlier in the unit. The children draft, edit and refine their own poems before reflecting on their response to the unit as a whole.

Prior learning

This unit assumes that the children can already:

- talk together and use drama techniques to explore poems
- identify and respond to the themes in a poem
- select words and language imaginatively when creating their own poems
- create, edit, refine and evaluate their own poems.

Key aspects of learning

Communication: Communicate through own poems, expressing a viewpoint and / or creating an atmosphere.

Creative thinking: Use language imaginatively, creating unusual and surprising images.

Evaluation: Evaluate poems against success criteria; edit and revise first drafts; comment constructively on own and others' work; compare two poets' styles.

Self-awareness: Discuss personal preferences; reflect on own progress and learning.

Progression in poetry

In this unit the children will:

- explain the impact of figurative and expressive language, including metaphor
- use language imaginatively to create surreal, surprising, amusing and inventive poetry
- use imagery to create poems based on real or imagined experience.

Cross-curricular links

PSHE: Discussions around the different cultures in our society

Science: Links to the seasons; links to work on recipes

PHASE 1: READING POEMS THAT USE POWERFUL IMAGERY (3 DAYS)

Session 1

We are learning to …	Resources
• use talk to explore a poem • understand how poets use language for effect (PNS Strands 1.3, 8.3) **Assessment Focuses** AF (R): 5	*Year 6 Poetry Collection* ITP: P1.1

Shared teaching

- Explain that, in the first week of this unit, the children will be reading poems by Ted Hughes that describe animals and the natural world, using powerful images. Share the learning objectives.
- Show Screen 1 of '*Dog*' (ITP P1.1) and focus on the images of sleeping dogs. *What words would you use to describe the sleeping dogs? What similes could you use?* The children Mind Map ideas using structures such as 'like a … ', 'as if … ', etc. Scribe their suggestions and use them to start the Learning Wall.
- Read *Dog* by Ted Hughes (page 4), as the children follow in their books. Talk Partners discuss the poem freely in an exploratory way. Prompt as necessary. *What do you think of the descriptions of the sleeping dog? What about the comparisons in the poem? Are any of them like the ones you thought of?*
- Remind the children of the terms 'simile' and 'metaphor' and discuss examples in the poem, e.g. 'a loaf of bread'; 'a sack of snoring dog'; 'like a log'; 'like a miner'. *Which comparisons are particularly powerful? Which ones compare the dog to an object?* (E.g. loaf of bread, sack, log.) Annotate the poem on Screen 2 of ITP P1.1 with the children's responses. Introduce and explain the term 'personification'. *How is the dog compared to a person?*
- Encourage the children to suggest terms to identify different sound patterns in the poem. Remind them about: rhyme schemes, e.g. couplets; alliteration (repeated sounds at the start of adjacent words); and onomatopoeia (words that sound like what they mean).
- The children help you annotate the poem further with notes about the sound patterns in the poem, using the terms discussed.

Independent and Guided

- The children work in groups to discuss and make notes on other poems by Ted Hughes which have similar features to *Dog*. They explore the poems' images, then investigate sound patterns, following the whole-class model used to discuss *Dog*. Avoid using *Jellyfish* or *Woodpecker* as these will be explored in detail in Session 2.

ooo Discuss at least three other poems by Ted Hughes from *Year 6 Poetry Collection*. If possible, include Ted Hughes poems from other books.

oo Discuss at least two other poems by Ted Hughes from *Year 6 Poetry Collection*. (T)

o As above, discussing at least one other poem. (TA)

Plenary

- Recap the learning objectives.
- Ask the groups to share one of the poems they discussed. *What images and sound patterns did you enjoy most in the poem?*
- Show the annotated poem on ITP P1.1. Encourage the children to compare it with the sound patterns they found in other poems. *Did Ted Hughes use similar language?*

Assessment pointers

- S&L: group work will show how far the children can express and respond to opinions.
- AF5 (R): group work will show how far the children can identify various features in the use of language.

Session 2

We are learning to ...	Resources
• use talk to explore a poem • understand how poets use language for effect (PNS Strands 1.3, 8.3) **Assessment Focuses** AF (R): 5	*Year 6 Poetry Collection* ITP: P1.2, P1.3 PCM: P1.1, P1.2, P1.3

Shared teaching

- Share the learning objectives. Explain that the children will be reading another Ted Hughes poem that uses powerful images to describe an animal.
- Show Screen 1 of '*Jellyfish*' (ITP P1.2) and focus on the images. *Now that you know Ted Hughes' style from the poem* Dog, *what words do you think he might use to describe a jellyfish? Can you think of any strong images?* Encourage the children to avoid images that are weak or have been used too often before.
- Scribe the children's images of jellyfish to add to the Learning Wall.
- Read *Jellyfish* by Ted Hughes (page 9).
- Talk Partners discuss the poem freely in an exploratory way. Prompt as necessary. *What do you think of the images? Are they what you expected or did they surprise you? Were the images strong ones?*
- Discuss metaphors in the poem, e.g. 'a chandelier', 'a slob', 'a blob', and the children's responses to them. Focus on the verb 'waltzes' in the second line and discuss the comparison with a dancer.
- *Which comparisons use personification to make the jellyfish sound like a person? Does it make a difference that the poem is in the first person so the creature is telling us what it is like?* Annotate the poem on Screen 2 of ITP P1.2 with the children's responses.
- *Can you find any sound patterns in the poem?* Allow the children Think Time to look for examples of rhyme (in triplets) and alliteration ('beached and bare'; 'being just a blob'). Use their responses to annotate Screen 2 ITP P1.2 further.

Independent and Guided

- In groups, the children annotate *Woodpecker* by Ted Hughes (page 10). They explore the poem's images and sound patterns, then make notes about the poem.

ooo Use 'Poem features 1' (PCM P1.1).

oo Use 'Poem features 2' (PCM P1.2). (TA+)

o Use 'Poem features 3' (PCM P1.3). (T+)

Plenary

- Recap the learning objectives and share the children's responses to *Woodpecker* from their exploratory group talk.
- Show and annotate '*Woodpecker*' (ITP P1.3) with the children's suggestions for use of rhyme, alliteration, onomatopoeia, metaphor and personification in the text.
- Ask for examples of any other interesting uses of language the children have identified. Record suggestions on ITP P1.3.
- *If you could ask Ted Hughes any questions about the poem, what would they be?*

Assessment pointers

- S&L: group work will show how far the children can adopt group roles, drawing ideas together and promoting effective discussion.
- AF5 (R): group work will show how far the children are able to identify use of language and make simple comments on the poet's choice of words.

Session 3

We are learning to ...	Resources
• use talk to explore a poem • understand how poets use language for effect (PNS Strands 1.3, 8.3) **Assessment Focuses** AF (R): 5; AF (W): 2	*Year 6 Poetry Collection* ITP: P1.4

Shared teaching

- Share the learning objectives. Explain that the children will be reading a Ted Hughes poem that uses powerful images in a different way from the poems read so far.
- Show 'Autumn' (ITP P1.4). Play the slideshow of images of autumn with accompanying music. *How do the images and music make you feel?*
- Replay ITP P1.4 while reading *The Seven Sorrows* by Ted Hughes (pages 6–7).
- The children Think-Pair-Share their responses to the poem and its images and patterns.
- *Is there anything you didn't understand?* Clarify any puzzles, e.g. Stanza 2, 'the woodland of gold': the dead pheasant with golden feathers stands for the whole autumn woodland; Stanza 3, 'ground of the picture': there is a golden background to the birds gathering in the evening sky; Stanza 4, 'catacombs': an underground cemetery.
- Read the poem again. *What do you like about it? What don't you like?*
- Ask for any patterns that the children have identified. Make a list to add to the Learning Wall. *Which patterns are different from the ones in other Ted Hughes poems you have read?* (E.g. there is no rhyme as the poem is in free verse; the poem is in seven stanzas, one for each sorrow; alternate stanzas have the same second line: 'is the slow goodbye'.)
- *What do you notice about the images in the poem?* (E.g. each stanza paints a different image; the images are powerful and unusual.)
- *What other uses of language can you find in the poem?* (E.g. alliteration, personification, simile, metaphor.) Add to the Learning Wall.

Independent and Guided

- The children work in pairs to express their responses to *The Seven Sorrows* through creative writing or artwork.

ooo Write about the coming of autumn from the point of view of one of the creatures in the poem. Write in prose or free verse, using strong images and avoiding clichés.

oo Write about the person with the wrinkled face who looks through the window in Stanza 7. Write in prose or free verse, using fresh and interesting comparisons to explain who the person is, what they see and how they feel about autumn. (T+)

o Write other images to describe autumn. If there is time, illustrate the images. (TA+)

Plenary

- Talk Partners share their writing or artwork created in response to *The Seven Sorrows*, explaining their written or pictorial images.
- Create a wall display, or multimedia presentation, using the children's writing and artwork alongside *The Seven Sorrows*.
- Recap the learning objectives.

Assessment pointers

- S&L: pair work will show how well the children can express and explain relevant ideas.
- AF5 (R): responses to questioning will show how far the children can comment on the poet's use of language.
- AF2 (W): independent work will show how well the children can produce appropriate texts to develop features of poems.

Session 4

We are learning to ...	Resources
• write poems that use surprising and powerful images (PNS Strands 9.5) **Assessment Focuses** AF (W): 7	*Year 6 Poetry Collection* ITP: P1.5, P1.6

Shared teaching

- Share the learning objectives. Explain to the children that, in this session, they are going to write a poem as a whole class using *The Seven Sorrows* as a model.
- Reread '*The Seven Sorrows*' by Ted Hughes (pages 6–7). Explain that the children are now going to write a similar poem about the seven joys of spring.
- Show 'Spring' (ITP P1.5). Play the slideshow of images of spring with accompanying music. *How does it make you feel?*
- *What images did you spot in the presentation? What other images to do with spring would you have included?* The children Mind Map ideas. Encourage them to choose strong fresh images, rather than tired clichés such as lambs or bunny rabbits. Add a mind map diagram of their responses to the Learning Wall.
- Use Modelled Writing to draft the opening stanza of the class poem using free verse on 'The Seven Joys of Spring' (ITP P1.6).
- Focus on the image of the daffodil on ITP P1.5. Allow Think Time, then ask the children to write a description of it, using a comparison or personification if they wish. Use their suggestions to compose the next stanza of the class poem on ITP P1.6, writing in loose, free verse.
- Refer to the mind map diagram on the Learning Wall. *Can you suggest an image for the third stanza?* Select from the children's ideas and use Modelled Writing to compose the third stanza on ITP P1.6.

Independent and Guided

- The children work in groups to draft more stanzas for the whole-class poem. They use a loose, free verse style that does not need to rhyme. They follow the structure started on ITP P1.6 and try to use comparisons and personification, referring to the mind map on the Learning Wall for ideas.

(ooo) Draft the next four stanzas. Include a powerful simile to end the final stanza.

(oo) Draft the next two or three stanzas. (TA+)

(o) Draft a stanza for the fourth joy of spring. (T+)

Plenary

- The groups perform their draft stanzas for the class.
- Take feedback. *Do they use strong and fresh images of spring?*
- Choose stanzas from several different groups to complete the poem. Complete ITP P1.6 and save it for use in Session 5.
- Replay the slideshow on ITP P1.5, while reading the class poem as an accompaniment.
- Recap the learning objectives. *Does our poem use powerful words and images?*

Assessment pointers

- S&L: group work will show how well the children can adopt group roles, drawing ideas together and promoting effective writing.
- AF7 (W): contributions to the class poem will show how far the children can select vocabulary that is effective and appropriate to the content of the poem.

Session 5

We are learning to ...	Resources
• write our own poems that use surprising and powerful images • present our work for an audience using handwriting • present our work for an audience using ICT (PNS Strands 9.5, 12.1, 12.2) **Assessment Focuses** AF (W): 1	*Year 6 Poetry Collection* ITP: (P1.6), P1.7, P1.8 PCM: P1.4

Shared teaching (1)

- Share the learning objectives. Explain that the children are going to write their own poems using powerful words and images, following the model of *The Seven Sorrows*.
- Recap the features and patterns of *The Seven Sorrows* identified in Session 3. Refer to the list on the Learning Wall.
- Recall annotated 'The Seven Joys of Spring' (ITP P1.6). *How many of these features did our class poem have? Which ones were not used?*
- Explain that the children are going to write a similar poem about either summer or winter. They should try to use most of the features that are in *The Seven Sorrows*, but not necessarily all of them. Remind the children that the most important feature is the use of strong and fresh images, rather than weak and tired ones.
- Show 'Seasonal poem' (ITP P1.7) and discuss the success criteria. Add any other criteria the children suggest. Add the success criteria to the Learning Wall.
- Show 'Summer and winter' (ITP P1.8). Show the summer and winter pictures. *What other images to do with summer and winter would you have included?* Talk Partners share ideas for possible images to use in their poems.

Independent and Guided (1)

- The children write about 'The Sorrows of Winter' or 'The Joys of Summer', using as many of the features of Ted Hughes' poem as they can, e.g. similes and metaphors, personification and strong images.

(ooo) Draft an eight stanza poem, alternating images of winter sorrows and summer joys. (T+)

(oo) Draft a seven stanza poem about either summer or winter.

(o) Use 'The Four Sorrows of Winter' (PCM P1.4) to draft a poem. (TA+)

Shared teaching (2)

- Talk Partners exchange drafts and comment on how well their partner's draft meets the success criteria on ITP P1.7. Remind the children to refer to the list of features on the Learning Wall.

Independent and Guided (2)

- The children work independently to edit and improve their writing based on their feedback. They finalise their poems using handwriting or ICT to ensure the presentation is suitable for an audience. Support the children with an identified need. (T/TA)

Plenary

- Invite some, or all, of the children to perform their poems. Encourage the class to identify features that match the success criteria. Highlight poems which match up well with the features of Ted Hughes' poem.
- Recap the learning objectives.

Assessment pointers

- S&L: pair work will show how sensitively the children can give and respond to opinions.
- AF1 (W): written drafts and final poems will show how well the children can choose and develop relevant ideas with imaginative detail.

Session 6

We are learning to ...	Resources
• examine a performance of a poem • understand how poets use language for effect (PNS Strands 2.2, 8.3) **Assessment Focuses** AF (R): 5	*Year 6 Poetry Collection* *For Word* (film)

Shared teaching

- Share the learning objectives.
- Explain that, in the second week of this unit, the children will be reading poems by Benjamin Zephaniah about the power of words.
- *Imagine a world without words, where you use body language to communicate. What reasons to be grateful for words can you think of?* Allow Think Time, then compare and discuss the children's responses.
- Watch *For Word* to see Benjamin Zephaniah perform this poem. *Listen for the different reasons to be grateful for words.*
- Talk Partners discuss the theme of the poem. *How did Benjamin Zephaniah's reasons compare with your own?* Encourage the children to discuss the performance and the effect it had on them.
- Read *For Word* by Benjamin Zephaniah (page 9). Discuss performance poetry. *How do you think performance poetry is different to written poetry?* (E.g. the use of gestures, tone of voice, etc.) *What do you think this adds to the poem?* Explain that as a live performance, often the poem may be slightly different to the written version. *Why do you think this is? Do you think it is important?*
- *Did anyone spot the pun in the title?* ('Foreword', which is the term for an introductory chapter in a book.)
- *What is unusual about the layout of the poem on the page?* Take suggestions and add a list of features on the Learning Wall. ('Thank you' or 'Thanks' is written in bold at the start of each stanza; 'Thanx' in line 6 is an example of 'words I make myself'; 'words' is written in a different font or style in every line; fonts sometimes relate to what is being said, e.g. capital letters, script style or word art.)
- *Why do you think the poet set out the poem like this?* (to try to capture on the page the lively and expressive way he performs it)
- Watch *For Word* again. The children follow the text in their books as they listen to the performance. *How do the two match up?*
- Discuss the way the poet speaks the poem from memory like a rap, rather than reading it from a book.

Independent and Guided

- In pairs, the children draft more lines for the poem, using handwriting or ICT to set them out in the same style as the original. The children use rhyming dictionaries if possible.

ooo Draft another stanza. (T)

oo Draft another six lines.

o Draft another four lines. (TA)

Plenary

- Ask some of the pairs to perform their new lines or stanzas in a similar way to Benjamin Zephaniah. *Do the additional lines sound like the original? Are they amusing?*
- Recap the learning objectives.
- Add the children's work to the Learning Wall alongside the poem.

Assessment pointers

- S&L: pair work will show how well the children collaborate to develop ideas.
- AF5 (R): responses and pair work will show how well the children can identify features of the poet's language and understand the effect.

Session 7

We are learning to ...	Resources
• compare different poets • understand how poets use language in performance and on the page (PNS Strands 8.3) **Assessment Focuses** AF (R): 5	*Year 6 Poetry Collection* *Poetics* (film) PCM: P1.5

Shared teaching (1)

- Share the learning objectives. Explain that, during this session, the children will be reading another poem by Benjamin Zephaniah. This poem is about the power of poetry.
- Watch *Poetics* to see Benjamin Zephaniah perform this poem. *Listen for what he has to say about poetry in the poem.*
- Talk Partners discuss the theme of the poem. *What are Benjamin Zephaniah's views about the power of poetry?* Encourage the children to talk about Benjamin Zephaniah's performance of the poem and the effect it had on them.
- Refer to Benjamin Zephaniah's view that poems are everywhere. *What does he mean by that?* (E.g. that you can find poetry all around you, all the time in everyday life; that there are all kinds of poems; that there are poems in all of us.)
- Read *Poetics* by Benjamin Zephaniah (pages 10–11).
- Discuss why Benjamin Zephaniah set out the text of the poem in this way. (E.g. to try to capture on the page the way he performs the poem.)

Independent and Guided

- The children work in groups to annotate the text of the poem for performance using 'Performance poem' (PCM P1.5). The children watch *Poetics* again, making notes about interesting presentation and language features. They then practise performing the poem as a group.

ooo Use PCM P1.5. Include the use of a musical instrument in the performance.

oo Use PCM P1.5. Decide what beat to use for the performance. (T+)

o Use PCM P1.5. (TA+)

Shared teaching (2)

- Invite some of the groups to perform their versions of the poem.
- Encourage the other children to listen carefully to the performances. *What rhythm or beat did they use for reading the poem? Did it sound like rap, reggae, hip hop or something else?* Ask the performers how helpful their notes were in performing the poem.
- Discuss the similarities between Benjamin Zephaniah's poems *Poetics* and *For Word. Are they poems for the ear or poems for the page?*
- Encourage the children to compare Benjamin Zephaniah's poems to Ted Hughes' poems. *What is different about their themes? What is different about their use of language? Whose poems do you prefer?*

Plenary

- Recap the learning objectives.
- Discuss the performances the children have seen throughout the unit. *Which was your favourite performance?*

Assessment pointers

- S&L: pair work will show how well the children collaborate to develop ideas.
- AF5 (R): responses to questioning and group work will show how far the children can identify and explain some of the features of the poet's use of language.

Session 8

We are learning to ...	Resources
• debate a poem's theme • understand how poets use language for effect (PNS Strands 1.2, 8.3) **Assessment Focuses** AF (R): 5	*Year 6 Poetry Collection* ITP: P1.9 PCM: P1.6

Shared teaching (1)

- Share the learning objectives.
- Show 'A recipe' (ITP P1.9). Read the example recipe. Discuss the structure and highlight the different parts of the recipe.
- Identify the use of language in the recipe, especially how verbs are used. *Where are the verbs placed?* (at or near the beginning of lines) Annotate these features on ITP P1.9.
- Explain that, in this session, the children will be reading a poem by Benjamin Zephaniah that uses free verse instead of rhyme, and is written in the form of a recipe.
- Read *The British* by Benjamin Zephaniah (pages 6–7). Explain any unfamiliar vocabulary, e.g. the names of tribes and nationalities.
- Encourage the children to point out any recipe features they recognise in the first few lines of the poem.

Independent and Guided

- In pairs, the children annotate the text of the poem on 'Recipe poem' (PCM P1.6), marking any recipe features they find. They refer to the annotated recipe text on ITP P1.9 for support and note any words or phrases that particularly appeal to them. Support the children with an identified need. (T/TA)

Shared teaching (2)

- Take feedback. Use an enlarged copy of PCM P1.6 to collate the recipe features the children have found. Add this to the Learning Wall.
- *Which features of the poem are not usually found in recipes?* (E.g. the names of different nationalities; the numbers used; vocabulary such as 'melting pot', 'languages', 'unity', 'understanding', 'respect'; expressions such as 'allow time to be cool'.)
- Discuss why these non-recipe features are present in the poem. As a class, debate the message of the poem expressed in the last line. *What is the poem saying? What do you think about this?*

Plenary

- *What do you think about the comparison of racial integration in Britain to following a recipe? Is it a surprising image? Is it a powerful image?* Encourage the children to discuss whether they feel this is an effective way for Benjamin Zephaniah to communicate his message.
- Recap the learning objectives.
- *Do you prefer this style of poem or the two rhyming, rap-style poems by Benjamin Zephaniah you read previously?* Encourage the children to explain their reasons referring, to the language and imagery used.

Assessment pointers

- S&L: pair work will show how well the children can express and explain relevant ideas.
- AF5 (R): group discussions will show how far the children can identify language features used and comment on the effect of these choices.

PHASE 4: WRITING POEMS USING SURPRISING AND AMUSING IMAGERY (2 DAYS)

Session 9

We are learning to ...	Resources
• write poems that using surprising and powerful images (PNS Strands 9.5) **Assessment Focuses** AF (W): 7	*Year 6 Poetry Collection* ITP: (P1.4, P1.5, P1.8), P1.10 PCM: (P1.6), P1.7

Shared teaching

- Share the learning objectives. Explain to the children that, in this session, they are going to write a poem as a class using *The British* by Benjamin Zephaniah (pages 6–7) as a model.
- Reread the poem.
- Explain that the children will write a 'recipe poem' about a season of the year. Remind them that this is the same theme they used for the whole-class poem 'The Seven Joys of Spring' in Session 4.
- Recall the slideshows on 'Autumn' (ITP P1.4) and 'Spring' (ITP P1.5), and the images on 'Summer and winter' (ITP P1.8). Discuss and agree on a season to write about, e.g. the British winter.
- Recap the language and structure used in recipe writing from Session 8, referring to annotated 'Recipe poem' (PCM P1.6) on the Learning Wall.
- Use Modelled Writing to draft the opening of the recipe poem. Use 'Recipe poem' (ITP P1.10) or create your own version.
- *What other images of the season could be used? How could we use the language and structure of a recipe to include them?* Talk Partners discuss ideas.
- Take feedback. Demonstrate writing more lines of the poem on ITP P1.10. Use Think Alouds to model editing and improving the language and structure as you write. Save the changes.
- Invite suggestions for vivid images of the season to include in the poem. Discuss examples of tired images to avoid, e.g. log fires, Jack Frost, a blanket of snow, etc. Encourage the children to think of surprising and powerful images in the style of Benjamin Zephaniah instead of common clichés.

Independent and Guided

- The children work in groups to draft more lines for the whole-class poem using a free verse style that does not have to rhyme. They follow the recipe structure and language used on ITP P1.10 and refer to *The British* by Benjamin Zephaniah as a model . They can also view images from ITP P1.4, ITP P1.5 or ITP P1.8 for appropriate ideas.

ooo Include a note and a warning at the end of the poem. (T+)

oo Use as many different recipe verbs as possible.

o Use 'Recipe poem 1' (PCM P1.7). (TA+)

Plenary

- Invite the groups to share their draft lines. Agree on which of these contributions to use to complete the whole-class poem on ITP P1.10.
- Read the whole-class poem. *How could it be improved? Are the images of the season used in the poem powerful ones?*
- Use Think Alouds to make any revisions to ITP P1.10 and save the changes for use in Session 10.
- Recap the learning objectives.

Assessment pointers

- S&L: group work will show how well the children can adopt group roles, drawing ideas together and promoting effective planning.
- AF7 (W): contributions to the whole-class poem will show how far the children can choose effective vocabulary.

Session 10

We are learning to ...	Resources
• write poems that use surprising and powerful images • write and edit imaginative recipe poems (PNS Strands 9.5) **Assessment Focuses** AF (W): 1	*Year 6 Poetry Collection* ITP: (P1.10), P1.11 PCM: (P1.6, P1.7), P1.8

Shared teaching (1)

- Share the learning objectives. Explain that the children are going to write their own seasonal recipe poems, following the model of *The British* by Benjamin Zephaniah (pages 6–7).
- Recap the language and structure used in recipe writing, referring to annotated 'Recipe poem' (PCM P1.6) on the Learning Wall.
- Reread the whole-class poem from annotated 'Recipe poem' (ITP P1.10). *How many of the recipe features does this poem have?*
- Explain that the children are going to write a similar poem about another season of the year in Britain. They should use recipe features and include surprising and powerful images of their chosen season.
- Show 'Writing a recipe poem' (ITP P1.11) and discuss the success criteria. *Are there any more you would like to add?*

Independent and Guided (1)

- The children work independently to choose a season different to the one used in Session 9 and draft a recipe poem, referring to *The British* as a model for their writing.

ooo Include an appropriate note and warning at the end of the poem.

oo Use 'Recipe poem 2' (PCM P1.8). (TA+)

o Use a clean copy of 'Recipe poem 1' (PCM P1.7). (T+)

Shared teaching (2)

- Talk Partners discuss and provide feedback on each other's first drafts, using the success criteria on ITP P1.11.
- Remind the children to refer to the notes on the Learning Wall. *Has your partner used the features of a recipe? Have they included some surprising and powerful images of the season?* The children suggest Two Stars and a Wish for their partner's poem.

Independent and Guided (2)

- The children work independently, editing and improving their poems based on the feedback received. They proofread their writing and check the spelling. The children finalise their poems using handwriting or ICT. Support the children with an identified need. (T/TA)

Plenary

- Invite the children to perform their poems. Encourage the class to identify features that meet the success criteria. Highlight poems which match up well with the features of *The British.*
- Create a display of all the children's poems alongside the original poem to share with other audiences.
- Recap the learning objectives and review the unit as a whole. *Which poems did you enjoy most? Do you prefer Ted Hughes' or Benjamin Zephaniah's style? What did you learn while writing your poems? What was most difficult?* Encourage the children to review their own progress. *What are you most proud of? What do you need to improve?*

Assessment pointers

- S&L: poetry readings will show how far the children can shape their speech to engage listeners.
- AF 1 (W): written drafts and final poems will show how well the children can choose relevant content and develop ideas with imaginative detail.

Poem features 1

1. Underline the features of the poem using the key. Choose a colour for each feature.

Woodpecker

Ted Hughes

Woodpecker is rubber-necked
But has a nose of steel.

He bangs his head against the wall
And cannot even feel.

When Woodpecker's jack-hammer head
Starts up its dreadful din
Knocking the dead bough double dead
How do his eyes stay in?

Pity the poor dead oak that cries
In terrors and in pains.
But pity more Woodpecker's eyes
And bouncing rubber brains.

Key

- Rhyme scheme ☐
- Alliteration ☐
- Onomatopoeia ☐
- Metaphors ☐
- Personification ☐

2. Write about anything that puzzles you or that you want to know more about.

____

____

____

Poem features 2

1. Underline the features of the poem using the key. Choose a colour for each feature.

Woodpecker

Ted Hughes

Woodpecker is rubber-necked
But has a nose of steel.

He bangs his head against the wall
And cannot even feel.

When Woodpecker's jack-hammer head
Starts up its dreadful din
Knocking the dead bough double dead
How do his eyes stay in?

Pity the poor dead oak that cries
In terrors and in pains.
But pity more Woodpecker's eyes
And bouncing rubber brains.

Key

- Rhyme scheme ☐
- Alliteration ☐
- Onomatopoeia ☐

2. Write about anything that puzzles you or that you want to know more about.

______

______

______

Poem features 3

1. Underline the features of the poem using the key. Choose a colour for each feature.

Woodpecker

Ted Hughes

Woodpecker is rubber-necked
But has a nose of steel.

He bangs his head against the wall
And cannot even feel.

When Woodpecker's jack-hammer head
Starts up its dreadful din
Knocking the dead bough double dead
How do his eyes stay in?

Pity the poor dead oak that cries
In terrors and in pains.
But pity more Woodpecker's eyes
And bouncing rubber brains.

Key

Alliteration ☐
(e.g. terrible trouble, big, bouncing ball)

Onomatopoeia ☐
(e.g. crunch, smash, slurp)

Personification ☐
(the wind that weeps and moans)

2. Write about anything that puzzles you or that you want to know more about.

____

____

____

The Four Sorrows of Winter

Write each stanza and draw a picture to illustrate it.

The first sorrow of winter

Is ____________________

____

____

____

The second sorrow of winter

Is ____________________

____

____

____

The third sorrow of winter

Is ____________________

____

____

____

The fourth sorrow of winter

Is ____________________

____

____

____

Performance poem

Watch Benjamin Zephaniah perform *Poetics*. Make notes about the performance. Practise performing the poem together as a group.

Poetics

Benjamin Zephaniah

There's a poem on your face
There's a poem in the sky
There's a poem in outta space
There are poems passing by,
There are poems in your dreams
There are poems in your head
Sometimes I cannot get to sleep
Cause there are poems in me bed.

There's a poem in me tea
There are poems on me toast
I have found much poetry
In the place I love the most,
There's a poem right in front of you
Get to know its rhyme,
If you are not sure what to do
Just call it poem time.

There's a poem in me shoes
There's a poem in me shirt
When the poem meets the blues
It can really, really hurt,
Other poems make you grin
When they dribble off your chin
Some poems think they are great
So they like to make you ...

Wait
I see poems in your teeth
I see poems in me cat
I hear poems underneath
Going rata tat tat tat,
This one has not finished yet
It keeps coming on the beat
It is soggy and it's wet
But it's also very sweet.

There are poems for the **ear**
There are poems for the page
Some poems are not quite clear
But they get better with age,
There are poems for the hip
There are poems for the hop
Everything is poetic
Poetry will never stop.

There are poems on your **fingers**
There's a poem on your nose
If you give it time to linger
It will grow and grow and grow,
There's a poem in you beautiful
Can't you see it
It's right

There,
I think it's so incredible
There are poems
Everywhere.

Think about:

- gestures
- tone and volume of voice
- movement
- facial expression

Recipe poem

Highlight any recipe features you find in this poem. Underline your favourite words or phrases.

The British

Benjamin Zephaniah

Serves 60 million

Take some Picts, Celts and Silures
And let them settle,
Then overrun them with Roman conquerors.

Remove the Romans after approximately four
hundred years
Add lots of Norman French to some
Angles, Saxons, Jutes and Vikings, then stir vigorously.

Mix some hot Chileans, cool Jamaicans, Dominicans,
Trinidadians and Bajans with some Ethiopians,
Chinese, Vietnamese and Sudanese.

Then take a blend of Somalians, Sri Lankans, Nigerians
And Pakistanis,
Combine with some Guyanese
And turn up the heat.

Sprinkle some fresh Indians, Malaysians, Bosnians,
Iraqis and Bangladeshis together with some
Afghans, Spanish, Turkish, Kurdish, Japanese
And Palestinians
Then add to the melting pot.
Leave the ingredients to simmer.

As they mix and blend allow their languages to flourish
Binding them together with English.

Allow time to be cool.

Add some unity, understanding and respect for the
future
Serve with justice
And enjoy.

Note: All the ingredients are equally important. Treating one ingredient better than another will leave a bitter, unpleasant taste.

Warning: An unequal spread of *justice will damage the people and cause pain.*

Give justice and equality to all.

Name: ______________________ Date: ______________ P1.7

Recipe poem 1

Use the framework to write your own recipe poem.

Title: ______________________

Serves ______________________

Take some ______________________
Then sprinkle with ______________________
And allow to settle.

Mix some ______________________
Then take ______________________
And leave the ingredients for ______________________

Allow time to ______________________
Serve with ______________________
And enjoy.

Name: ______________________ Date: ______________ P1.8

Recipe poem 2

Use the framework to write your own recipe poem.

Title: ______________________

Serves ______________________

Take some ______________________

Add ______________________

Then ______________________

And allow to settle.

Mix some ______________________

Then take ______________________

Combine with ______________________

And leave ______________________

Allow time to ______________________

Then ______________________

Serve with ______________________

And enjoy.

Note: ______________________

Warning: ______________________

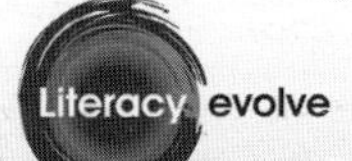

Poetry Unit 2

BENJAMIN ZEPHANIAH / TED HUGHES (Poetic voice)

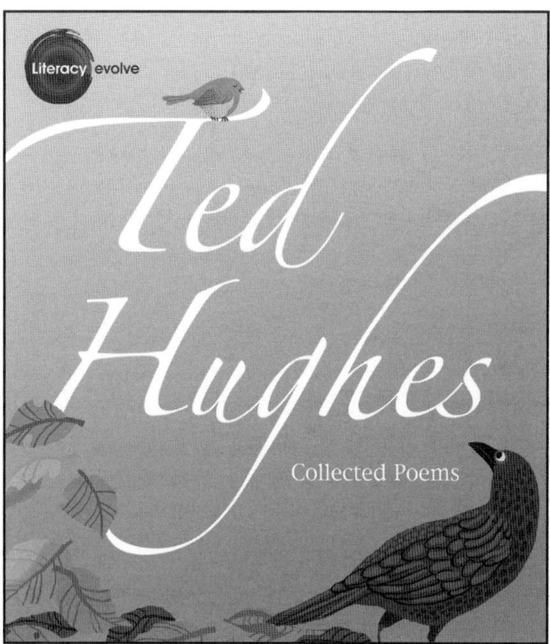

Medium term plan (1 week)	
Phase	**Learning Outcomes**
Phase 1: Reading poems that express the writer's voice (3 days)	• Children can identify and discuss a poet's views. • Children can comment on a poet's use of language to express their views and persuade the reader.
Phase 2: Exploring an issue and writing a shared poem (1 day)	• Children can use talk to discuss an issue. • Children can contribute to a shared poem to express their views on an issue.
Phase 3: Writing and performing a poem about an issue (1 day)	• Children can write their own poems to express their views on an issue and perform these poems.

Poetry Unit 2

BENJAMIN ZEPHANIAH/TED HUGHES

Big picture

The children explore several poems that tackle a similar issue, debating the issues as a class and responding to the images using drama techniques. They examine how the poet in each case uses language to persuade the reader, and evaluate how persuasive the poems are. The children work together to discuss issues that they feel strongly about as a class, before choosing one to create a whole-class poem about. They evaluate each other's contributions to the class poem and consider how persuasive and powerful the poem is overall. They then have the opportunity to explore issues that they individually feel strongly about, before writing, editing and refining their own poems.

Prior learning

This unit assumes that the children can already:

- talk together and use drama techniques to explore the issues in poems
- comment on the language choices that poets make, with some experience of evaluating how persuasive they are
- create their own poems, with some experience of writing on an issue about which they feel strongly.

Key aspects of learning

Communication: Explore issues with other group members; express views orally; communicate a point of view in the form of a poem.

Evaluation: Evaluate own and published poems according to how persuasive they are.

Self-awareness: Express their own views on issues, including those which they feel strongly about. Reflect on their own learning and progress.

Social skills: Work together to discuss issues, responding sensitively to others' points of view; comment constructively on others' work.

Progression in poetry

In this unit the children will:

- interpret poems, explaining how the poet creates shades of meaning; justify own views and explain underlying themes
- explain the impact of figurative and expressive language, including metaphor
- use imagery to create poems based on real or imagined experience; select pattern or form to match meaning and own voice.

Cross-curricular links

Geography: Links could be made to work on human impact on the environment.

PSHE: Some of the issues explored may overlap with those discussed in PSHE.

PHASE 1: READING POEMS THAT EXPRESS THE POET'S VOICE (3 DAYS)

Session 1

We are learning to ...	Resources
• use talk to explore a poem • explore how poets use language to communicate their views (PNS Strands 1.3, 8.3) **Assessment Focuses** AF (R): 5	*Year 6 Poetry Collection* *Talking Turkeys!* (film) ITP: P2.1 PCM: P2.1

Shared teaching

- Share the learning objectives and explain that, in this unit, the children will be reading poems that communicate poets' thoughts and feelings about various issues in powerful ways.
- Watch *Talking Turkeys!* to see Benjamin Zephaniah perform this poem. Discuss performance poetry. *How do you think performance poetry is different to written poetry? What do you think this adds to the poem?* Explain that as a live performance, often the poem may be slightly different to the written version. *Why do you think this is?*
- Read *Talking Turkeys!* by Benjamin Zephaniah (pages 4–5), as the children follow in their books. Discuss the use of non-standard English such as 'yu', 'dis', 'dem' and clarify any unfamiliar language.
- *What issues does Benjamin Zephaniah give his views about in the poem?* (E.g. vegetarianism/veganism; cruelty to animals; human greed and waste, particularly at Christmas time.)
- Talk Partners discuss these issues in an exploratory way. *How do you feel about eating meat? Do you think humans are wasteful?*
- As a class, debate the issues more formally, ensuring that both sides of the arguments are represented. If necessary, put forward the other side of the case yourself, encouraging the children to respond and to explain their thoughts and feelings.
- *How has Benjamin Zephaniah used poetry to communicate his thoughts and feelings about the issue? Why do you think he decided to write a poem and not a non-fiction text or an opinion article in a newspaper?*
- Discuss the features used in the poem to make the argument more memorable, e.g. rap-style rhythm, rhyme, personification, non-standard English. Make a list to start the Learning Wall.

Independent and Guided

- In groups, the children watch *Talking Turkeys!* again and make notes about the language and structure used to communicate the poet's message.

(ooo) Use 'Poem with a message' (PCM P2.1). Focus on the use of non-standard English.

(oo) Use PCM P2.1. Highlight the uses of personification in the poem that make the turkeys seem human. (TA+)

(o) Use PCM P2.1. Underline all the rhymes in the poem and try to find a pattern. (T+)

Plenary

- Show '*Talking Turkeys!*' (ITP P2.1). Invite the groups to share their ideas about the use of rhyme, personification and non-standard English.
- Watch *Talking Turkeys!* again. *What impact does the performance have on the audience?*
- Recap the learning objectives. As a class, evaluate how effective the poem is in expressing the poet's views about the issues raised and persuading others to share them.

Assessment pointers

- S&L: group work will show how far the children can express and respond to opinions.
- AF5 (R): responses will show how far the children can identify language features and the effect of the poet's choices.

Session 2

We are learning to ...	Resources
• use talk to explore a poem • explore how poets use language to communicate their views (PNS Strands 1.3, 8.3) **Assessment Focuses** AF (R): 5	*Year 6 Poetry Collection* ITP: P2.2

Shared teaching

- Share the learning objectives and explain that the children are going to read another poem that communicates thoughts and feelings about an issue, this time by Ted Hughes.
- Read *Work and Play* by Ted Hughes (pages 8–9).
- Clarify any unfamiliar imagery. (E.g. 'the serpent of cars': the long line of cars looks like a snake; 'the barbed harpoon ... ': the swallow is like a spearhead made in a hot forge then dipped in water; 'disgorges its organs': holidaymakers fall out of cars like a snake's insides; 'like tomatoes': red from sunbathing; 'transistors': portable radios; 'the hand stretched': a swallow's nest under a roof.)
- Discuss the contrast between the language used to describe the swallow's activities (the phrases sound graceful, joyful, dynamic) and the humans' activities (the phrases sound sluggish, messy, miserable). *What issue is Ted Hughes writing about?* (How we have more leisure time than the swallow but turn that play into work, or don't really enjoy or appreciate it.) Talk Partners discuss this issue in an exploratory way.
- As a class, debate the issues more formally, ensuring that both sides of the argument are represented. If necessary, put forward the other side of the case yourself.
- *Can you see any links between the themes and issues in* Talking Turkeys! *and* Work and Play? Allow Think Time for the children to consider their responses before sharing them.
- *How has Ted Hughes used poetry to communicate his thoughts and feelings? What features are different from Benjamin Zephaniah's poem?* (E.g. free verse; stanzas with long lines for the swallow, shorter lines for the humans; powerful metaphors and similes.) Add notes to the Learning Wall.
- Recap the work on powerful imagery in Ted Hughes' poems from Unit 1.

Independent and Guided

- In groups, the children use drama and dance to investigate the powerful images in *Work and Play*. Each group dramatises one stanza, using Improvisation, gesture and movement. Support the children with an identified need. (T/TA)

Plenary

- The groups present their performances of the stanzas. Encourage the children to evaluate the effectiveness of the performances, especially the use of movement and gesture.
- Show 'Powerful verbs' (ITP P2.2). Click on the 'Swallows' to highlight the text about swallows. *Which is the most powerful?* Repeat for the holidaymakers and compare. *Which images have the most impact?*
- Recap the learning objectives.
- Evaluate how effective the poem is in expressing the poet's views and persuading others to share them.

Assessment pointers

- S&L: drama pieces show how far the children can sustain roles and scenarios to explore the poem.
- AF5 (R): responses to questioning will show how far the children are aware of the effect of the poet's language choices.

Session 3

We are learning to ...	Resources
• explore how poets use language to communicate their views (PNS Strand: 8.3) **Assessment Focuses** AF (R): 6	*Year 6 Poetry Collection* ITP: P2.3 PCM: P2.2

Shared teaching (1)

- Share the learning objective.
- Explain that, in this session, the children will be reading another poem by Ted Hughes expressing his view on a different issue.
- *Who has a cat as a pet? Do you enjoy stroking it and having it on your knee, purring? How does this make you feel?*
- Read *Cat* by Ted Hughes (page 5). Encourage the children to focus on the feelings described. *Does the poem do a good job of describing the feeling you get from having a cat purring on your lap?*
- Discuss any language in the poem that is unclear, e.g. 'neon-lit': lit by a bright, unnatural light; 'video glow': flickering light from TV screens.
- Ted Hughes describes the cat as having certain 'powers'. The children Think-Pair-Share what these powers might be.
- Draw out a few examples of the language used to describe the human world in the first few stanzas, e.g. 'tired and flat', 'too much town', etc. *How is the animal world described?*

Independent and Guided

- In groups, the children continue to compile lists of words to summarise what the poem *Cat* is saying about the animal and human worlds.

ooo Complete 'Comparing worlds' (PCM P2.2). Then create a list of words to describe the animal world. (T+)

oo Complete PCM P2.2.

o As above. (TA+)

Shared teaching (2)

- The children share their lists of words. Show and complete 'Natural and human worlds' (ITP P2.3) by adding their contributions.
- *What do you think the poem is saying about the two worlds?* (E.g. living in the artificial environment of the human world in the city can make us feel tired, ill and depressed. Contact with an animal like a cat can refresh and revive us by putting us back in touch with the animal world.)

Plenary

- Recap the learning objective.
- As a class, evaluate how effective *Cat* is in expressing the poet's views and persuading others to share them.
- Compare the poem *Cat* with *Work and Play*. *Is the issue the same: the contrast between animal and human worlds?* Discuss whether *Cat* is written in the same way as *Work and Play*. (E.g. *Cat* uses rhyme not free verse and has less imagery.)
- *Which poem is more persuasive? Which did you enjoy reading most?*

Assessment pointers

- S&L: group work will show how far the children can engage with others, draw ideas together and promote discussion.
- AF6 (R): responses to questioning will show how far the children are able to identify the poet's purpose and viewpoint and comment on the overall effect this has on the reader.

PHASE 2: EXPLORING AN ISSUE AND WRITING A SHARED POEM (1 DAY)

Session 4

We are learning to ...	Resources
• use talk to explore a poem • write our own poems to express our views (PNS Strands 1.3, 9.5) **Assessment Focuses** AF (W): 1, 7	*Year 6 Poetry Collection* ITP: P2.4 PCM: P2.3

Shared teaching

- Share the learning objectives.
- Explain that, in this session, the children will be reading another poem by Benjamin Zephaniah that communicates his thoughts and feelings about an issue in a powerful way. Then they will write a whole-class poem using the same model.
- Read *Christmas Wise* by Benjamin Zephaniah (page 3).
- Discuss any unfamiliar language and the use of non-standard English such as 'fe', 'loads a', 'dat', etc.
- *What issues are raised in the poem? Are there any links with the poems* Talking Turkeys! *and* Work and Play? The children Think-Pair-Share using exploratory talk.
- Discuss the structure and language used in *Christmas Wise*. Create a list of features to add to the Learning Wall. (E.g. it uses a mixture of free verse and rhyme; uses a mixture of non-standard and standard English; puts key words in bold; uses the structure of the popular song *All I want for Christmas is Me Two Front Teeth.*) *How does it compare to* Talking Turkeys! *and* Work and Play?
- Explain that the children are now going to write a whole-class poem about an issue they feel strongly about. Discuss and agree on an appropriate topic, e.g. bullying, racism, wildlife conservation, etc.
- Use Modelled Writing to draft the opening lines in standard or non-standard English, using free verse with occasional rhymes, on 'Finding a voice' (ITP P2.4).
- Take suggestions from the children for the next few lines and demonstrate choosing from the ideas put forward. Add the selected contributions to ITP P2.4. Save the annotations.

Independent and Guided

- In groups, the children continue the poem using the *Christmas Wise* model and referring to the list of features on the Learning Wall.

●●● Complete the poem.

●● Continue the poem for at least another six lines. (T+)

● Use 'Christmas poem 1' (PCM P2.3). (TA+)

Plenary

- Listen to the draft lines from each group and compare them to the features on the Learning Wall. *Do they follow the model of* Christmas Wise? Take feedback.
- As class, choose successful lines to complete the whole-class poem, adding the new lines to ITP P2.4. Save the annotations.
- Read or perform the final version of the poem.
- Recap the learning objectives.
- *How effective is the poem in expressing your views? How well do you think it will persuade others to share your views?*

Assessment pointers

- S&L: group work will show how well the children can adopt group roles, drawing ideas together and promoting effective writing.
- AF1, 7 (W): contributions to the whole-class poem will show how well the children can select and develop relevant ideas to produce imaginative texts, using effective vocabulary.

PHASE 3: WRITING AND PERFORMING A POEM ABOUT AN ISSUE (1 DAY)

Session 5

We are learning to ...	Resources
• write our own poems to express our views • present our work for an audience using handwriting • present our work for an audience using ICT (PNS Strands 9.5, 12.1, 12.2) **Assessment Focuses** AF (W): 1	*Year 6 Poetry Collection* ITP: (P2.4), P2.5 PCM: P2.4

Shared teaching (1)

- Share the learning objectives. Explain that the children are going to write their own poems on an issue that they feel strongly about.
- *What issues could you write about?* Encourage the children to Mind Map ideas and add their suggestions to the Learning Wall.
- Talk Partners discuss what they plan to write about.
- Remind the children that they could follow the model of *Christmas Wise* by Benjamin Zephaniah (page 3). Recall annotated 'Finding a voice' (ITP P2.4) and reread the class poem to remind the children of the format. Alternatively, the children could use another format, such as *Work and Play* by Ted Hughes (pages 8–9).
- Encourage the children to avoid rhyme or any form that is too restrictive, as they need to focus on expressing their views.
- Talk Partners discuss how they will write about their chosen issue.

Independent and Guided (1)

- The children work independently to write a first draft of their poem.

●●● Use one of the free verse models from the poems studied, or create a free verse format. (TA+)

●● As above. (T+)

● Use 'Christmas poem 2' (PCM P2.4).

Shared teaching (2)

- Show 'Writing poems about issues' (ITP P2.5) and discuss the success criteria. *Are there any more that you would like to add?*
- Talk Partners provide feedback on their partner's first draft. Encourage the children to comment on how well the drafts express the writer's views on the issue and how well they meet the success criteria.

Independent and Guided (2)

- The children reflect on their own writing, editing and improving their poems based on the feedback from their partner. They proofread their writing and check the spelling. The children then finalise their poems using handwriting or ICT. Support the children with an identified need. (T/TA)

Plenary

- Talk Partners share their final poems. *Has your partner improved their first draft? Have they expressed their views clearly and persuasively?*
- Ask some of the children to perform their poems to the class. Highlight examples that match the success criteria.
- Create a class poetry book called *Finding a Voice*, using all the children's poems alongside Ted Hughes' and Benjamin Zephaniah's.
- Recap the learning objectives and review the unit as a whole. *Which poems did you enjoy most? What did you learn while writing about issues?* Encourage the children to review their own progress. *What are you most proud of? What do you need to improve?*

Assessment pointers

- S&L: pair work will show how sensitively the children can express and respond to opinions.
- AF1 (W): written drafts and final poems will show how well the children can choose relevant content and develop ideas with imaginative detail.

Poem with a message

Make notes about the language and structure the poet uses to communicate his message.

Talking Turkeys

Benjamin Zephaniah

Be nice to yu turkeys dis christmas
Cos turkeys jus wanna hav fun
Turkeys are cool, turkeys are wicked
An every turkey has a Mum.
Be nice to yu turkeys dis christmas,
Don't eat it, keep it alive,
It could be yu mate an not on yu plate
Say, Yo! Turkey I'm on your side.

I got lots of friends who are turkeys
An all of dem fear christmas time,
Dey wanna enjoy it, dey say humans destroyed it
An humans are out of dere mind,
Yeah, I got lots of friends who are turkeys
Dey all hav a right to a life,
Not to be caged up an genetically made up
By any farmer an his wife.

Turkeys jus wanna play reggae
Turkeys jus wanna hip-hop
Can yu imagine a nice young turkey saying,
'I cannot wait for de chop'?
Turkeys like getting presents, dey wanna
watch christmas TV,
Turkeys hav brains an turkeys feel pain
In many ways like yu an me.

I once knew a turkey called
Turkey
He said 'Benji explain to me please,
Who put de turkey in christmas
An what happens to christmas trees?'
I said, 'I am not too sure turkey
But it's nothing to do wid Christ Mass
Humans get greedy an waste more dan need be
An business men mek loadsa cash.'

Be nice to yu turkey dis christmas
Invite dem indoors fe sum greens
Let dem eat cake an let dem partake
In a plate of organic grown beans,
Be nice to yu turkey dis christmas
An spare dem de cut of de knife,
Join Turkeys United an dey'll be delighted
An yu will mek new friends **'FOR LIFE'**.

Comparing worlds

Answer the questions about *Cat* by Ted Hughes.

In what other ways can animals comfort humans?

What words and phrases are used to describe the human world?

How does the cat offer comfort?

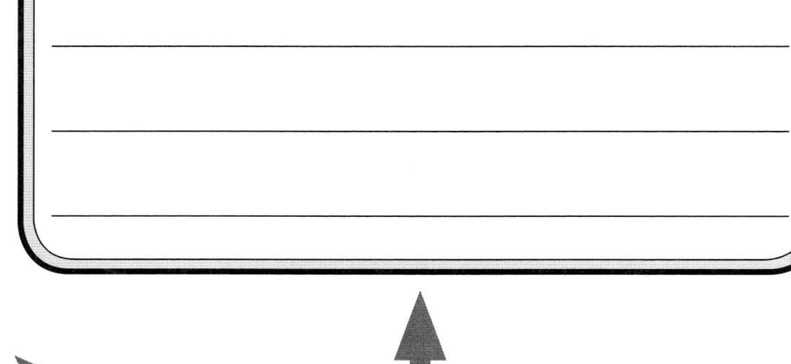

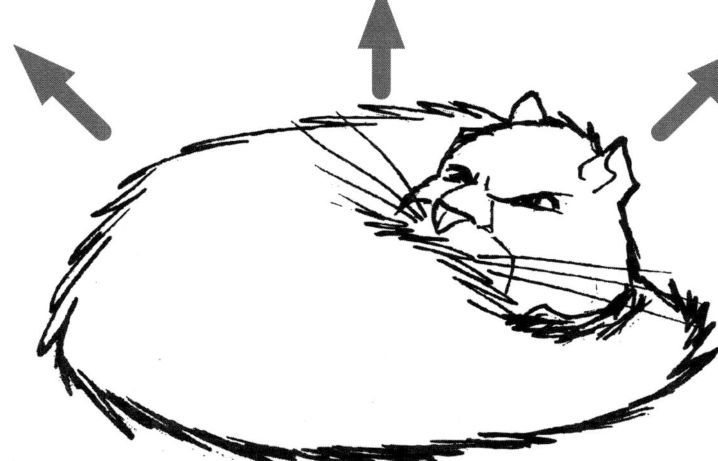

Christmas poem 1

Write the first few lines of your whole-class poem in the style of *Christmas Wise*. Then continue the poem.

Title: ______________________

____

____

____

All I **want** for Christmas is ______________________

I don't **want** ______________________

I **won't** be ______________________

All I **want** for Christmas is ______________________

No more ______________________

I don't **want** ______________________

All I **want** for Christmas is ______________________

But I reckon ______________________

Name: ______________________ Date: ____________ **P2.4**

Christmas poem 2

Write a poem in the style of Benjamin Zephaniah about an issue that you feel strongly about.

Title: ______________________

All I **want** for Christmas is ______________________

I don't **want** ______________________

I **won't** be ______________________

All I **want** for Christmas is ______________________

No more ______________________

I don't **want** ______________________

All I **want** for Christmas is ______________________

No more ______________________

I don't **want** ______________________

All I **want** for Christmas is ______________________

But I reckon ______________________

Poetry Unit 3

BENJAMIN ZEPHANIAH / TED HUGHES (Revision)

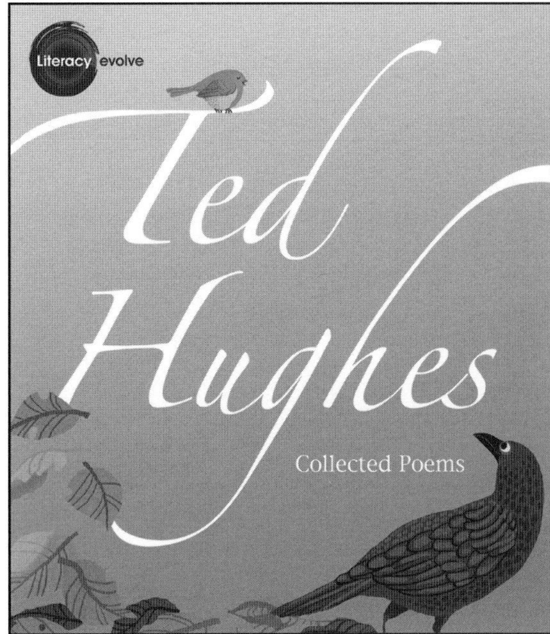

Medium term plan (2 weeks)	
Phase	**Learning Outcomes**
Phase 1: Reading and evaluating poems (7 days)	• Children can identify language features and comment on their effect. • Children can perform and evaluate the effect of a choral reading. • Children can construct their own questions about a poem. • Children can comment on how point of view is conveyed in a poem.
Phase 2: Answering test questions about poems (3 days)	• Children can identify different question types and answer questions on a poem. • Children can evaluate good and weak features of answers to test questions.

Poetry Unit 3

BENHAMIN ZEPHANIAH/TED HUGHES

Big picture

This unit is designed to provide revision sessions around poetry. The children revise knowledge of similes and metaphors and highlight key aspects of language in various poems. They record first impressions, puzzles and patterns and share their likes and dislikes about various poems. They prepare and evaluate choral performances and consider how these help their understanding of poems. They create their own questions about poems and reflect on how talking about poems helps them to understand them better. They consider the impact of non-standard English and how point of view is expressed. They answer questions on poems, evaluate answers and consider features of good test answers.

Prior learning

This unit assumes that the children can already:

- identify language features such as simile and metaphor
- talk together to explore poetry and prepare performances
- begin to recognise the different types such as inference and deduction.

Key aspects of learning

Enquiry: Form questions about poems and find evidence to answer them.

Evaluation: Evaluate poetry performances, answers to comprehension questions and their own and others' work.

Self-awareness: Express their personal views on poetry.

Social skills: Work effectively in pairs and groups to identify language features and prepare a performance

Progression in poetry

In this unit the children will:

- interpret poems by answering inferential questions and justifying own views
- explain the impact of expressive language such as simile and metaphor
- in performance, vary aspects of the performance to create impact and convey meaning
- discuss different forms and describe their impact on the reader
- discuss the poet's viewpoint and explain and justify interpretation.

Cross-curricular links

Geography: Explore the different locations described in the poems.

PSHE: Dicsuss topical issues; the impact of humans on the environment, racism, diversity.

Science: Links to the seasons.

PHASE 1: READING AND EVALUATING POEMS (7 DAYS)

Session 1

We are learning to ...	Resources
• use talk to explore a poem • explore how poets use language for effect (PNS Strands 1.3, 8.3) **Assessment Focuses** AF (R): 4, 5	*Year 6 Poetry Collection* ITP: P3.1, P3.2, P3.3 PCM: P3.1

Shared teaching

- Explain that, in this unit, the children will revise techniques for reading poetry, beginning with poems by Ted Hughes.
- Share the learning objectives.
- *What can you remember about Ted Hughes?* Allow Think Time, then invite the children to share recollections. Recap the poems read in Poetry Units 1 and 2: *Dog, The Seven Sorrows, Work and Play* and *Cat, Woodpecker* and *Jellyfish*.
- Explain that the poem the children will be reading in this session uses very powerful imagery.
- Show 'Simile or metaphor?' (ITP P3.1). Recap the definitions of 'simile' and 'metaphor'. *Which of these phrases are similes? Which are metaphors?* Take feedback and drag the phrases into the correct box.
- Talk Partners create two more similes about being hot or cold.
- Read *The Warm and the Cold* by Ted Hughes (pages 10–11) , as the children follow in their books, listening to the language.
- Show 'First impressions' (ITP P3.2). Talk Partners reread the poem, discussing and recording their impressions in a grid similar to ITP P3.2.
- Take feedback, beginning with puzzles in the language of the poem, e.g. 'viol', 'vice', 'tide-rip', 'mammoth of ice'. Make notes on ITP P3.2.
- The children share their likes and dislikes, encouraging them to give evidence from the poem to back up their preferences.
- Ask the children to share any patterns or language features they found.

Independent and Guided

- Groups annotate the poem to identify different aspects of language.

(three-dot icon) Use 'Language' (PCM P3.1). Highlight the use of metaphor, personification, rhymes and similes. (T+)

(two-dot icon) Use PCM P3.1. Highlight rhyming words and similes.

(one-dot icon) Use PCM P3.1. Highlight rhyming words and particularly effective words or phrases. (TA+)

Plenary

- Show '*The Warm and the Cold*' (ITP P3.3). Ask the groups to point out the similes from the poem and highlight them on ITP P3.3. Discuss the patterns, e.g. alternate lines rhyme, except in the last two stanzas; there are five similes starting with 'like' in the first three stanzas, etc.
- Discuss any puzzles about the similes used. Explain that there is not necessarily one correct meaning, since images can mean different things to different readers. Encourage the children to share their own images, e.g. 'like smiles on a nurse': something comforting; 'like money in a pig': something precious kept safe in a piggy bank.
- Recap the learning objectives and reread the poem.
- Talk Partners refer back to their impressions grid. *Have your impressions of the poem changed? How have your feelings changed?*

Assessment pointers

- S&L: group work will show how well the children can adopt group roles and express relevant ideas.
- AF4, 5 (R): responses to questioning will show how far the children understand the structure of the poem and how far they are able to identify effective language.

Session 2

We are learning to ...	Resources
• use talk to explore a poem • understand how poets use language for effect (PNS Strands 1.3, 4.2) **Assessment Focuses** AF (R): 2, 3	*Year 6 Poetry Collection* ITP: P3.4

Shared teaching

- Share the learning objectives. *What is meant by a choral reading?*
- Organise a whole-class choral reading of *The Warm and the Cold* by Ted Hughes (pages 10–11). Divide the class into three groups: group 1 reads the introductory four lines in each of the first three stanzas; groups 2 and 3 read alternate lines for the remaining eight lines of the first three stanzas; group 2 reads the fourth stanza; group 1 reads 'A star falls'; group 3 reads the final stanza.
- As a class, rehearse and then perform the choral reading, encouraging suggestions from each group for how to improve the performance.
- Evaluate the effect. *How does the choral reading help you hear patterns in the poem?* Explain that the children are going to use what they have learned to answer some questions about the poem.
- Show 'Comprehension questions' (ITP P3.4). Discuss questions 1 to 3 in turn, explaining that these questions test how well the children understand the information and ideas in the poem. Talk Partners discuss their answers, referring to the text.
- Discuss the children's responses and add agreed answers to ITP P3.4.
- Explain that the next questions will test how well the children can use inference. *Can you work out what the poem means when it does not tell you in a straightforward way?* Talk Partners discuss questions 4 to 6 in a similar way. Record agreed answers on ITP P3.4.

Independent and Guided

- In pairs, the children write questions about the poem *The Warm and the Cold*. Then pairs join together to ask and answer questions, referring to evidence from the poem in their answers.

ooo Write five questions to test inference.

oo Write five questions to test either information retrieval or inference. (TA+)

o Write two or three questions to test information retrieval. (T+)

Plenary

- Ask some of the pairs to share their questions and answers. *Do the answers contain evidence from the poem?*
- Recap the learning objectives. *Did reading the poem aloud help you to answer the comprehension questions?*

Assessment pointers

- S&L: pair work will show how well the children can express and explain relevant ideas.
- AF2, 3 (R): answers to questions will show how well the children can retrieve, infer or interpret information, events or ideas from the poem and refer to the text.

Session 3

We are learning to ...	Resources
• use talk to explore a poem • understand how poets use language for effect (PNS Strands 1.3, 8.3) **Assessment Focuses** AF (R): 4, 5	*Year 6 Poetry Collection* ITP: (P3.2), P3.5

Shared teaching (1)

- Share the learning objectives. Explain that the children are going to read another poem by Ted Hughes.
- Read *Leaves* by Ted Hughes (pages 2–3). Share first impressions of the poem. *What is the mood and style? What words and phrases give you this impression?*
- Allow time for the children to reread *Leaves* independently. *What season does the poem describe?* Talk Partners identify words that tell them it is describing autumn.
- *What mood does the poet create?* (E.g. serious, sombre tone.) *Which words create this mood?* Allow Think Time for the children to find answers, e.g. 'shroud', 'grave', 'mourner', 'weep'.

Independent and Guided

- Pairs use the structure on 'First impressions' (ITP P3.2) to explore their likes, dislikes and the puzzles and patterns in *Leaves*.

ooo Copy the grid from ITP P3.2. Make notes of relevant words and phrases from the poem in each section.

oo As above. (T)

o Make notes of likes and dislikes in *Leaves*. (TA)

Shared teaching (2)

- Take feedback about the children's impressions of *Leaves*. Show and annotate '*Leaves*' (ITP P3.5), highlighting different aspects with different colours. Save the annotations for future sessions.
- Begin with any puzzles about the language, e.g. 'glottle': noise made at the back of the throat.
- Discuss any puzzles arising from the images, e.g. 'I study the bible right down to the bone': a crow pecking bones looks like a person studying his bible.
- Discuss the children's likes and dislikes. Encourage them to give evidence from the poem to back up their preferences.
- The children share any patterns they see in the poem, focusing particularly on repetition and rhyming.

Plenary

- Recap the learning objectives. *Did talking about the poem help you to understand it better?*
- Point out that in test situations the children will not be able to discuss the poem. *What techniques could you use when working in silence?* Make a list of good suggestions to add to the Learning Wall, e.g. noting down questions on the test paper; 'hearing' the poem in their heads while reading; looking out for rhymes, rhythm and other patterns; rereading texts, etc.

Assessment pointers

- S&L: pair work will show how well the children can express and explain relevant ideas.
- AF4, 5 (R): written notes will show how far the children understand the poem's structure and the way language is used to create mood.

Session 4

We are learning to ...	Resources
• give a choral reading to help our understanding of a poem • identify how poets use familiar ideas and structures in their poetry (PNS Strands 4.2, 7.2) **Assessment Focuses** AF (R): 2, 3	*Year 6 Poetry Collection* ITP: P3.6 PCM: P3.2, P3.3

Shared teaching

- Share the learning objectives.
- Organise a whole-class choral reading of *Leaves* by Ted Hughes (pages 2–3). Select ten pairs or ten individual children to play the ten 'characters' (e.g. 'apple', 'pear') in the stanzas; the rest of the class acts as the narrator. The whole class reads the first line of the poem; the narrators read the first line of each of the other nine stanzas; the chosen 'characters' read their lines; all the children read the last line of the poem together.
- Rehearse and perform the choral reading. As the children rehearse, ask each group for suggestions for how they could improve the reading.
- Evaluate the impact of the choral reading. *Did you notice anything new in the poem by reading it in this way?*
- Show *'Who Killed Cock Robin?'* (ITP P3.6). Organise a choral reading of this nursery rhyme in a similar way.
- Talk Partners compare the nursery rhyme to the poem. *What is similar and what is different?* (E.g. they both use the same pattern of rhyme; the creatures in the nursery rhyme are all animals, mostly birds; the poem uses the same questions, but the answers are different; there are some questions in the nursery rhyme that don't appear in the poem; the nursery rhyme uses speech marks; the ending of the nursery rhyme has a different structure to the other stanzas.)
- Discuss the changes Ted Hughes made to the nursery rhyme. *Why has he made the changes?* (E.g. to write about the death of the leaves.) *What effect does it have on readers if they know the original nursery rhyme already?*

Independent and Guided

- In pairs, the children answer questions about the poem *Leaves*.

ooo Complete 'Questions about *Leaves* 1' (PCM P3.2). Then write two more inferential questions. (TA+)

oo Complete PCM P3.2.

o Complete 'Questions about *Leaves* 2' (PCM P3.3). (T+)

Plenary

- The children compare the Ted Hughes poems read in this unit: *Leaves* and *The Warm and the Cold. Which did you enjoy most?* Remind them to back up their preferences with reference to the texts.
- Recap the learning objectives. *How did reading the poems aloud help you to compare them?*

Assessment pointers

- S&L: pair work will show how well the children can recount ideas and listen and respond to others.
- AF2, 3 (R): written outcomes will show how far the children are able to retrieve, infer or interpret information, events and ideas from the poems and refer to the text.

Session 5

We are learning to ...	Resources
• understand how poets uses language for effect (PNS Strands 8.3) **Assessment Focuses** AF (R): 3,5	*Year 6 Poetry Collection* ITP: (P3.2), P3.7 PCM: P3.4

Shared teaching

- Share the learning objective. Explain that in the next few sessions, the children will be reading poems by Benjamin Zephaniah.
- *What can you remember about Benjamin Zephaniah?* Allow Think Time before taking feedback. Recap the poems read in Poetry Units 1 and 2: *For Word, Talking Turkeys!, The British, Christmas Wise.*
- Explain that the first poem the children will read is about being hot and cold, like *The Warm and the Cold* by Ted Hughes, but it is written in a very different way. *Based on what you already know about Benjamin Zephaniah, how might he describe hot and cold?*
- Read the title of *Jamaican Summers* by Benjamin Zephaniah (page 2). The children close their eyes and picture whatever image this title suggests to them. Read the rest of the poem.
- Discuss first impressions of the poem. *Did the poem fit with the image you imagined?* Explore responses and reasons.
- Recall 'First impressions' (ITP P3.2). Talk Partners reread the poem in their books, then explore their responses, recording their impressions in a grid similar to ITP P3.2.
- *What did you notice about the language of the poem?* Discuss any puzzles about the language and the use of non-standard English. *Why is non-standard English used?* Explain to the children about Jamaican Creole, and how the poet is recreating that distinctive speech pattern in writing.
- The children share their likes and dislikes about the poem. Encourage them to give evidence from the text to support their preferences.
- Encourage the children to identify patterns in the poem, such as repetition and rhyme.
- Show 'Jamaica' (ITP P3.7). Discuss the country's location, climate, geography and language. *Was Benjamin Zephaniah's poem successful in giving you a strong image of what Jamaica is like?*

Independent and Guided

- The children work in groups to explore the language of the poem.

ooo Compile a glossary for the Jamaican Creole words in the poem. Then create a standard English version of the poem. (T+)

oo Complete 'Questions about *Jamaican Summers*' (PCM P3.4).

o As above. (TA+)

Plenary

- Ask different groups to share their answers to the questions and their 'translations' of the poem.
- *What do you think of the poem in standard English? Which version do you prefer? What has been lost in the 'translation'?* Talk Partners discuss, then give feedback.
- Recap the learning objective. *How did Benjamin Zephaniah use language to create effects in this poem? What stood out to you about his choice of language?*

Assessment pointers

- S&L: group work will show how well the children can adopt group roles and express relevant ideas.
- AF3, 5 (R): translations into standard English and responses to questioning will show how well the children can interpret the language in the poem and understand the effect on the reader.

Session 6

We are learning to:	Resources
• compare and evaluate different poems and performances, expressing preferences and giving reasons (PNS Strands 4.3) **Assessment Focuses** AF (R): 2, 3, 4, 5, 6	*Year 6 Poetry Collection* *Jamaican Summers* (film) ITP: P3.8

Shared teaching (1)

- Share the learning objective. Explain to the children that, in this session, the children will compare poems and performances.
- Watch *Jamaican Summers* to see Benjamin Zephaniah perform this poem. Talk Partners discuss the performance. *Does it help you appreciate the poem more to hear it read in the voice of the poet?*
- Explain that as a live performance, often the poem may be slightly different to the written version.
- Explain that in groups, the children are going to create their own performances of the poem. Show '*Jamaican Summers*' (ITP P3.8), adding suggestions for how groups might perform the poem, dividing the lines so that some are spoken by groups and some by soloists.

Independent and Guided (1)

- In groups, the children create and rehearse their own performances of *Jamaican Summers,* using the arrangements discussed or their own ideas. Support the children with an identified need. (T/TA)

Shared teaching (2)

- Watch the group performances of *Jamaican Summers.* Ask the children to give Two Stars and a Wish to evaluate each performance.
- Discuss how the performances varied. *Which did you prefer?*
- Talk Partners read and compare *Jamaican Summers* with *The Warm and the Cold.*
- Take feedback. Use Modelled Writing to show how to refer to specific aspects in the text, e.g. *in Ted Hughes's poem the animals shelter from the cold:* 'the badger in its bedding/Like a loaf in the oven', *whereas in Benjamin Zephaniah's poem, the people shelter from the heat:* 'People chill out in de shade/Sleep under trees'.
- Remind the children that when answering longer questions, they need to make two or three points and offer evidence to support them.

Independent and Guided (2)

- The children write about which poem they prefer and why.

ooo Work independently to compose a written response. Then invent a question to compare another aspect of the two poems.

oo Work independently to compose a written response. (TA+)

o Work in pairs to compose a written response. (T+)

Plenary

- Share the children's responses. *Did you refer to evidence from the text?*
- Recap the learning objective. *What have you learned about comparing and evaluating poems?*

Assessment pointers

- S&L: group work and poetry performances will show how well the children effectively collaborate and understand the poem.
- AF2, 3, 4, 5, 6 (R): oral and written responses will show how well the children can infer or interpret information from poems and understand the structural features, use of language, and poets' viewpoints.

Session 7

We are learning to ...	Resources
• identify viewpoint in a poem (PNS Strands 7.2) **Assessment Focuses** AF (R): 4, 6	*Year 6 Poetry Collection* *Walking Black Home* (film) ITP: (P3.2)

Shared teaching

- Share the learning objective. *What do we mean by viewpoint?*
- Explain that the children are going to read another poem by Benjamin Zephaniah which is very different from *Jamaican Summers.* Remind them that some of his poems express his views on certain issues.
- Watch *Walking Black Home* and see Benjamin Zephaniah perform this poem. Talk Partners discuss their first impressions of the poem, then read *Walking Black Home* by Benjamin Zephaniah (page 8).
- Talk Partners discuss their responses to the poem and make lists of likes and dislikes and any puzzles and patterns they notice. If necessary, recall 'First impressions' (ITP P3.2) for reference.
- Address any puzzles about the language in the poem, e.g. *Why is 'was' written 'waz' in line one?*
- Take feedback on the children's likes and dislikes. Prompt them to give evidence from the poem to support their preferences, referring back to what they learned in Session 6.
- Discuss the issue in the poem: people being discriminated against in everyday life because of the ethnic group to which they belong. Identify the viewpoint of the poet and his purpose in writing the poem.
- *Can you see any patterns in the poem?* (E.g. the first and last words are in bold; lines 4 and 8 rhyme; lines 16 and 19 rhyme; there are short lines with gaps in between.)
- The children Think-Pair-Share why the poem is written in this way. *What effect does it have on the reader? How does it persuade them to share the poet's strong feelings about the issue?*

Independent and Guided

- The children compose different types of questions about *Walking Black Home.*

ooo Work in pairs to compose questions based on the poet's viewpoint, including at least two which require longer answers. (T+)

oo Work in pairs to compose questions which focus on the use of language and interpreting information.

o Work as a group to compose questions based on retrieving information and the structure of the poem. (TA)

Plenary

- Ask some of the pairs to ask their questions. Develop answers orally as a class, highlighting good examples of references to the text.
- Recap the learning objective.
- Compare the two poems by Benjamin Zephaniah studied in this unit. *How are* Jamaican Summers *and* Walking Black Home *different? What was the poet's purpose in each poem? What effect did each one have on you as a reader?*

Assessment pointers

- AF4, 6 (R): responses to questioning and independent work, will show how far the children understand the poet's views, the poem's structure and the effect of the text on the reader.

Session 8

We are learning to ...	Resources
• explore themes in stories and poems • understand how poets use language for effect • answer test questions about poems (PNS Strands 3.2, 7.2, 8.3) **Assessment Focuses** AF (R): 2, 3, 6	*Year 6 Poetry Collection* PCM: P3.5

Shared teaching

- Share the learning objectives. Explain that the children will be answering questions about the poem *Walking Black Home* by Benjamin Zephaniah.
- Talk Partners recall the poem. *What can you remember about* Walking Black Home*?*
- Explain to the children that having previously explored the poem as a class should help them to provide fuller answers to the questions. Remind them that in a test situation they will not be able to discuss their answers with others.
- Make a list of the different kinds of questions the children may face on a reading comprehension paper: information retrieval questions (finding the answer directly in the text); inferential questions (working out the answer from information implied in the text); deductive questions (using reason to come to an answer based on information in the text and prior knowledge); evaluative questions (comparing or evaluating text). Add the list to the Learning Wall.
- Encourage the children to generate examples of the different questions, e.g. information retrieval, inferential, deductive and evaluative. Discuss tips for answering these questions, e.g. remember that multiple choice questions often include 'red herrings' which use a word or two from the text but are not the correct answer.
- Remind the children to look carefully at the questions and consider how much detail is needed in their answer.

Independent and Guided

- The children work individually to answer test questions about *Walking Black Home*. They try to answer as many questions as they can within a set period of time and in any order they wish.

ooo Use 'Questions about *Walking Black Home*' (PCM P3.5).

oo As above. (TA+)

o As above. (T+)

Plenary

- Talk Partners share responses and compare their answers.
- As a class, discuss the children's answers to each question on PCM P3.5 in turn. Agree on which answers are the most appropriate, explaining how to improve them if necessary. Refer to the text of the poem for evidence to support the answers.
- Recap the learning objectives.
- Ask the children which of the test questions they found the most difficult and why. *How could you do better next time you have a timed test? What could you improve?*

Assessment pointers

- AF2, 3, 6 (R): written responses to test questions will show how far the children are able to understand and retrieve information, deduce, infer and interpret information and comment on a poet's purpose and viewpoint.

Session 9

We are learning to ...	Resources
• explore themes in stories and poems • understand how poets use language for effect • explore different types of test questions about poems (PNS Strands 3.2, 7.2, 8.3) **Assessment Focuses** AF (R): 2, 3, 4, 5, 6	*Year 6 Poetry Collection* ITP: P3.9, P3.10

Shared teaching (1)

- Share the learning objectives. Explain that the children will be answering questions about poems and evaluating other example answers. They will decide which answers they think are good and explore ways to improve weak answers.
- Reread *Cat* by Ted Hughes (page 5), which the children looked at in Poetry Unit 2. *Read the poem to yourself as if in a test. What can you remember about the ways to read poetry when taking a test?* Refer to the list from Session 3 on the Learning Wall and review the points, e.g. 'hearing' the words in their heads; looking out for rhymes, rhythm and other patterns; rereading texts; writing down questions.
- Show 'Multiple choice questions' (ITP P3.9). Talk Partners discuss each question in turn and decide which answer they think is correct. Take feedback, then reveal the answers.
- Show 'Answering test questions' (ITP P3.10). Discuss the questions shown on screen, but do not reveal the example answers yet.

Independent and Guided

- The children work independently to write as full an answer as possible to the questions on ITP P3.10 about the poem *Cat*. Support the children with an identified need. (T/TA)

Shared teaching (2)

- Talk Partners discuss their answers. Encourage the children to look for specific references to the text rather than generalisations.
- Reveal the example answers on ITP P3.10. Read through the two examples for each question. *Which answer do you think is the most effective?* Talk Partners discuss their opinions.
- Share ideas about which of the answers are good or weak. *How do they compare with your own answers?* Refer to specific points, e.g. in the second answer for Question 1, the word 'repeating' from the question is used again in the answer and the explanation is very general. *Could more detail be added?*
- Allow the children time to review and improve their own answers. If these are already strong, encourage them to improve the weaker answers on ITP P3.10.

Plenary

- Recap the learning objectives. *What have you learned about answering multiple choice questions? What features make a good answer to the longer response questions? What will you remember for next time?*

Assessment pointers

- S&L: pair work will show how well the children can recount ideas and listen and respond to others.
- AF2, 3, 4, 5, 6 (R): responses to test questions will show how far the children are able to retrieve, deduce and infer information, comment on the structure of texts and a poet's use of language, purpose and viewpoint.

Session 10

We are learning to ...	Resources
• understand how poets use language for effect • answer test questions about poems (PNS Strands 3.2, 8.3) **Assessment Focuses** AF (R): 2, 3, 4, 5, 6	*Year 6 Poetry Collection* ITP: (P3.10), P3.11 PCM: P3.6, P3.7

Shared teaching

- Share the learning objectives. Explain that, in this session, the children will be answering test questions about poems and identifying some useful tips to help them with these kinds of questions.
- Recap some of the features of good and weak test answers from Session 9. Recall 'Answering test questions' (ITP P3.10) to remind the children of examples of successful answers.
- *What tips would you give for answering test questions effectively?* Talk Partners discuss their ideas.
- Take feedback and draw up a list of class tips to add to the Learning Wall. Show 'Tips for success' (ITP P3.11). *Are there any tips here that we haven't thought of? Do you feel more confident about answering test questions now?*

Independent and Guided

- The children read the poems *Dog* and *Cat* by Ted Hughes (pages 4–5). They work independently to complete 'Questions about *Dog*' (PCM P3.6) and 'Questions about *Dog* and *Cat*' (PCM P3.7). If appropriate, organise this activity under test conditions. Support the children with an identified need. (T/TA)

Plenary

- Discuss each question in turn on PCM P3.6 and PCM P3.7 and agree on what kind of answer is required. Refer to the list of class tips on the Learning Wall and ITP P3.11 each time to reinforce the tips for success.
- Invite some of the children to share their answers and encourage the other children to give feedback. Explain that you will provide individual feedback on the children's test answers after the session.
- *Which test questions did you find the most difficult? How could you improve your answers in the future?* Encourage the children to reflect on their answers and to evaluate how successful they were.
- Recap the learning objectives and the unit as a whole. *What is the most important thing you have learned in this unit?* Remind the children to refer to the tips for success on the Learning Wall and ITP P3.11 to help them in future tests.

Assessment pointers

- AF2, 3, 4 (R): written responses to test questions will show how far the children are able to retrieve information, deduce and infer information and comment on the structure of texts.
- AF5, 6 (R): written responses to test questions will show how far the children can comment on a poet's use of language, purpose and viewpoint.

Name: ______________________ Date: ______________ **P3.1**

Language

Use the key to highlight different kinds of language in the poem.

Key

Metaphors	☐	Rhymes	☐	Effective words	☐
Personification	☐	Similes	☐		

The Warm and the Cold

Ted Hughes

Freezing dusk is closing
Like a slow trap of steel
On trees and roads and hills and all
That can no longer feel.
But the carp is in its depth
Like a planet in its heaven.
And the badger in its bedding
Like a loaf in the oven.
And the butterfly in its mummy
Like a viol in its case
And the owl in its feathers
Like a doll in its lace.

Freezing dusk has tightened
Like a nut screwed tight
On the starry aeroplane
Of the soaring night.
But the trout is in its hole
Like a chuckle in a sleeper.
The hare strays down the highway
Like a root going deeper.
The snail is dry in the outhouse
Like a seed in a sunflower.
The owl is pale on the gatepost
Like a clock on its tower.

Moonlight freezes the shaggy world
Like a mammoth of ice –
The past and the future
Are the jaws of a steel vice.
But the cod is in the tide-rip
Like a key in a purse.
The deer are on the bare-blown hill
Like smiles on a nurse.
The flies are behind the plaster
Like the lost score of a jig.
Sparrows are in the ivy-clump
Like money in a pig.

Such a frost
The flimsy moon
Hast lost her wits.

A star falls.

The sweating farmers
Turn in their sleep
Like oxen on spits.

Name: ____________________ Date: ____________

Questions about *Leaves* 1

Answer the questions about *Leaves* by Ted Hughes.

a. Which season is the poem describing? How do you know this?

b. What is the effect of the repetition in the line 'Me, me, me says the marrow, the marrow'?

c. Who will make a 'shroud' for the leaves?

d. The river says it will 'dig their grave'. Explain what the poet meant by this.

e. Find two phrases that show how the wind is similar to a 'chief mourner'. Explain what this means.

f. Why does the swallow say it must pack and be off?

g. Why is it appropriate for the sunset to lower the coffin?

Questions about *Leaves* 2

Answer the questions about *Leaves* by Ted Hughes.

a. Who killed the leaves? Circle your answer.

the apple the pear the crow the sunset

b. What job did the wind say it would do in the poem?

c. Why does the pear complain about the leaves dropping?

d. Which three animals are mentioned in the poem?

e. What kind of pattern is used in the line 'gear grinding glottal'?

personification ☐ rhyme ☐ simile ☐ alliteration ☐

f. Which season is the poem describing?

g. Explain in your own words what happens to the leaves in this poem.

Questions about *Jamaican Summers*

Answer these questions about the poem *Jamaican Summers* by Benjamin Zephaniah.

a. What are the two meanings of 'cool' ? (Stanza one)

____

____

b. Why do parents tell their children to drink a lot? (Stanza two)

____

____

c. What does 'chill out' mean? (Stanza three)

____

d. Which season seems to be very short in Jamaica? (Stanza four)

____

e. Write these lines in standard English.

'Drink yu mountain water' ______________________________

____

'Yu muss drink a lot' ______________________________

____

'Or travel fe miles
To find cool breeze' ______________________________

____

'Let me give yu a warning me friend' ______________________________

____

Questions about *Walking Black Home*

Answer these questions about *Walking Black Home* by Benjamin Zephaniah.

a. Why was it a bad day for the poet? Tick the correct answer.

It was raining. ☐ No one smiled at him. ☐

He couldn't get a taxi. ☐ He hadn't had lunch. ☐

b. Why did he have to walk for many miles?

____

____

c. Why didn't he smile back at people?

____

d. How did he feel after walking so far?

____

____

e. What is the mood of the poet in the poem? Use evidence from the text to support your answer.

____

____

____

f. Why wouldn't he turn back?

____

____

g. Why do you think Benjamin Zephaniah wrote this poem?

____

____

____

Name: ______________________________ Date: ______________

Questions about *Dog*

Answer as many of the questions as you can about *Dog* by Ted Hughes.

a. Circle **two** things the dog in the poem likes to do.

racing sleeping exercising eating digging

b. What is the only other thing the dog wakes up for?

____

c. Why does the poet compare the dog to 'a sack' and 'a log' in lines 5 and 6?

____

____

d. What does 'gobble and chomp' mean in line 12?

____

____

e. The poet starts half of the lines in the poem with the word 'He'. What effect does this have?

____

____

f. In line 15, the poet says that the dog 'flops flat, and digs down deep'. Why is this a good way to describe how the dog goes to sleep?

____

____

____

g. What do you think the poet's view of the dog is?

____

____

____

Questions about *Dog* and *Cat*

Answer as many of the questions about *Dog* and *Cat* by Ted Hughes as you can. Find evidence to support your answers.

a. How is the pattern of rhyming different in each poem?

____

____

____

b. The sleeping cat is compared to 'a battery', 'a leopard', 'a tiger'. The sleeping dog is compared to 'a sack', 'a log', 'a miner'. Why does the poet choose these different comparisons?

____

____

____

____

c. Which poem uses the most alliteration? ______________________

Give an example. ______________________

____

____

d. Explain how each poem gives a different feeling about the pet. You will need to think about how the pet is described and the poet's view of the pet.

____

____

____

____

____